ICSA Study Text

Risk Management

ICSA Study Text

Risk Management

Dr Simon Ashby

The Governance
Institute

First published 2019
Published by ICSA Publishing Ltd
Saffron House
6–10 Kirby Street
London EC1N 8TS

Typeset by Patricia Briggs

British Cataloguing in Publication Data
A catalogue record for this book is available from the British Library.

ISBN   978-1-86072-751-1

Contents

How to use this study text

This study text has been developed to support the Risk Management module of the ICSA's qualifying programme and includes a range of navigational, self-testing and illustrative features to help you get the most out of the support materials.

The text is divided into three main sections:

◆ introductory material
◆ the text itself
◆ reference material.

The sections below show you how to find your way around the text and make the most of its features.

Introductory material

The introductory section includes a full contents list and the aims and learning outcomes of the qualification, as well as a list of acronyms and abbreviations.

The text itself

Each part opens with a list of the chapters to follow, an overview of what will be covered and learning outcomes for the part.

Every chapter opens with a list of the topics covered and an introduction specific to that chapter.

Chapters are structured to allow students to break the content down into manageable sections for study. Each chapter ends with a summary of key content to reinforce understanding.

Features

The text is enhanced by a range of illustrative and self-testing features to assist understanding and to help you prepare for the examination. You will find answers to the 'Test yourself' questions towards the end of this text. Each feature is presented in a standard format, so that you will become familiar with how to use them in your study.

These features are identified by a series of icons.

The text also includes tables, figures and other illustrations as relevant.

Reference material

The text contains a range of additional guidance and reference material, including a glossary of key terms and a comprehensive index.

Stop and think

Test yourself

Making it work

Case study

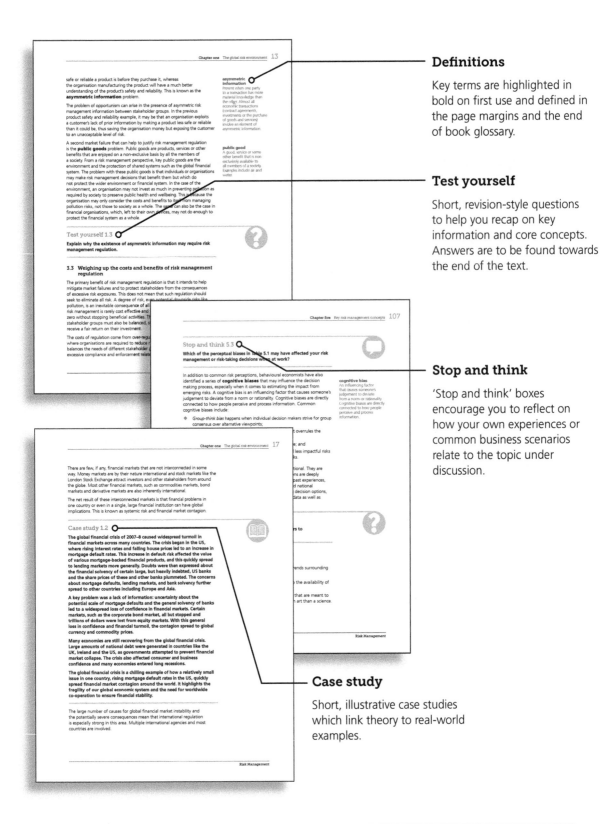

Definitions

Key terms are highlighted in bold on first use and defined in the page margins and the end of book glossary.

Test yourself

Short, revision-style questions to help you recap on key information and core concepts. Answers are to be found towards the end of the text.

Stop and think

'Stop and think' boxes encourage you to reflect on how your own experiences or common business scenarios relate to the topic under discussion.

Case study

Short, illustrative case studies which link theory to real-world examples.

About the author

Dr Simon Ashby is an Associate Professor at Plymouth Business School. Prior to this, he worked as a financial regulator for the UK Financial Services Authority (writing policy on risk management) and as a senior risk manager in a number of top UK financial institutions, designing and implementing risk management frameworks.

Simon has a PhD in corporate risk management from the University of Nottingham and has published many academic papers and industry reports on risk, governance, financial services regulation, banking and insurance. His current research interests include board-level risk management, cyber risk, risk culture and operational risk management.

Simon is a fellow and former chairman of the Institute of Operational Risk, and a director and audit and risk committee chair of Plymouth Community Homes.

Acknowledgements

The publisher would like to acknowledge the contributions of
Julia Graham and Eve Sorokina during the creation of this work.

Acronyms and abbreviations

ACCA	Association of Certified Chartered Accountants
AI	artificial intelligence
AIRMIC	Association of Insurers and Risk Managers
ALARM	Association of Local Authority Risk Managers
ALARP	as low as reasonably practical
ALCO	asset and liability committee
ALM	assets and liabilities management
AML	anti-money laundering
BCBS	Basel Committee on Banking Supervision
BCCI	Bank of Credit and Commerce International
BIS	Bank for International Settlements
BoE	Bank of England
BOFIA	Banks and Other Financial Institutions Act
BSI	British Standards Institute
CAMA	Companies and Allied Matters Act
CCAR	capital analysis and review
CCR	counterparty credit risk
CEO	chief executive officer
CFT	countering financing of terrorism
CLS	continuous linked settlement
COBIT	Control Objectives for Information and Related Technologies
Coco	contingent convertible
COSO	Committee of Sponsoring Organizations of the Treadway Commission
CRO	chief risk officer
CSR	corporate social responsibility
EA	Environment Agency

EBA	European Banking Authority
EC	European Commission
ECB	European Central Bank
ECJ	European Court of Justice
EPA	Environmental Protection Agency
ERM	enterprise risk management
ESG	environmental, social and governance
EU	European Union
FATF	Financial Action Task Force
FCA	Financial Conduct Authority
FRC	Financial Reporting Council
FSB	Financial Stability Board
GDPR	General Data Protection Regulation
GFSC	Guernsey Financial Services Commission
GRC	governance, risk and compliance
HAZOP	hazard and operability summary
HR	human resources
HSE	The UK Health and Safety Executive
IA	information assurance
IHSA	Irish Health and Safety Authority
ILO	International Labour Organization
IMF	International Monetary Fund
IOR	Institute of Operational Risk
IRM	Institute of Risk Management
ISA	Investments and Securities Act
ISACA	Information Systems Audit and Control Association
ISE	Irish Stock Exchange
ISO	International Organization for Standardization
IT	information technology
JFSC	Jersey Financial Services Commission
KPI	key performance indicator
KRI	key risk indicator
KYC	know your customer
LCR	liquidity coverage ratio
LIBOR	London Interbank Offer Rate

LSE	London Stock Exchange
MLRO	money laundering reporting officer
NCA	National Crime Agency
NED	non-executive director
NHS	National Health Service
NSFR	net stable funding ratio
OECD	Organisation for Economic Co-operation and Development
PAS	publicly available specification
PCDD	Preventive, Corrective, Directive, Detective
PEST	Political, Economic, Social and Technological
PLC	public limited company
PMI	Project Management Institute
PPI	payment protection insurance
PRA	Prudential Regulatory Authority
PRINCE2	PRojects IN Controlled Environments:.
QCA	Quoted Companies Alliance
RAG	red, amber, green
RCSA	risk and control self-assessment
RIDDOR	Reporting of Injuries, Diseases and Dangerous Occurrences Regulations
RMIS	Risk Management Information Systems
RST	reverse stress test
SAR	Suspicious Activity Report
SRM	sustainability risk management
SWD	solvent wind down
SWIFT	structured what if technique
UAE	United Arab Emirates
VaR	value at risk
VW	Volkswagen

Part one

Risk frameworks

Overview

Risk is a diverse area covering a wide range of activities, including health and safety, environmental pollution, information security, quality and performance, compliance and organisational solvency. In this part, we explore the various frameworks that underpin the management of risk in organisations.

Chapter one provides a helicopter view of the global risk environment. It covers the importance of risk management, as well as the various regulations and standards that influence the management of risk in organisations.

Chapter two explains the various corporate governance frameworks that influence the management of risk within organisations at an international and national scale. These include the OECD and World Bank principles on corporate governance, EU regulations and the UK and Irish corporate governance codes.

Chapter three provides more detail on the sector-specific regulatory frameworks that exist, including frameworks for health and safety management, protecting the global financial system, and the prevention of environmental pollution.

Chapter four investigates the components that make up a typical risk management framework. It also considers the international and national standards that help to support the design and implementation of risk management frameworks.

Chapter five looks at some key risk management concepts, explores the definition of risk and risk management, and explains some ways in which risks can be classified and categorised.

Chapter six explains how the risk management discipline has evolved during the twentieth century and how different risk management practices can be deployed to make an organisation more valuable.

Chapter seven explores the basic risk management process of identifying, assessing, monitoring and controlling risk. It then extends this to the concept of enterprise risk management.

Chapter eight concludes Part One with an overview of the practical governance and compliance arrangements that organisations use to ensure that their risk management objectives are embedded into day-to-day operations.

Learning outcomes

At the end of this part, you will be able to:

◆ Appreciate the importance of risk management and associated risk management, governance and compliance frameworks.

◆ Understand the business benefits of risk management.

◆ Explain the various international and national regulations that influence the management of risk in organisations, including the risk management elements of corporate governance regulations and codes.

◆ Consider the reasons for risk management regulations and standards, as well as the role that regulators play in ensuring the effective management of risk in organisations.

◆ Understand the role of international and national risk management standards in helping organisations to develop effective risk management frameworks.

◆ Explain how risk and risk management may be defined.

◆ Identify a variety of categories of risk within organisations.

◆ Consider the role of risk management in organisations from a variety of perspectives.

◆ Identify the components of the standard risk management process and enterprise risk management.

◆ Demonstrate the elements of an effective risk management framework, including roles and responsibilities.

◆ Understand the role and importance of governance and compliance from a risk management perspective.

Chapter one
The global risk environment

Contents

1. Introduction

This chapter outlines the global environment within which risk management is conducted. This environment consists of stakeholders, regulatory agencies and standard setting bodies, all of whom have an interest in ensuring the effectiveness of organisational risk management activities. These stakeholders, agencies and standard setters are increasingly global in nature. For example, multinational organisations have consumers across many countries; even country-specific organisations may have shareholders and creditors from outside their country of operation. Many international regulatory agencies and standard setters exist, such as the International Organization for Standardization (ISO).

The chapter considers how and why an organisation and its diverse range of stakeholders derive value from effective risk management. It explores why organisations may not always manage risk as effectively as possible – or as their stakeholders might prefer. It outlines why this forms the rationale for risk management guidelines and regulations, and organisations' internal risk management compliance activities.

The chapter ends with an overview of the global regulatory environment for risk management, as well as the key international regulations and good practice standards.

2. The importance of risk management: a stakeholder approach

Whether consciously or not, all organisations manage risk. Every activity that an organisation performs and every decision it makes involves risk.

Risk is an essential part of any organisation and the management of risk is essential to help preserve and create value for stakeholders. Little is certain in the world in which organisations operate, meaning that almost every decision that is made will have multiple potential outcomes. Organisations exist to meet the needs of their stakeholders. They inevitably make risky decisions (decisions that could result in a range of potential outcomes) that generate stakeholder value, while at the same time reducing the risk of adverse events such as pollution, injury or bankruptcy. To fulfil this need organisations must take risks that can yield positive benefits for stakeholders and reduce risks that could cause financial or physical harm. Balancing these two goals is far from easy.

Risk is both an input into the strategic decision making process and an output. From an input perspective, the risk exposures that exist will influence the types of strategy that are chosen. For example, an organisation might launch a new product to exploit a new market or choose to merge to help address an increase in the cost of regulation or survive in a competitive marketplace. From an output perspective, strategic decisions may create risks that need to be managed (such as health and safety risks or environmental risks).

Risk management may be an essential activity but that does not mean all organisations manage these risks effectively or devote sufficient resources to risk management. Managing an organisation effectively, including the adequate management of risk, requires significant time and financial resources: employees, managers or directors do not always appreciate the value of this investment. The media is full of stories of **risk events** that have affected organisations and their stakeholders, causing injury, disruption and financial loss. Day after day, these serve as a strong reminder of the importance of effective risk management.

risk event
A random discrete occurrence which may affect, positively or negatively an organisation.

Stop and think 1.1

Reflect on the types of decision that organisations have to make (strategic and operational decisions). What outcomes might arise from these decisions? Think of as many positive and negative outcomes as you can and write them down.

2.1   The organisation as a nexus of global stakeholders

Organisations serve to meet the needs of multiple stakeholder groups, including consumers, creditors, owners, shareholders and third parties. These stakeholders can come from a variety of different countries, whether the organisation itself is internationally active or not. In addition, the actions of organisations can have international consequences (such as pollution). Meeting the needs of these stakeholders in relation to risk, or more specifically the risks they may want an organisation to take and the risks that they do not wish it to take, is a key way in which risk management can create and preserve value.

Organisations meet the needs of their stakeholders through setting objectives that provide an appropriate balance between risk and return and by ensuring that these objectives are achieved. This includes managing the risks which may threaten the achievement of these objectives, such as competition or **compliance risks**. How an organisation balances risk and return, and the degree to which it manages the risks associated with implementing its objectives, will depend on the risk attitudes and preferences of these stakeholders.

compliance risk
The risk of criminal sanction or a financial or reputation loss as a result of actual or perceived non-compliance with all applicable laws, regulations, standards, guidelines and codes of conduct.

Each of these stakeholder groups 'invest' in the organisation with their time, skills, money or something less tangible like their health and wellbeing. Stakeholders expect returns like salaries, safe and reliable products and services, or interest payments to meet the cost of these investments. They also expect the organisation to be managed in such a way that these returns are delivered in a consistent manner without any unpleasant surprises. For example, employees will expect the organisation to remain in business to ensure that their salary is paid. They will also expect to be kept safe when at work. Customers expect to receive goods and services that are safe and reliable and expect product guarantees to be honoured. Creditors will be concerned that the organisation remains solvent to ensure that loan capital is paid back with the agreed rate of interest.

Figure 1.1 illustrates the main stakeholder groups that have an explicit or implicit contract with a typical organisation. The stakeholders in the outer ring are termed external stakeholders because they are outside the organisation. The stakeholders in the inner circle are termed internal stakeholders because they are employed by or own the organisation. In all cases, each group wants to be reasonably assured that the agreements and reasonable expectations are being met. Effective risk management supports this.

Shareholders and owners are less easy to classify. For large quoted companies, such as public limited companies, they are generally viewed as external stakeholders. For smaller companies with smaller numbers of owners or partners, especially where these owners are involved in the management of the organisation, they are considered to be internal.

Stop and think 1.2

Identify the main stakeholder groups for an organisation of your choice. In each case, reflect on why each group might require the organisation to invest in effective risk management. This need might be related to personal safety, financial security, financial returns, product reliability or similar.

Reflect on what each group expects from the organisation, what uncertainties exist in this regard, and how they could be managed. Is a risk for a stakeholder the same risk for the organisation itself?

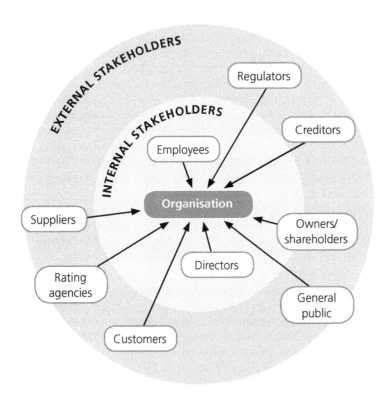

Figure 1.1 The organisation as a nexus of contracts with global stakeholders

Test yourself 1.1

Identify the key risks that the following stakeholder groups will wish to have managed effectively:

◆   **creditors**

◆   **customers**

◆   **employees.**

2.2   A shareholder perspective on risk management

Most stakeholders are inherently **risk averse**. They prefer certainty to risk and will sacrifice some of their wealth or income to achieve this certainty.

Like any other stakeholder, the average shareholder is inherently risk averse but that does not mean they will demand the same level of risk reduction as other stakeholder groups. This is because shareholders have different objectives to some other stakeholder groups and because they have their own tools to manage risk. Shareholders may not behave in a risk-averse way for three reasons:

risk averse
A reluctance to take or to be exposed to risk. Individuals, groups or organisations that are risk averse will, all things being equal, prefer certainty to risk and will typically require some form of financial premium in order to take risk.

asymmetric returns
Present when the gains or losses from a risky investment or other economic decision are not equal. For example, the gains associated with positive outcomes may exceed the losses associated with negative ones, or vice versa.

1. **Asymmetric returns**: shareholders many receive dividends and they may benefit from an increase in the value of the shares that they hold, allowing them to be sold for a profit. There is no theoretical limit on the size of these returns, meaning that they could be 100%, 1,000% or more. Generally, risk and return are positively correlated. The more risk an organisation takes, the more return it can generate: a return that should translate into increased dividends and share values. Shareholders may value an increase in risk, providing that there is the prospect of higher returns. Such an increase in risk may result in a higher chance of bankruptcy, but shareholders are often protected from this because of their limited liability.

2. *Limited liability*: the shareholders of most companies, whether public or private limited companies, have limited liability. In the event that the company becomes insolvent or goes bankrupt, shareholder liability is limited to the value of their investment stake. Limited liability shareholders cannot be forced to provide additional funds once they have invested in a company, as would be the case if shareholders had unlimited liability.

3. *The diversification of risk*: shareholders often choose to create diversified portfolios of investments. They purchase shares in multiple companies or some other form of investment asset (for example, bonds, commodities or property). Through diversification, shareholders can insulate their investment portfolio from company-specific risk events such as fires, frauds or a decline in sales. Diversification can be understood via the well-known proverb 'do not put all your eggs in one basket'.

risk neutral
An indifference to risk. A risk-neutral individual, group or organisation will be unconcerned about exposure to risk and is indifferent to risk or certainty, providing the expected returns from these two different states is identical.

risk preferring
A liking for risk and risk taking. Individuals, groups or organisations that are risk preferring will, all things being equal, prefer risk to certainty and will typically pay a financial premium or suffer some other kind of non-financial cost (such as to their health) in order to take risk.

Asymmetric payoffs and limited liability combined with diversification means that shareholders may at times behave in either a **risk neutral** or even **risk preferring** way. The potential to achieve a diversified portfolio of investments can explain why shareholders may be risk neutral, choosing to base their investment decisions solely on expected returns, rather than the potential volatility of these returns. Limited liability supports effective diversification in this regard. However, it can also create a situation where shareholders are risk preferring.

Real world scenarios where shareholders encourage companies to act in a risk preferring way are very rare. Many shareholders would find such conduct to be unethical and smaller shareholders can rarely achieve fully diversified portfolios. Equally shareholders may be unwilling to risk previous gains in the value of their shares where an organisation has been successful. Nevertheless, risk preferring behaviour on the part of shareholders is possible and was considered a factor in the global financial crisis of 2007–8.

The global financial crisis of 2007–8 provides an example of how shareholders may at times behave in ways that are considered irresponsible as a result of their limited liability. Evidence of this is provided in a UK government review of the actions of shareholders in the lead up to the crisis. This case serves as an example of the types of conflict that can exist between stakeholders.

Case study 1.1

"Experience in the recent crisis phase has forcefully illustrated that while shareholders enjoy limited liability in respect of their investee companies, in the case of major banks the taxpayer has been obliged to assume effectively unlimited liability. This further underlines the importance of discharge of the responsibility of shareholders as owners, which has been inadequately acknowledged in the past." (Walker, 2009, page 12)

Prior to the financial crisis some banks, such as Northern Rock in the UK and Lehman Brothers and Bear Stearns in the US, increased shareholder returns by exploiting high risk investment opportunities such as sub-prime lending and mortgage-backed derivatives. These investments generated high levels of return, but when the economies in the US and Europe slowed down in 2007, the level of risk exposure was great and these banks were forced to declare bankruptcy.

In terms of shareholder pressure it was alleged that well-diversified institutional shareholders (pension funds and hedge funds) encouraged these and other banks to take high levels of risk to increase their quarterly profits to generate dividends and higher share prices. Low interest rates prior to 2007 meant that the only way to generate a high level of profit was to take excessive levels of credit (lending) and financial market risk.

The shareholders of a failing organisation may also encourage it to take high levels of risk in an attempt to improve its fortunes. A contemporary example of risk preferring which is intentional and not unethical is technology start-ups, which are increasingly common in the digital age.

Although there are reasons why shareholders may be risk neutral or even risk preferring, in practice most will value effective risk management. This may be because of ethical concerns and a desire to protect employees, third parties or customers from harm. It may also be because of concerns about:

◆ bankruptcy costs
◆ the effect of cash flow fluctuations on opportunities for growth.

Higher levels of risk taking by an organisation may result in the expectation of higher returns, but there are no guarantees. Bankruptcy could occur with higher levels of risk, along with its associated costs. Growth opportunities may be missed, meaning lower returns in the future.

Bankruptcy costs
High levels of risk taking may result in financial distress and ultimately bankruptcy. In theory, shareholders should be indifferent to bankruptcy, providing that the organisation can be sold and they receive back their investment stake. In practice, shareholders rarely get back the money they have invested and almost certainly will not receive any of the appreciation they may

have received on this investment (though well informed investors may be able to sell their shares before they start to fall in value).

When an organisation becomes bankrupt it can incur a range of costs. These may include legal costs, other administration costs and legal liability claims. In addition, the organisation will lose the value of any goodwill (such as brand value) that has been built up over time. It also may have to sell assets at far below their market value.

Bankruptcy costs significantly decrease the chance that shareholders are repaid the capital that they have invested in a company. While they may have limited liability, they will still want to get back the funds that they have invested. Shareholders will typically value risk management activity that can help to prevent the costs associated with bankruptcy.

Cash flow fluctuations

Almost all risks will affect an organisation's cash flows. Gains from risk taking will help to increase the level of cash flowing into an organisation. In contrast, losses from risk taking will result in cash flowing out of the organisation.

Fluctuations in cash flows can be very disruptive. A large, unexpected loss – such as a fire or major fraud – could mean that there are insufficient funds to invest in profitable opportunities such as new product development or process efficiencies via the purchase of a new IT system. From a cost perspective, large and unexpected losses may necessitate high-cost debt finance or lead to other financing and contractual costs, such as late payment charges.

In contrast, companies with stable cash flows will be able to invest for the future and control their costs, generating higher profits and dividends for shareholders over the long term.

risk premium
The rate of return required for risk taking. The higher the level of risk exposure, the higher the risk premium.

Shareholders will typically require much higher rates of expected return from organisations with less stable cash flows. This is known as the **risk premium** or 'cost of risk'. The extra return is required to compensate for the higher level of cash flow volatility associated with increased risk. This is why venture capital organisations may choose to invest in high risk start-up companies, because they estimate that the level of return they should receive is sufficient to compensate them for the greater degree of cash flow volatility.

2.3 Managing conflicts of interest between stakeholders

Just because stakeholders are typically risk averse, that does not mean that they will be averse to the same risks or have equal levels of risk aversion. One way to understand this is to remember that different stakeholders may have different risk objectives. Shareholders look to maximise their dividends and the share price. Creditors want the security of knowing that their loan will be repaid with the agreed level of interest and consumers will prioritise safe, reliable products and services. Conflicts regarding the preferred type and level of risk exposure may arise even in the case of organisations that do not have shareholders. For example, employees may be less concerned about the health and safety of the organisation's customers than their own health and safety, and vice versa.

Where conflicts exist between stakeholder groups, risk management takes on a new objective: to further protect and create value by managing these conflicts and increasing the overall level of stakeholder satisfaction. Effective risk management is needed to help balance the conflicting interests of different stakeholder groups, weighing up different priorities and assessing the costs and benefits of different risk management decisions and risk exposure levels. The board and senior management are very important here, as they are the ones who have to make these difficult decisions. These decisions will influence the riskiness of the strategy that the board chooses for the organisation, along with the level of investment in risk management to help ensure that organisational objectives are met. Company secretaries and other governance professionals (as well an organisation's specialist risk management staff, where present) have a role to play in supporting these decisions to ensure that any legal, regulatory or ethical concerns are considered.

Test yourself 1.2

Explain the conflicts of interest that can exist between shareholders and creditors.

3. Reasons for risk management regulation

The risk management decisions of an organisation are subject to a range of regulations. Common regulations include health and safety regulation, environmental regulation and legal liability regulations (such as compulsory insurance for employee and public liability).

Certain industries, such as financial services, are subject to additional risk management regulation aimed at protecting the overall financial system and preventing financial or legal misconduct (protecting consumers from being mis-sold financial products that do not meet their needs). Much of this regulation is now global, as global financial markets become more interconnected.

The case for regulation is not clear, even given the importance of effective risk management for organisations and their stakeholders and allowing for occasional conflicts of interest. Compliance with regulation can also be very time consuming and expensive. However, regulation is necessary because organisational stakeholders are not always able to ensure an optimal level of risk management on their own, primarily because of issues around self-regulation and market failures.

3.1   The problem of self-regulation

One regulatory option is to have a self-regulatory system, where a group of organisations or professionals agree to set and enforce specific risk management standards. Co-ordination and enforcement may be managed by a trade association or institute to help prevent the collapse of the self-regulatory agreement.

Professional regulation in areas such as law and medicine often include an element of self-regulation that may cover aspects of risk management practice by these professionals. Risk management activities such as customer complaint handling can be self-regulatory in some countries, such as the Advertising Standards Authority in the UK.

The advantage of self-regulation is that the regulation is agreed and enforced by those being regulated. This should ensure that the regulation is appropriate and proportionate, cutting down on the costs of compliance. The disadvantage is that self-regulation is hard to sustain because of the limited incentives to enforce such an agreement. Organisations may be reluctant to punish their contemporaries because they may be next to receive enforcement action. Many self-regulatory systems fail – such as financial services self-regulation in the UK in the 1980s and early 1990s – and are replaced by statutory regulation, enforced by a government-appointed regulatory body.

Stop and think 1.3

Research the case of food labelling self-regulation in the UK. Consider the benefits of self-regulation and reflect on why increased levels of government regulation has been introduced, regarding the level of nutritional information required.

3.2   Market failures

Stakeholders need efficient markets to ensure that their risk preferences are reflected in the risk management decisions made by organisations. For example, customers need to have a clear understanding of the health and safety or quality risks associated with the use of a particular product if they are to decide whether to purchase it at a given price or even to choose to pay a higher price for a safer product. Equally, a prospective employee's decision to work for a company may be affected by the associated health and safety risks. They may demand higher wages for a higher risk job or decide that the job is too risky at any price. From a financial risk perspective, employees and creditors must be able to assess the risk of bankruptcy before deciding how much to charge for their time and skills (in the case of employees), or loan interest (in the case of creditors).

A key factor that is needed to ensure market efficiency is information. Stakeholders need to know the types and degrees of risk to which they will be exposed in order to generate market incentives for effective risk management. This can be hard to achieve in practice. Customers are unlikely to know how safe or reliable a product is before they purchase it, whereas the organisation manufacturing the product will have a much better understanding of the product's safety and reliability. This is known as the **asymmetric information** problem.

The problem of opportunism can arise in the presence of asymmetric risk management information between stakeholder groups. In the previous product safety and reliability example, it may be that an organisation exploits a customer's lack of prior information by making a product less safe or reliable than it could be, thus saving the organisation money but exposing the customer to an unacceptable level of risk.

A second market failure that can help to justify risk management regulation is the **public goods** problem. Public goods are products, services or other benefits that are enjoyed on a non-exclusive basis by all the members of a society. From a risk management perspective, key public goods are the environment and the protection of shared systems such as the global financial system. The problem with these public goods is that individuals or organisations may make risk management decisions that benefit them but which do not protect the wider environment or financial system. In the case of the environment, an organisation may not invest as much in preventing pollution as required by society to preserve public health and wellbeing. This is because the organisation may only consider the costs and benefits to itself from managing pollution risks, not those to society as a whole. The same can also be the case in financial organisations, which, left to their own devices, may not do enough to protect the financial system as a whole.

asymmetric information
Present when one party to a transaction has more material knowledge than the other. Almost all economic transactions (contract agreements, investments or the purchase of goods and services) involve an element of asymmetric information.

public good
A good, service or some other benefit that is non-exclusively available to all members of a society. Examples include air and water.

Test yourself 1.3

Explain why the existence of asymmetric information may require risk management regulation.

3.3   Weighing up the costs and benefits of risk management regulation

The primary benefit of risk management regulation is that it intends to help mitigate market failures and to protect stakeholders from the consequences of excessive risk exposures. This does not mean that such regulation should seek to eliminate all risk. A degree of risk, even potential downside risks like pollution, is an inevitable consequence of all organisational activity. Excessive risk management is rarely cost effective and few risks can be reduced to zero without stopping beneficial activities. The reasonable needs of different stakeholder groups must also be balanced, such as the need for shareholders to receive a fair return on their investment.

The costs of regulation come from over-regulation or ineffective regulation, where organisations are required to reduce risk below the optimum level that balances the needs of different stakeholder groups or where organisations face excessive compliance and enforcement related costs without much benefit.

Over-regulation is relatively rare, but different groups of stakeholders have conflicting opinions on this. In all cases compliance costs can be considerable and these costs may both decrease the profitability of an organisation and increase the price of goods and services. Compliance costs include the cost of maintaining a compliance function or providing information to regulators. This means that the stakeholder groups that regulation is designed to protect may end up paying some or all of the associated costs of compliance.

Stop and think 1.4

Identify the regulations that affect the risk management decisions of an organisation of your choice. At a minimum this should include information on health and safety and environmental regulations.

Identify for one of these areas of regulation the benefits and costs for the various stakeholders. Do the benefits outweigh the costs?

3.4 The role of compliance management

Compliance management ensures that an organisation's risk management arrangements and decisions are consistent with all applicable laws and regulations. This will often include ensuring that the organisation does not expose vulnerable stakeholders to excessive levels of risk.

4. The global regulatory environment for risk management

The global risk environment for organisations contains a range of international laws and regulations that address the management of risk. The number and complexity of these laws and regulations has grown significantly in the past few years, especially after the global financial crisis and the subsequent sovereign debt crisis, In addition, many of the local laws and regulations are influenced by international laws and regulations. An organisation may be indirectly affected by a particular international law or regulation, even if they are not directly under its purview.

In addition to formal laws and regulations, there are also international standards for risk management. These standards have also grown in their number and complexity. These standards primarily help to share good practice, improving the effectiveness of risk management within organisations and delivering further value to their stakeholders. These standards also help organisations to comply with international and local laws and regulations.

4.1 The need for international regulation and standards

International regulations and standards are required because risk exposures often cross national boundaries. The removal of trade barriers, easier travel and tools like the Internet mean that organisations are now more multinational in terms of their operations and markets. Major risks to public goods like the environment or the financial system can have far-reaching effects. Diverse risks may be connected: for example, major environmental pollution events and weather events may affect financial markets across the world. In addition, problems in financial markets and institutions can affect the supply of credit and cause global economic problems, as is still happening in the wake of the global financial crisis.

The interconnected world has also led to the development of international standards for risk management. There is much to learn from risk management experiences around the globe, as good risk management practice in one country or organisation is likely to be useful for improving practice elsewhere.

Test yourself 1.4

Identify the reasons why international environmental risk management regulation is needed.

4.2 International regulation and standards in relation to risk management

Many international regulations and standards cover key areas such as governance, the environment, financial stability, and health and safety. They are only indirectly focused on risk management in organisations. The following key areas are subject to international regulations and standards that have relevance in a risk management context:

◆ corporate governance

◆ environmental regulation

◆ financial stability

◆ health and safety.

Corporate governance
Effective corporate governance is an important element in today's business environment. Weak corporate governance can lead to corruption, costly scandals, organisational failure and even systemic breakdowns that damage the interests of all stakeholder groups. International regulations and standards on corporate governance help to promote sustainable economic growth on a global level, ensuring that stakeholders are treated fairly and that organisations have cost-effective access to global capital markets. Without good governance access to global capital would be limited.

One of the most influential international standards on corporate governance is the G20/ Organisation for Economic Co-operation and Development (OECD) 2015 Principles of Corporate Governance. These principles are often referenced by countries developing local governance codes or guidelines and have been adopted by international agencies such as the World Bank and Financial Stability Board (FSB). The principles exist to provide a worldwide benchmark for good corporate governance practice and supervisory assessments of this practice. The principles cover issues such as the design of effective corporate governance arrangements, ensuring the fair treatment of shareholders and other stakeholder groups, and the disclosure of corporate governance and associated risk management information on key risk exposures.

Environmental regulation

Environmental risks such as ground, water and air pollution, along with global warming, do not respect national borders and are therefore a key part of the global risk environment. National regulation and standards in an area of significant global concern requires careful co-ordination to ensure that weaknesses in one national regulatory regime are not exploited to the detriment of stakeholders in other nations.

Organisations that may cause pollution risk events or who contribute in other ways to environmental concerns may be subject to international laws and regulations on environmental risk management. These laws and regulations cover, among other things, the following areas:

◆ air quality
◆ water quality
◆ waste management
◆ contaminant clean-up
◆ chemical safety.

While making and executing strategic business decisions, organisations should ensure that they comply with these international rules and regulations as otherwise they may face fines (or worse). This is an integral part of good risk management. International law and associated environmental regulation is complex. It consists of legally binding treaties and subsidiary protocols, such as the Kyoto Protocol on climate change. For most organisations these laws and protocols are incorporated into national regulation or in the case of the European Union (EU), EU Directives. This means that, except in complex multinational enterprises, it may not be necessary for organisations to understand in detail these international laws and regulations.

Financial stability

The stability of the global financial system is a key source of risk for both financial and non-financial organisations. For non-financial organisations, a stable global financial system is necessary to ensure that they continue to have access to capital resources to help finance their activities. Financial system instability can trigger worldwide economic problems, restricting access to consumer and government credit, threatening the safety of saving deposits and disrupting payment systems. Ultimately, these problems can cause major economic recessions and even economic collapse of businesses and nations alike.

There are few, if any, financial markets that are not interconnected in some way. Money markets are by their nature international and stock markets like the London Stock Exchange attract investors and other stakeholders from around the globe. Most other financial markets, such as commodities markets, bond markets and derivative markets are also inherently international.

The net result of these interconnected markets is that financial problems in one country or even in a single, large financial institution can have global implications. This is known as systemic risk and financial market contagion.

Case study 1.2

The global financial crisis of 2007–8 caused widespread turmoil in financial markets across many countries. The crisis began in the US, where rising interest rates and falling house prices led to an increase in mortgage default rates. This increase in default risk affected the value of various mortgage-backed financial products, and this quickly spread to lending markets more generally. Doubts were then expressed about the financial solvency of certain large, but heavily indebted, US banks and the share prices of these and other banks plummeted. The concerns about mortgage defaults, lending markets, and bank solvency further spread to other countries including Europe and Asia.

A key problem was a lack of information: uncertainty about the potential scale of mortgage defaults and the general solvency of banks led to a widespread loss of confidence in financial markets. Certain markets, such as the corporate bond market, all but stopped and trillions of dollars were lost from equity markets. With this general loss in confidence and financial turmoil, the contagion spread to global currency and commodity prices.

Many economies are still recovering from the global financial crisis. Large amounts of national debt were generated in countries like the UK, Ireland and the US, as governments attempted to prevent financial market collapse. The crisis also affected consumer and business confidence and many economies entered long recessions.

The global financial crisis is a chilling example of how a relatively small issue in one country, rising mortgage default rates in the US, quickly spread financial market contagion around the world. It highlights the fragility of our global economic system and the need for worldwide co-operation to ensure financial stability.

The large number of causes for global financial market instability and the potentially severe consequences mean that international regulation is especially strong in this area. Multiple international agencies and most countries are involved.

The key international agencies are as follows:

◆ the OECD;
◆ the World Bank;
◆ the International Monetary Fund (IMF);
◆ the FSB
◆ the Bank for International Settlements (BIS).

The primary source of regulation for global financial stability risks are the Basel Accords. Under the patronage of BIS, these arrangements are negotiated by the Basel Committee whose membership comes from representatives of the G20 countries. The Basel Accords are adopted by most countries around the world.

The Basel Committee has produced a wide range of publications on the subject of financial market stability over the years. The main Basel Accord is now in its third iteration, known as Basel III. The Accords are focused on internationally active banks, as they are a key source of financial market instability. However, most countries apply the Accords to a wider range of financial institutions. The requirements of the Accords can affect non-financial organisations via the availability of credit and the terms on which credit can be offered.

The Basel Accords include requirements relating to capital resources and risk management practices. Their aim is to prevent financial crises through effective risk management, but if that fails, the capital resource requirements help to provide a financial buffer. The strictness of these requirements has increased significantly since the global financial crisis of 2007–8. Banks now hold significant levels of cash as capital to ensure that funds are available to pay for most of the losses that they may incur.

Health and safety
The protection of human rights is a major focus for international law and regulation. This includes protecting people from work-related sickness, disease, and injury and from harmful actions of organisations located near to their homes.

Overall responsibility for international health and safety regulation rests with the International Labour Organization (ILO). The ILO produces a wide range of standards and codes of practice. It also works to address areas of international concern, such as forced labour and child labour.

4.3 Global regulatory principles

Risk management and compliance regulations across the world come in various forms. The nature of these regulations can affect the costs of compliance and the strictness with which they are enforced. The main types of regulation are:

◆ rules
◆ guidance
◆ principles and outcomes based regulation
◆ risk-based regulation.

Rules

Rules are direct legal requirements. The contravention of a rule will lead to enforcement action in most cases which could result in a fine, imprisonment, or some other civil or criminal sanction.

Very few international regulations are rules. International bodies rarely have the legal authority necessary for rule-making powers. As a result, it is up to individual countries and their governments to turn international regulations into rules that are then enforced by their own local agencies.

Guidance

Guidance includes standards or codes of practice. Guidance need not be complied with as strictly as rules. It is up to an organisation to decide how to interpret and implement guidance.

Guidance usually reflects established good practice, such as established practices for the effective management of health and safety risks. Organisations that decide to ignore guidance may be required to explain why – similar to the 'comply or explain' approach to corporate governance regulation adopted in countries like the UK.

Most international regulation is produced as guidance. Individual countries or groups of countries like the EU may then decide whether or not to turn this guidance into legally enforceable rules.

Stop and think 1.5

Compare and contrast the costs and benefits of rules versus guidance. Why do some areas of regulations (such as financial services capital requirements and hazardous industry regulations) rely on rules, while others (such as corporate governance regulations) are guidance-based?

Principles and outcomes-based regulation

Principles and outcomes-based regulation relies on relatively high-level regulatory principles and associated outcomes, such as 'consumer protection' or 'maintaining financial stability'. The aim is to minimise the volume of detailed rules and guidance and to allow organisations more freedom when deciding how to apply the principles or how to achieve the intended outcomes in specific areas of regulation.

Principles and outcomes-based regulations work best when dealing with complex or dynamic risk management issues, where there is no agreed good practice or where good practice has not yet emerged. A further aim is to minimise the volume of detailed rules and guidance and to allow organisations more freedom when deciding how to comply with specific areas of regulation. Principles and outcomes regulation can lead to a lack of clarity about how to comply.

Financial services risk management regulation is often principles and outcomes-based, as is corporate governance regulation. This is because the best way to

principles and outcome-based regulation
Regulation that relies on high-level principles and desired regulatory outcomes, such as 'consumer protection' or 'maintaining financial stability'.

manage the risks associated with these areas varies according to the nature, scale and complexity of an organisation.

Risk-based regulation

Risk-based regulation may be combined with rules, guidance and principles and outcomes-based regulation. The idea is that the higher the degree of risk, the stricter the level of regulation that is applied. This means that lower risk organisations will generally be subject to lighter touch regulation than high risk ones.

Risk-based regulation is common in financial services risk management regulation, as well as areas like health and safety. For example, in the context of health and safety, an organisation working in chemical processing is subject to much greater safety regulation than one working in the service sector. This includes a greater volume of regulatory intervention and more severe penalties for non-compliance.

5. International risk management standards

In addition to targeted international regulations for specific areas of risk, such as financial stability or environmental pollution, there are a number of global standards for the practice of risk management more generally.

The idea behind these standards is to help organisations evaluate and improve the effectiveness of their risk management arrangements by sharing good practice on a global scale. Stakeholders may encourage organisations to follow these standards. Organisations often use them to help benchmark their practices and find ways to improve the effectiveness of their risk management arrangements.

5.1   ISO 31000:2009 and 2018

The ISO provides a wide range of standards to help improve management practices. The ISO 31000 standard provides guidelines for managing risk in all types of organisations, regardless of their size, activities or industry sector.

This standard covers the essential aspects of risk management practices in organisations. It provides a set of principles, a management framework, and a process that can be used to evaluate and further improve the organisation's risk management arrangements. This supports the achievement of an organisation's objectives and the creation and preservation of value to its stakeholders.

The standard is used by regulators, external and internal auditors, risk management professionals and company secretaries/governance professionals to help improve the management of risk against an international benchmark for good practice.

In addition to the core standard, the ISO also provides a number of additional documents in this family, such as:

1.   ISO Guide 73:2009 (Risk Management Vocabulary), which provides a collection of terms and definitions in relation to the management of risk.

2.   IEC 31010:2009 (Risk management – Risk assessment techniques), which looks at the use of a range of risk assessment techniques and concepts.

3.   ISO/TR 31004:2013 (Risk management – Guidance), to assist the implementation of ISO 31000.

The core ISO 31000 guidance was updated in 2018, to become ISO 31000:2018. The supplementary documents have not yet been updated. The 2018 update does not change the core philosophy of the original 2009 standard but is shorter and more concise with the intention to make the various concepts easier to understand. It also places greater emphasis on top management leadership in the creation and preservation of organisational value through risk management. There is a greater focus on the integrated nature of risk management, whereby organisations should review and regularly update their risk management practices to take account of new and changing risks, such as cyber and terrorism risks.

Test yourself 1.5

Why is an international standard on risk management needed?

5.2   COSO enterprise risk management framework 2004 and 2017

The Committee of Sponsoring Organizations of the Treadway Commission (COSO) is a joint initiative of five private sector organisations in the USA:

1.   the American Accounting Association

2.   the American Institute of Certified Public Accountants

3.   Financial Executives International

4.   the Investment Management Association

5.   the Institute of Internal Auditors.

COSO was created to provide thought leadership on risk management, internal control and fraud deterrence to help improve organisational performance and governance. COSO may be a US-based organisation but its influence is global. Many organisations and regulatory agencies around the world base their governance and risk management practices on the guidance provided by COSO.

The initial focus of COSO was on financial reporting and supporting US corporate governance regulation but its remit has grown since its creation in 1985. In 2004 COSO launched its initial guidance on what was termed **enterprise risk management**. This guidance was designed to support organisational stakeholders by improving risk management practices, ensuring that organisations achieve their strategic objectives and balancing the needs of different stakeholder groups into the long term.

enterprise risk management
Enterprise risk management is a process, effected by an entity's board of directors, management and other personnel, applied in strategy setting and across the enterprise, designed to identify potential events that may affect the entity, and manage risk to be within its risk appetite, to provide reasonable assurance regarding the achievement of entity objectives.

Since 2004, COSO has provided a number of thought leadership papers on different aspects and applications of risk management practice, including board oversight, cyber risk management and risk assessment. In 2017, COSO released a major update to its enterprise risk management framework (COSO, 2017), which highlights the importance of considering risk in both the strategy setting process and in driving the performance of an organisation. As such, it takes important steps toward ensuring risk is managed as an integrated part of managing an organisation.

5.3   ISO 19600:2014 (Compliance Management Systems)

ISO 19600:2014 is the international standard for compliance management systems. The standard is closely related to ISO 31000:2018 and is designed to help improve compliance management practices in organisations.

The standard has been designed as general guidance and does not cover specific issues in relation to specific areas of compliance (such as health and safety compliance and so on). The content of the standard includes:

◆   the role of the board and senior management in providing leadership for compliance management;

◆   the roles of other organisational functions, including the risk function and the compliance function;

◆   drafting a compliance management policy;

◆   agreeing compliance objectives and plans;

◆   communication and training;

◆   the operation of effective compliance management systems;

◆   the evaluation of compliance management performance; and

◆   dealing with non-compliance and improving the effectiveness of compliance management.

Chapter summary

◆   Organisations exist as a nexus of stakeholders including employees, suppliers, creditors and in the case of limited companies, shareholders.

◆   Effective risk management can add significant value for an organisation's stakeholders. Value is created by helping an organisation to achieve its objectives and protecting risk averse stakeholders from financial or physical harm.

◆   Despite the value enhancing benefits of risk management, organisations do not always invest the level of resources necessary to ensure effective risk management. This is because different stakeholder groups can have different risk preferences. Only some groups are risk averse, others can be risk neutral or even risk preferring in certain contexts, notably shareholders.

◆   Conflicts can exist between stakeholders where their preferences for risk differ. In particular, an organisation may not value risk management activities aimed at reducing risk where investors are well-diversified limited liability shareholders.

◆   Risk management regulation is used to help manage the conflicts that can exist between stakeholders. Although market forces can be used to help resolve conflicts, imperfections exist in these forces, notably asymmetric information and public good problems.

◆   Risk management regulation is common in areas such an environmental protection, health and safety and financial stability. Regulation may be country specific but international regulation is very common in the 21st century.

◆   International regulation is often principles-based and risk-based. This allows it to be adapted to different situations and organisations.

◆   In addition to international regulations, a range of international standards exist for risk management. The aim of these standards is to improve the effectiveness of risk management in organisations around the world.

Chapter two
Regulatory frameworks

Contents

1. Introduction

This chapter outlines the various corporate governance regulations that influence risk management practices in an organisation at a national level. It focuses on corporate governance regulations because they are an important element of the work done by company secretaries and other governance professionals. Corporate governance regulations also contain rules, guidance and principles that can have a major impact on risk management practices in an organisation.

2. The link between risk management practices and corporate governance regulation

Corporate governance is the system and related processes by which an organisation is directed and controlled. Effective corporate governance should ensure that an organisation is directed and controlled in a manner that meets the needs and expectations of its stakeholders. This can be achieved by setting strategic objectives which meet stakeholders' needs and expectations, as well as by implementing measures to identify, assess, monitor and control the various risks which could threaten the achievement of these objectives.

Already you should see one key link between corporate governance and risk management – to identify and control the sources of risk that may either support or threaten the proper establishment and achievement of an organisation's objectives. A well governed organisation should take all reasonable steps to ensure it determines the right to effectively, efficiently, and economically achieve its objectives. The discipline of risk management supports these activities with a range of tools and techniques that can be used to identify, assess, monitor, and ultimately control the risks to these objectives. These risks comprise the whole spectrum of uncertainty around the organisation's objectives, whether already chosen or still under consideration, and might include:

◆ risks that may affect the ability of an organisation to continue as a going concern, such as the establishment of a new form of subsidies, a large fraud or financial mismanagement;

◆ risks to the reputation of an organisation, such as the breakthrough of a new invention or a major scandal;

◆ risks which affect the continuity of the organisation's operations, such as the loss of a key outsource service provider; and

◆ other risks that may positively or adversely affect an organisation's objectives in relation to the non-financial needs of its stakeholders, such as ensuring their health and safety.

Good governance should effectively manage, not eliminate risk. Even a well governed organisation may encounter risk events which threaten the achievement of its objectives. As the effects of risk can never be completely eliminated, organisations need to build both resilience and agility in all their activities, enabling them to adequately respond to changes in circumstances or to deal with the consequences of unforeseen events.

Case study 2.1

The Volkswagen (VW) emissions scandal, which came to light in 2015, is an example of a risk management control-related failure in governance. This scandal has led to significant negative publicity and has resulted in some very large fines in several countries. Volkswagen's share price fell as a result of the crisis and VW removed diesel cars from sale in America for a time.

Staff within VW developed an electronic 'defeat' device that allowed certain types of VW cars (mostly diesels) to provide false emission test results, making these cars appear to be more environmentally friendly than they were in normal use.

All organisations should have effective risk management controls in place to help prevent staff misconduct. In VW's case these controls were ineffective. This means that although those involved in developing or encouraging the development of the device must share some of the blame for their behaviour, the event is more about the failure of senior management and board to ensure that appropriate policies, procedures, incentive arrangements and other relevant risk management tools were in place to ensure that such extreme staff misconduct did not occur in the first place. This failure of senior management is a failure of corporate governance.

Another link between corporate governance and risk management relates to the 'directed' element of corporate governance. For a board or senior management to appropriately determine the strategic objectives of an organisation, they will need to have a good understanding of the environment in which the organisation operates. They will also need to understand the capabilities of the organisation to function effectively within this environment and to exploit any opportunities that may be present. The environment will include a range of risks, including risks relating to customer demand, technology development or political change. It is up to the board and senior management to direct the strategy of the organisation in such a way that opportunities related to these risks can be exploited without unduly threatening its financial viability.

Good governance should ensure the long-term sustainability of an organisation, where value – be this profits, surpluses, environmental protection or some other social benefit – is generated through the exploitation of opportunities that contribute to the organisation's mission but which do not create an excessive level of risk or related financial failure, reputational damage or similar.

From a corporate governance perspective, the failure to exploit opportunities can be as destructive as a failure to manage the risks associated with opportunities that are exploited. The case of Kodak and the digital camera is a well-documented example of a failure to exploit a valuable opportunity.

Case study 2.2

Kodak was the market leader in photography prior to its invention of digital cameras. Despite inventing digital photography, Kodak missed many opportunities to develop it into a marketable product. Instead, Kodak decided to continue to focus on its established market of traditional film-based products.

It has been alleged that Kodak attempted to keep digital photography a secret. Although Kodak conducted market research which highlighted its potential the company failed to make the right strategic choices.

This failure in strategic decision making is as much a failure in corporate governance as the VW scandal. It is also an example of ineffective risk management. With effective risk management arrangements in place Kodak could have been able to identify, assess, monitor and control the risks associated with developing digital photography and those associated with not doing so.

The following quote from the UK Financial Reporting Council (FRC), the organisation tasked with overseeing UK corporate governance regulation, sums up these links between risk management and corporate governance:

"Good stewardship by the board should not inhibit sensible risk taking that is critical to growth. However, the assessment of risks as part of the normal business planning process should support better decision-taking, ensure that the board and management respond promptly to risks when they arise, and ensure that shareholders and other stakeholders are well informed about the principal risks and prospects of the company." (FRC, 2014, p1)

Stop and think 2.1

Reflect on the two connections between corporate governance and risk management. One of these connections relates to limiting risk exposure via the control of risks to an organisation's strategic objectives. The other relates to strategic level risk taking and may involve a significant increase in certain types of risk where there are opportunities to exploit.

What are the potential conflicts that may exist between these two areas of linkage, where one is about limiting risk and the other about increasing risk? How might these conflicts be resolved within an organisation? Can you think of any real world examples where organisations have either succeeded or failed to manage these conflicts and the consequence of this?

One example to consider is the global financial crisis where some banks, under pressure to generate higher profits, made risky but profitable strategic changes such as moving heavily into sub-prime lending or allowing customers to self-certify their income when applying for a loan but did not develop appropriate controls to manage the associated risks.

Test yourself 2.1

Corporate governance is concerned with how organisations are directed and controlled. Explain how risk management can be used to support the control and direction of organisations.

3. UK regulations: the Corporate Governance Code

Most countries have corporate governance regulations. In almost all cases, these regulations contain rules and guidance relating to risk management. The UK's Corporate Governance Code contains a significant amount of guidance on risk management, particularly on the role of the board and senior management in supporting and overseeing risk management activity.

Although the UK Corporate Governance Code is primarily aimed at public limited companies (PLCs) with a premium listing on exchanges like the London Stock Exchange (LSE), its influence goes far wider than this. Many other UK organisations comply voluntarily with the Code or follow regulations and standards that are closely related to the contents of the Code. One such standard is BS 13500 (Delivering Effective Governance of Organisations), which provides a framework that organisations can use to assess and improve their corporate governance activities on a continuous basis.

3.1 A brief history of UK corporate governance regulation

2017 marked the 25th anniversary of the UK Corporate Governance Code. In 1992, the Cadbury Report was published. This was a response to growing concerns about the standards of financial reporting and board/senior management accountability in the wake of various governance and risk management scandals, such as the failure of the Bank of Credit and Commerce International (BCCI) and the Maxwell Communication Corporation.

The Cadbury Report developed a set of principles for good corporate governance, which were incorporated into the LSE's Listing Rules. The report introduced the concept of 'comply or explain' which is the foundation of corporate governance regulation in the UK and in many other countries.

The key recommendations of the Cadbury Report were as follows:

◆ the CEO and chair roles should be separated;

◆ boards should have at least three non-executive directors (NEDs); and

◆ each board should have an audit committee made up of non-executive directors.

internal control
The systems and processes used by an organisation to ensure that organisational objectives are fulfilled and that related policies and procedures are complied with. In this context organisational objectives may include maintaining operational efficiency, protecting financial, social, and environmental performance, and ensuring compliance with legal and regulatory requirements.

Subsequent reports and committees, notably Greenbury in 1995, Hampel in 1998 and Higgs in 2003, built on the principles outlined in the Cadbury Report and extended into areas such as directors' remuneration and the appointment of a senior independent director to represent shareholder concerns. From a risk management perspective, the key milestone was the 1999 Turnbull Report. Turnbull provided additional guidance for boards on **internal control**, to ensure that sensitive issues such as financial controls and related controls in areas such as fraud and other crimes were given proper consideration by boards. This guidance was updated in 2005 and in 2014 with the publication of the FRC's Risk Guidance document.

The current version of the UK Corporate Governance Code was published in 2016 and is available from the FRC. The code includes a number of explicit principles related to risk management within organisations, particularly the role of the board in terms of risk management.

In February 2017, the FRC announced a fundamental review of the UK Corporate Governance Code. The code will remain principles based, but new requirements are expected in areas like risk management. This includes the management of softer risk issues such as **organisational culture** and **risk culture**, as well as practices for ensuring long-term financial performance and the disclosure of risk management information to stakeholders.

3.2   The 'comply or explain' approach

The UK Corporate Governance Code has always been built on a 'comply or explain' approach. This means that organisations subject to the principles and guidance contained within the code are not required to follow its contents in a strict rule-based way. An organisation may decide not to comply or to amend specific principles to better suit its situation. When organisations decide not to comply or to amend a principle, they are expected to explain publically why they have made such a decision. This requirement to explain ensures that stakeholders are kept informed of the organisation's governance arrangements and the reasons why these arrangements may not follow precisely the principles contained within the code.

For example, on the sudden loss of its CEO a board may decide that the chair is best qualified to take over the role for a brief period, to allow a new CEO to be recruited. This is clearly not compliant with the need to separate the roles of CEO and chair, but it may be tolerated by the organisation's stakeholders for a time due to the exceptional circumstances involved.

The advantages of this 'comply or explain' approach are that organisations are provided with clear principles in relation to their corporate governance practices but at the same time they are allowed a degree of flexibility in how they may apply them in their specific situation. This flexibility is appropriate, given the wide variety of contexts that organisations operate within and the diversity of their activities and operating environments.

organisational culture
The values, beliefs and assumptions that are shared by the employees of an organisation and which influence how these employees perceive the world around them, behave and make decisions.

risk culture
The values, beliefs and assumptions that are shared by the employees of an organisation and which influence how these employees perceive risk and make risk management decisions.

Stop and think 2.2

What are the potential disadvantages of a 'comply or explain' approach to corporate governance? Reflect on the incentives that organisations may have to develop weak systems of governance, along with the incentives and capabilities of boards to ensure effective governance.

Consider also whether shareholders and other stakeholders have the power they need to ensure effective compliance with governance regulations.

Test yourself 2.2

Explain the advantages and disadvantages of a 'comply or explain' approach to corporate governance regulation.

3.3 Key risk management regulations from the current UK Corporate Governance Code

The risk management provisions contained within the UK Corporate Governance Code are as follows.

principal risks
A single risk or a combination of risks that affects the performance, future prospects or reputation of an organisation to a significant degree. These include risks that could threaten the business model, future performance, solvency or liquidity.

◆ The board is responsible for managing the **principal risks** an organisation is willing to take in the pursuit of its strategic objectives. The board is also responsible for ensuring that the organisation has sound risk management and internal control systems. This should include mechanisms to monitor the soundness of these systems and reviewing the effectiveness of these systems at least annually.

◆ Non-executive directors should scrutinise management performance, including the robustness of the organisation's financial controls and risk management systems.

◆ A board audit committee or a separate board risk committee should normally be in place to support the work of the board on internal control and risk management.

◆ Information on the organisation's principal risks and the soundness of its risk management and internal control systems should be provided in the annual report.

◆ The board's work on risk management should include consideration of the organisation's appetite for risk, as well as embedding the desired culture and the related risk culture. The board should also consider the risks associated with strategic change and other major change initiatives, as well as the effectiveness of an organisation's crisis management and business continuity arrangements.

Principal risks are large scale risks to the achievement of an organisation's strategic objectives which may threaten the business model, future performance, the solvency (capital and other financial resources) and liquidity (cash flows) of an organisation. Board members clearly need to pay particular attention to these principal risks, but the UK Governance Code makes it clear that boards are responsible for overseeing the management of all risks. A board will usually delegate the management of tasks with less significant risks to lower management in the organisation.

Test yourself 2.3

What are the main risk management related principles within the UK Corporate Governance Code?

3.4 Corporate governance in organisations without a premium listing

Although the UK Corporate Governance Code was developed for PLCs on exchanges such as the LSE, many other organisations comply with some or all of the contents of the Code. A voluntary code has been developed by the Quoted Companies Alliance (QCA) for small to medium-sized companies quoted on alternative investment markets, securities exchanges and derivative exchanges. The QCA code adopts all the key elements of the UK Corporate Governance Code but adapts it to meet the needs of small to medium-sized companies.

There are specific (corporate) governance regulations and codes for public organisations, not-for-profit organisations (such as housing associations) and charities, as well as industry sectors like financial services (see Chapter 3). These regulations and codes are often adapted from the principles contained within the UK Corporate Governance Code.

Stop and think 2.3

Choose a public sector, not-for-profit or charity organisation that you are familiar with. Investigate whether this organisation is expected to comply with corporate governance regulation and whether this includes clauses on risk management.

What are the specific corporate governance regulations on risk management that this organisation is expected to comply with? Are they significantly different from the risk management related principles in the UK Corporate Governance Code?

4. Irish regulations: the Irish Companies Act 2014 and system of corporate governance

Irish corporate governance regulations are very similar to those in the UK. For the most part they are based on the UK Governance Code.

4.1 The Companies Act 2014

The Irish Companies Act 2014 came into force on 1 June 2015 with a transitional period until 30 November 2016. The Act helped to bring Irish company law up-to-date and is the largest piece of substantive statute law in Irish history. The Act set out a completely new legal architecture for corporate governance in Ireland.

The Act includes the normal requirements expected in relation to modern company law, including the requirement to file accounts, shareholder rights and the responsibilities of board members. The Act also requires companies, on a 'comply or explain' basis, to adopt appropriate compliance measures and to prepare a statement of compliance with company and tax law in their annual financial statements. The Act also provides a basis for related EU directives, such as the EU anti-money laundering and market abuse regulations.

The Act is in the process of being updated. A recent change is the Companies (Accounting) Act 2017, which put into law the EU Accounting Directive.

4.2   The Irish system of corporate governance

Corporate governance requirements exist for various types of company in the Republic of Ireland. The main requirements are applied to public companies listed on the Irish Stock Exchange (ISE).

Since the Irish Stock Exchange Act of 1995, the listing rules of the ISE have been based on the UK Corporate Governance Code (then known as the Combined Code on Corporate Governance). The Act included the adoption of the 'comply or explain' approach.

Additional corporate governance regulations for listed companies are laid out in the Irish Corporate Governance Annex. This includes two clauses on the role of the audit committee or risk committee, where appropriate. Companies are expected to include a 'meaningful description' of the work carried out by the audit or risk committee on risk management in their annual report.

Smaller companies listed on the Enterprise Securities Market may comply with the UK Corporate Governance Code and the related Irish Governance Annex on a voluntary basis, or the non-mandatory QCA Corporate Governance Code for Small and Mid-Size Quoted Companies.

As in the UK, Irish financial institutions are subject to additional risk management related corporate governance requirements (see Chapter 3).

5. European Union regulations

Developing a common EU approach to corporate governance and related risk management regulations is very challenging. Governance practices vary considerably; one notable difference is the composition of boards. Countries like the UK have a single unitary board. In contrast, countries like Germany have a dual board structure with two tiers: a management board that reports to the supervisory board. The supervisory board consists of external directors and itself reports to the shareholders or owners.

Developing a degree of consistency across the EU is necessary to facilitate the operation of the single market. It is also important to meet other objectives like the preservation of human rights, which includes factors such as health and safety, and the role of the board in ensuring that any risks related to the human rights of individuals are managed in an appropriate way. The EU has been following an action plan for corporate governance reform since 2003, which was updated in 2012. Much of this action plan does not focus directly on risk management practices but there are some relevant issues:

◆ the recruitment of independent directors who are free from any business, family or other relationship with the organisation to avoid conflicts of interest;

◆ enhanced disclosure requirements, which includes the disclosure of risk management policies; and

◆ enhancing the long-term sustainability of organisations by preventing excessive risk taking in the pursuit of short-term profits.

As in the Republic of Ireland and the UK, the focus of the EU's corporate governance work is on larger quoted companies. The approach adopted by the EU is very similar to the corporate governance regimes in the UK and Ireland, as the EU reforms were influenced significantly by the UK Corporate Governance Code. This includes the adoption of a 'comply or explain' approach.

Separate EU-wide corporate governance and related risk management regulations exist for financial organisations. These are more rule-based than in other sectors. This is to help maintain financial stability across Europe (see Chapter 3).

In addition, the EU has introduced regulations relating to financial crime and the financing of terrorism which may affect the governance and related risk management activities of some organisations. These regulations are based on the international standards adopted by the Financial Action Task Force (FATF).

There is no need for organisations to comply directly with the governance requirements set by the EU. Any EU regulations are adopted into the relevant domestic frameworks for corporate governance and risk management.

6. The G20/OECD Principles of Corporate Governance

The G20/OECD principles of corporate governance provide a worldwide benchmark for good corporate governance practice and for supervisory assessments of this practice. From a risk management perspective, the key principles are as follows.

◆ Ensuring that shareholders with a controlling interest do not force excessive risk taking to generate short-term returns because their limited liability may help to insulate them from the costs of this risk taking.

◆ Prevention of unethical or illegal practices through the use of whistleblowing controls.

◆ Public disclosure to ensure that stakeholders have information on all reasonably foreseeable material risks.

◆ The board is responsible for overseeing an organisation's internal control and risk management systems. This includes board level reviews of risk management policies and procedures and, where relevant, the creation of audit committees and risk committees to facilitate this work.

For organisations in countries like Ireland and the UK, these principles are incorporated in domestic corporate governance and related risk management regulations. The principles are also incorporated into the corporate governance regimes of other countries.

An OECD peer review report on risk management and corporate governance was published in 2014. This report reviewed the corporate governance and risk management frameworks of 27 legal jurisdictions, including India, Ireland, Saudi Arabia and the UK. The review found that, in general, risk management requirements are too focused on financial risk controls and should cover a broader range of risks to an organisation's (strategic) objectives, as is already the case in countries like Ireland and the UK.

The report found that risk governance standards in many countries are too 'high level' and perhaps could follow the more detailed provisions for financial institutions. It also concluded that more attention should be devoted to the management of potentially catastrophic sources of risk which can have large negative impacts on organisations and their stakeholders.

Test yourself 2.4

Why do organisations like the EU and OECD need to provide regulations on corporate governance and risk management?

7. World Bank corporate governance and financial reporting initiatives

The World Bank exists to provide financial and technical assistance to developing countries around the world. Its mission is to support economic development to end extreme poverty and to promote income growth for people on lower incomes.

The World Bank is a major provider of low interest loans. In addition, it provides knowledge sharing through policy advice, research and analysis. This includes corporate governance.

The World Bank recognises that effective corporate governance in private and public sector organisations is an essential element of a well-functioning market economy and can help to ensure an equitable allocation of financial and non-financial resources across stakeholder groups. Effective corporate governance can also help to protect markets and stakeholders from damaging risk events.

The World Bank's work on governance focuses on two key areas.

1. Promoting transparent and accurate financial reporting. From a risk management perspective, this should ensure that stakeholders have reliable information on which to assess the longer term performance of an organisation. This can support key activities such as corporate lending

and shareholder investments, providing creditors and investors with the confidence they need to invest.

2.   Improving the governance of state-owned enterprises, who are often providers of essential products and services to local communities and businesses. This ensures that state-owned enterprises are accountable for the quality of the products and services that they provide, as well as being free from corruption.

The World Bank provides a range of corporate governance services including advice and consultancy, training and learning programmes and diagnostic tools. The World Bank also provides data on issues such as corruption. More information is available via the World Bank website.

Stop and think 2.4

Why is corporate governance important for economic development? Take a look at the World Bank website to find out more.

8. Corporate governance regulations in other nations

Most countries have corporate governance regulations that contain clauses on risk management related topics. Some examples are provided below.

The Channel Islands

There are no generally applicable corporate governance regulations in the Channel Islands beyond the general fiduciary duties of directors that exist in company law and the requirement for directors to perform these duties with due care, skill and diligence. There are also company law requirements relating to the rights of shareholders and regulations in relation to rights of other stakeholders in areas like health and safety and the environment. Company law in the Channel Islands is generally based on company law in England and Wales.

Commercial organisations that are subsidiaries of parent companies in the UK, elsewhere in Europe or internationally must comply with some or all of the relevant regulations in the home state of their parent. This means that many Channel Island companies will take steps to comply with the elements of the UK Corporate Governance Code or associated QCA code for small to medium sized enterprises that they feel are relevant.

Specific corporate governance regulations exist for financial institutions operating in the Channel Islands, because of the effect that they can have on investor confidence and the stability of the financial system. These regulations are closely aligned to the EU and related UK corporate governance requirements for financial institutions. They are overseen by the relevant financial services commission (the Guernsey Financial Services Commission and the Jersey Financial Services Commission).

The United Arab Emirates

As in many jurisdictions, corporate governance regulations in the United Arab Emirates (UAE) focus on listed companies.

The latest corporate governance regulations from the UAE were issued in 2016. Unlike the UK, Republic of Ireland and much of the rest of Europe, these rules are not based on a 'comply or explain' principle and contravention of these rules can lead to significant fines (currently up to AED10,000,000). The UAE's corporate governance rules cover issues such as board composition, board committees, remuneration and audits. The rules also require companies to have social responsibility policies on protecting their local community and the environment. Effective internal control is required via risk management and compliance procedures and these controls must be reviewed annually. Crimes such as fraud, embezzlement and other financial crimes are subject to separate legal requirements.

There is no legal requirement for companies to have a company secretary or related governance professional but they are required to have a compliance officer.

As in most other jurisdictions, additional corporate governance and related risk management requirements exist for financial institutions.

Kenya

Company law and the associated corporate governance regulations are modelled on the UK regime, which includes the UK Corporate Governance Code. The latest Companies Act came into force in 2015 and this was extended in 2016 with new rules on competition, bribery and insurance.

The Kenyan Code of Corporate Governance for Issuers of Securities to the Public was issued in 2015 and came into force in March 2017. As in many countries, the code only applies to public listed companies. Implementation of the code is supported by the World Bank, which has helped to provide training on the code for executive and non-executive directors in Kenyan organisations.

The code includes rules that must be adhered to and good practice guidance that should be implemented on an 'apply or explain' basis, which is effectively the same as the 'comply or explain' approach. The mandatory requirements include a requirement for boards to implement an effective risk management framework, along with an effective system of internal control. There are also requirements for the establishment of an audit committee and an internal audit function. Additional guidance is provided on these requirements similar to that provided for the UK Corporate Governance Code.

Nigeria

Formal corporate governance regulation in Nigeria began with the 2003 Artedo Peterside Committee, which was set up by the Nigerian Securities and Exchange Commission. This committee developed a code of best practice for public companies in Nigeria. The code is voluntary and is designed to embed good business practices for boards and their auditors.

Compliance with the code is one of the requirements for listing with the Nigerian Stock Exchange. There are other codes for specific industries, such as banking, pensions and insurance. The mandatory aspects of corporate governance are contained within the Companies and Allied Matters Act (CAMA), Investments and Securities Act (ISA) and the Banks and Other Financial Institutions Act (BOFIA).

Mandatory requirements cover issues such as the powers of shareholders, financial reporting requirements and the requirement that public limited companies should have an audit committee. The main governance code provides minimum governance standards for listed companies and is maintained and supervised by the Securities and Exchange Commission. The governance code was last reviewed in April 2011.

The 'comply or explain' approach is used for all governance codes, except the rules-based Central Bank of Nigeria Code of Governance for Banks.

On risk management, the Securities and Exchange Commission Code of Corporate Governance states that the board of a company is responsible for the process of risk management and that it should form its own opinion on the effectiveness of this process. It also states that management is responsible for implementing and monitoring the risk management process and for embedding it into the day-to-day operations of the company.

Russian Federation

Corporate governance in the Russian Federation is formally regulated by:

◆ the Civil Code of the Russian Federation, which contains basic company law provisions;

◆ federal regulation on limited liability and joint stock companies; and

◆ central bank regulations on the issue of shares.

There is no specific regulation on corporate governance, although the Central Bank of the Russian Federation approved a new version of the Corporate Governance Code in March 2014. The Code sets out voluntary principles and recommendations for public joint stock companies, especially those who have shares traded on stock exchanges.

Although compliance with the Code is not mandatory, a company that wishes to list on a stock exchange or be included on a quotation list will usually be expected to comply with the Code. Only a few private joint stock companies and limited liability companies comply with the Code.

The Russian Federation code covers very similar elements to other governance codes, including:

◆ shareholder rights and the fair treatment of shareholders;

◆ the board of directors;

◆ the role of the company secretary;

◆ incentive arrangements (remunerations and payments to directors, the CEO and key management);

◆   risk management and internal controls, including the need for companies to maintain effective risk management and internal control systems and to review the effectiveness of these systems; and

◆   the disclosure of information.

Public joint stock companies and some other companies that must disclose business information publically must include information on how they comply with the Corporate Governance Code in their quarterly reports.

Given the voluntary nature of the code, the 'comply or explain' approach does not apply. Specific stock exchanges and other organisations active in financial markets determine how the Code applies to their specific context.

There are no mandatory reporting requirements for social, environmental or ethical issues. However, many leading public limited companies provide this information on a voluntary basis.

Test yourself 2.5

What are the problems with a voluntary corporate governance code?

Chapter summary

◆   Risk management and corporate governance are closely related. Effective risk management supports the internal control of organisations and ensures they achieve their strategic objectives.

◆   Effective risk management can support strategy development in organisations, helping boards and senior managers to develop strategies that are appropriate to the risk preferences of its stakeholders and the opportunities and threats that exist within its operating environment.

◆   Corporate governance regulation in many countries typically contains high-level reference to the importance of effective management of risk.

◆   The UK was one of the first countries to implement formal corporate governance regulation In response to various corporate scandals. The UK Corporate Governance Code is a cornerstone of corporate governance regulation and has influenced codes in many countries.

◆   The corporate governance regulation is often based on a 'comply or explain' approach. This allows organisations, who will often differ in terms of the nature, scale and complexity of their operations, a degree of flexibility on how to comply with the regulation and how to apply the various principles. As there are exceptions to this, you should check the approach used in the country in which you work.

◆   In the UK Corporate Governance Code, boards are expected to manage and report on the principal risks to which their organisation is exposed. They are also required to ensure that risk management arrangements for all other risks are appropriate and to review the effectiveness of these arrangements on a regular basis.

◆ The UK Corporate Governance Code applies to public limited companies listed on premium exchanges such as the London Stock Exchange. The corporate governance codes of most other countries also apply to listed companies only.

◆ Many smaller non-premium listed companies still comply with governance codes, though they are generally less comprehensive. The QCA Governance Code is an example of such a code.

◆ The OECD and EU have also produced corporate governance codes and regulations. These influence corporate governance and related risk management practice in organisations around the world.

◆ The World Bank provides support and guidance for developing countries on corporate governance and risk management.

◆ Additional governance regulations exist for financial institutions. These are often more prescriptive.

◆ Most countries have some form of corporate governance regulation. Many are based on the UK Corporate Governance Code. This includes countries like the Republic of Ireland, Kenya and Nigeria.

Chapter three
Sector regulators

Contents

1. Introduction

This chapter outlines the sector-specific risk management regulations that exist in different countries in:

- financial services
- health and safety
- environmental risk management.

The focus is on UK, Republic of Ireland and related EU regulations, as many other countries have similar sector-specific risk management regulations. Tables summarising the names of key sector-specific regulatory agencies in other countries and their approaches are provided.

2. Sector regulation on risk management for EU member states

The EU is a political and economic union of sovereign member states. The EU only gets involved in the regulation of risk management activities in sectors where risks cross member state boundaries. It also gets involved where the human rights of EU citizens are threatened and the protection provided by its human rights treaties and the European Court of Justice (ECJ) is considered to be insufficient.

EU regulations on risk management exist for the following areas:

◆ the stability of the financial services sector

◆ environmental protection

◆ health and safety.

In terms of health and safety, EU regulations cover areas including the safety of medicines, food safety and the health and safety of employees and consumers. Environmental protection includes the regulation and supervision of risk management practices in nuclear power stations and other environmentally hazardous activities.

EU sector regulations on risk management are documented and enforced through the use of EU directives. These directives are normally drawn up by representatives from member states with the support of the European Commission (EC), debated and voted on by the European Parliament, then finally agreed by the Council of Ministers.

One sector where the approach differs is financial services regulation for organisations within the Eurozone. The European Central Bank (ECB) has a central role in the documentation and enforcement of regulations that are not contained within EU directives. This allows financial services regulation to be updated easily to reflect changes in the risk environment and risk management practices.

2.1 The relationship between EU and member state regulation

With the exception of the ECB, the EU and its institutions do not normally have the authority to direct the risk management activities of organisations operating within member states. Once a directive is agreed, individual member states must take steps to make this directive law in their own jurisdictions. As a result, the sector risk management regulations that apply to an organisation in an EU member state may differ slightly from those included in the directive. Member states must ensure that organisations comply at a minimum with the rules in an EU directive but they can choose to go beyond these rules.

This means that organisations do not need to review specific EU directives. The relevant risk management regulations will be implemented by the government or appropriate regulatory agency in the EU member state in which they operate. Where an organisation operates in multiple EU member states, they may have to comply with slightly different regulations. Passporting arrangements are in place in certain areas, such as financial services. These arrangements allow organisations to only comply with the regulations set by their 'home' state. This is the state in which the majority of their operations and usually their head office are located.

2.2 The European Central Bank

The ECB is the central bank for all of the EU member states that have adopted the Euro. The ECB has responsibility for maintaining financial stability and

prudential regulation
Regulation that governs the financial soundness of financial institutions in order to protect the customers of these institutions and maintain financial stability.

conduct of business regulation
Regulation that governs the conduct of financial organisations, including financial institutions and any financial intermediaries which support the sale of financial products. Conduct of business regulation covers the production and supply of financial services (such as product mis-selling) and the conduct of financial market participants (such as insider dealing). Financial crimes such as money laundering and fraud also fall under conduct of business regulation.

this includes implementing and enforcing risk management regulations for all systemically important financial institutions which operate within the relevant member states.

A systemically important financial institution is any bank, insurance company, or other financial institution whose failure may affect the stability of the financial system and potentially trigger a financial crisis. Most large banks, insurers, and investment firms are considered to be systemically important.

The ECB's authority applies to all systemically important financial institutions operating in countries that have chosen to use the Euro as their main currency. It does not apply to financial institutions operating in countries such as the UK, because the UK is not part of the Eurozone.

UK-based systemically important financial institutions are regulated by the UK Prudential Regulatory Authority (PRA) and the Financial Conduct Authority (FCA), but any operations that they have within the Eurozone may fall under the jurisdiction of the ECB, depending on the nature and scale of these activities. The same applies to financial institutions from other non-Euro countries.

The ECB is accountable to the European Parliament, but has its own Governing Council, which is its main decision making body. The Governing Council oversees the sector risk management regulation that is implemented and enforced by the ECB.

The ECB is only responsible for risk management regulation that relates to financial stability (**prudential regulation**). All other risk management regulation, such as **conduct of business regulation**, is the responsibility of each individual member state, subject to any relevant EU directives.

Stop and think 3.1

Why is a single central bank required to regulate financial stability in the Eurozone? The ECB's website will help provide the answers.

Test yourself 3.1

Which organisations does the ECB regulate?

2.3   Other EU-wide risk management regulators

The EU has a range of agencies that that support the regulation of risk management and the implementation of related EU directives in one sector or another. These agencies include:

◆   European Agency for Safety and Health at Work
◆   European Atomic Energy Community
◆   European Aviation Safety Agency

◆ European Banking Authority

◆ European Chemicals Agency

◆ European Food Safety Authority

◆ European Insurance and Occupational Pensions Authority

◆ European Maritime and Safety Agency

◆ European Medicines Agency

◆ EU Agency for Network and Information Security.

Few of these agencies issue regulatory rules that must be complied with. Rules are contained within the relevant EU directives and are implemented by each member state through their own legal systems. Instead, these agencies issue guidance on how to comply in an effective way. This guidance will often cover risk management-related activities. Organisations operating in a sector covered by a particular agency should be familiar with the work of the agency in question. Agencies may also work in partnership with a member state regulator to support its supervisory and enforcement activities in relation to the rules contained within EU directives.

3. Financial services risk management regulation

The sector with the largest amount of risk management regulation is financial services. This is partly because of the effect that financial institutions can have on financial stability and partly because of high levels of information asymmetry between financial services institutions and their stakeholders. These asymmetries could lead to misconduct, in the form of mis-selling, market manipulation and financial crime.

Risk management regulation for financial institutions covers three main areas:

1. the financial solvency of financial institutions
2. financial market stability
3. the conduct of financial institutions, their employees and intermediaries.

Areas one and two are usually grouped together and termed prudential regulation, while area three is termed conduct of business regulation.

Financial services risk management regulation in most countries is influenced by a range of international agencies and agreements (see Chapter 1). This includes the Bank for International Settlements (BIS) and the Financial Stability Board (FSB), as well as the European Banking Authority (EBA) and ECB in the EU.

3.1 British financial regulators

The risk management activities of organisations operating within the financial services sector in the British Isles are regulated by a number of agencies:

◆ Prudential Regulatory Authority

◆ Financial Conduct Authority

◆ Financial Ombudsman
◆ Guernsey Financial Services Commission (GFSC), if operating in Guernsey
◆ Jersey Financial Services Commission (JFSC) if operating in Jersey
◆ Isle of Man Financial Services Authority, if operating in the Isle of Man.

The PRA, FCA and Financial Ombudsman regulate financial service sector organisations authorised to operate in the UK; they have no jurisdiction over organisations that are authorised to operate in the crown dependencies of Jersey, Guernsey and the Isle of Man. Organisations authorised to operate in the crown dependencies cannot provide financial services to UK or EU residents. This prevents an organisation from exploiting any regulatory loopholes.

Some of the above agencies do not only regulate financial institutions. Any organisation that is involved in some form of financial service, such as handling client money, providing financial advice or acting as a financial intermediary is likely to be regulated by one or more of these agencies (especially the FCA and Financial Ombudsman if operating in the UK). This includes law and accounting firms, estate agencies and car dealerships.

The Prudential Regulatory Authority

The PRA was created as part of the Financial Services Act 2012 and regulates around 1,500 banks, building societies, insurers, credit unions and larger investment firms. The PRA is part of the Bank of England and has three statutory objectives:

1. to promote the financial safety and soundness of the firms it regulates;
2. for insurers, securing an appropriate degree of protection for existing and potential future policyholders; and
3. facilitating effective competition.

The PRA is responsible for drafting regulatory policy and the supervision of the organisations that it regulates. The policy consists of rules and guidance, all of which is contained within the PRA Rulebook. The PRA Rulebook contains different provisions for different types of organisation (such as banks or insurers), as well as organisations that are subject to EU financial regulations and those that are not.

Much of the PRA's regulatory policy is influenced by EU directives. This will continue as long as UK financial institutions operate across the EU. Irrespective of the type of organisation or whether it is covered by EU directives, much of the policy in the PRA Rulebook is related to the practice of risk management. This policy includes:

◆ financial resources requirements relating to the capital buffers that must be maintained to protect against unexpected losses;
◆ the role of auditors and audit committees;
◆ other roles and responsibilities for risk management, including the board, senior managers and the risk management function;

- the management of specific types of risk, such as market, credit and operational risk;
- risk control in general; and
- risk reporting to external stakeholders.

The PRA supervises the organisations that it regulates to ensure that they comply with its rulebook. This supervision includes:

- demanding detailed financial and risk management reports;
- the review of risk management policies and other documents;
- visits to talk with board members, senior managers, risk management and audit professionals; and
- enforcement action, including fines, where necessary.

Company secretaries and governance professionals in organisations regulated by the PRA are likely to be involved in supporting their organisations to manage these supervisory activities.

The Financial Conduct Authority

The FCA was established in 2013 and regulates the financial conduct of around 56,000 financial and non-financial organisations. The aim of the FCA is to ensure that financial markets operate honestly and fairly so that all stakeholders, especially consumers, get a fair deal. This includes ensuring that stakeholders understand the financial risks that they are taking and their potential negative consequences.

The FCA is also involved in the prudential regulation of 18,000 smaller financial organisations. These organisations are not considered a threat to the stability of financial markets but their failure could cause their customers to suffer major financial losses. The FCA looks to protect these customers from these losses.

The FCA's three main objectives are as follows:

1. consumer protection;
2. protecting the integrity of financial markets from misconduct (such as insider trading); and
3. promoting competition in financial markets to ensure that consumers get a fair deal.

The FCA incorporates the UK Listing Authority, which regulates the issuing of securities including company shares and bonds.

The FCA issues regulatory policy and supervises firms to ensure that they comply with this policy. The FCA's regulatory policy and supervisory activities cover many risk management activities, including:

- roles and responsibilities for risk management, especially in relation to the management of conduct-related risks;
- the management of financial crime risks, including money laundering and terrorist financing;

◆ the management of other conduct-related risks including mis-selling, insider trading, market manipulation, protecting client money and unfair contract terms;

◆ compliance management;

◆ the purchase of professional indemnity insurance;

◆ whistleblowing; and

◆ disclosing the risks associated with financial products and investments.

Test yourself 3.2

Compare and contrast the objectives of the PRA and FCA.

Stop and think 3.2

Identify whether the organisation that you work for or another that you are familiar with is regulated by the Financial Conduct Authority. Usually this is made clear on the website and on any correspondence with external stakeholders like customers.

The Financial Ombudsman

The Financial Ombudsman helps to resolve disputes between financial organisations and their customers. Where the Financial Ombudsman decides that a customer has been treated unfairly, it has legal powers to put the situation right.

The Financial Ombudsman does not directly regulate the risk management activities of financial organisations, but it does issue judgements that can affect their risk management activities. The judgements that the Financial Ombudsman has made in relation to the mis-selling of payment protection insurance (PPI) is one example.

Case study 3.1

Payment protection insurance, also known as credit protection insurance and loan repayment insurance, is a form of insurance that provides funds to help repay a loan if a borrower dies, is ill or injured or loses their job.

PPI is a useful form of insurance and can be sold as a standalone policy or as an add-on to a mortgage, personal loan or some other form of debt such as an overdraft or credit card. In the UK the growth in popularity of PPI as an add-on product took place in the 1990s. Billions of pounds in premium income was generated.

Standalone PPI policies were not generally mis-sold but many add-on policies have been found to have been mis-sold. Mis-selling occurred because the contractual provisions of the policy made it very difficult to claim or because information was hidden from customers, such as the full cost of cover or claim limits. In some cases, customers were not aware that they had purchased PPI.

Concerns about PPI mis-selling began in the 1990s but it was not until 2005, when a super-complaint was brought by the Citizens Advice Bureau, that financial institutions were required to make changes to how they sold PPI and provide compensation to all affected customers.

It is estimated that financial institutions will have to pay up to £36 billion in re-paid premiums and compensation for mis-selling before the August 2019 deadline for claims. The scandal has led to significant changes in selling practices to avoid similar problems in the future. It has also forced financial institutions to hold back large sums of money in provisions for these claims.

Guernsey and Jersey financial services commissions and the Isle of Man
Crown dependencies such as the Bailiwicks of Jersey and Guernsey are not part of the EU or the UK's financial services regulatory regime and have their own sector regulations for financial services organisations. These jurisdictions balance attracting financial services organisations and investment against protecting consumers and ensuring financial stability. The level of regulation is generally lower than in the UK, Republic of Ireland and the rest of Europe.

Jersey and Guernsey each maintain their own individual systems of financial services regulation, as do all the other crown dependencies, such as the Isle of Man. These systems are based on EU and associated UK financial services regulation but not all of the requirements set out in EU directives and UK financial services regulations apply to financial institutions operating in these crown dependencies. UK and EU residents cannot generally access the services provided by financial institutions operating in crown dependencies, meaning that only customers residing outside of the UK and EU can use their services. This ensures that the financial institutions operating in crown dependencies do not directly threaten the welfare of UK and EU consumers or the UK and wider European financial system.

In Jersey, the creation of financial services regulation and its associated supervision is undertaken by the JFSC. Guernsey has the GFSC, while the Isle of Man has the Isle of Man Financial Services Authority.

3.2   Irish regulators

The prudential regulation of large systemically important financial institutions in the Republic of Ireland is undertaken by the ECB, as Ireland uses the Euro as its currency. Systemically important financial institutions includes all banks and some larger insurance companies and investment funds, but excludes sectors such as Irish credit unions, as the services they provide are on a small, local scale.

The prudential regulation of non-systemically important financial institutions, as well as all conduct of business regulation is undertaken by the Central Bank of Ireland. Much of this regulation is influenced by EU directives and is very similar in approach to that adopted by the PRA and FCA in the UK.

The Central Bank of Ireland regulates over 10,000 firms providing financial services in Ireland. As in other EU countries, this regulation is undertaken through risk-based supervision underpinned by the threat of enforcement action. The Central Bank of Ireland's objective is to ensure financial stability, consumer protection and market integrity. To achieve this objective the Bank has a range of regulatory powers in the areas of authorisation, supervision and enforcement. These enforcement powers include the ability to fine and to close down non-compliant financial organisations or to remove directors.

3.3   Financial services sector regulators in other countries

Most countries have financial services regulations and regulators. A significant amount of this regulation is similar in approach to that implemented in the EU. Table 3.1 provides a list of financial services regulators and their approaches to regulation.

4. Health and safety regulation

Most organisations in most countries are subject to health and safety regulation. Health and safety regulation exists to protect stakeholders from death, injury and ill health (whether physical or mental health). The key stakeholder groups that are protected are employees, customers and third parties. Third parties may include households who may live near an organisation and who may be affected by its activities, such as by noise, air, or ground pollution.

Health and safety regulation exists because the market-based incentives for appropriate levels of health and safety risk management are generally thought to be insufficient. Workers or customers could, for example, incentivise health and safety activities by demanding higher wages or paying a lower price if they believe their health or safety to be at risk. However, market-based incentives can be ineffective because of asymmetric information and public good problems (see Chapter 1).

Health and safety regulations generally cover the following risk management activities:

hazard
Anything that may cause physical or mental harm to an organisation's stakeholders. Common hazards include poisonous chemicals, electricity, working at height, working excessively long hours, trip hazards such as an open drawer and the utilisation of machinery.

- the identification and assessment of health and safety **hazards**, including determining who might be affected (employees, customers and so on) and how they might be affected (injury or ill-health);
- taking appropriate measures to control health and safety hazards to protect stakeholders from harm;
- recording health and safety incidents and reporting major incidents to the relevant regulatory agency; and
- implementing appropriate policies and procedures for all of the above.

Country or region	Financial regulator(s)	Approach
Africa	In Kenya, financial regulation is provided by the Central Bank of Kenya and the Capital Markets Authority. In other countries, the primary regulator for banks and non-banks is the central bank. This includes the Central Bank of Nigeria and the Bank of Ghana.	Similar to the EU and related UK approach to financial services regulation. Risk-based regulation and supervision is often used to ensure financial stability and protect consumers. This means that the focus is on larger, more complex financial institutions. Rules exist in relation to financial resources requirements and risk management.
The Caribbean	Each Caribbean state has its own agency for financial services regulation and supervision. This includes the Barbados Financial Services Commission, Central Bank of the Bahamas and the Financial Services Commission of Jamaica. Most states also have a central bank to oversee financial stability in general.	In the English-speaking Caribbean Islands the approaches adopted are similar to that in the UK. As in the crown dependencies, the level of prescriptiveness and the intensity of supervision are generally lower than the UK, to help attract inward investment and because most financial institutions in these states are relatively small and are not a threat to global financial stability.
Mauritius	Bank of Mauritius and the Financial Services Commission	The Bank of Mauritius regulates banks and the Commission regulates non-bank financial institutions. These organisations are responsible for both prudential regulation and conduct of business regulation. They operate in a similar way to EU and UK regulatory agencies.
Russian Federation	Central Bank of the Russian Federation	The central bank operates as the single regulator for all financial institutions and other financial services organisations in Russia. The bank covers both prudential regulation and conduct of business regulation. This includes capital resources and risk management requirements.
United Arab Emirates	The UAE Insurance Authority, Securities and Commodities Authority and the Dubai Financial Services Authority	The UAE Insurance Authority regulates insurance providers and intermediaries. The Securities and Commodities Authority covers financial markets and the Dubai Financial Services Authority regulates all activities within the Dubai International Financial Centre. The approach to financial services regulation is similar to that in the EU and UK.

Table 3.1 Financial services regulators in other countries and regions

Most countries manage their health and safety regulations via government-appointed agencies. These agencies draw their power from laws that enable them to:

◆ implement new rules and guidance on health and safety management processes or the control of specific hazards;

◆ supervise the health and safety management activities of organisations; and

◆ take enforcement action to address any non-compliance.

Test yourself 3.3

Why are market-based incentives for health and safety risk management often thought to be insufficient?

4.1　Health and safety agencies in the British Isles

As with the financial services sector there is one agency for the UK and separate agencies for each of the crown dependencies:

◆ the Health and Safety Executive (HSE) for the UK

◆ the Guernsey Health and Safety Executive

◆ the Health and Safety Inspectorate for Jersey

◆ the Health and Safety at Work Inspectorate for the Isle of Man.

The UK Health and Safety Executive
The HSE is an independent health and safety regulator that draws its powers from the Health and Safety at Work Act 1974. The Act gave the HSE its powers to create regulations, inspect health and safety practices in organisations and take enforcement action, such as issuing fines, where necessary.

The 1974 Act places expectations on employees and employers, but prime responsibility for providing a safe working environment rests with the employer – which means an organisation's management and directors. Employers are expected to ensure that employees are protected from hazards that may endanger their health and safety 'as far as reasonably practical'. This includes providing appropriate levels of protection against hazards including fire, 'slips, trips and falls', dangerous equipment, excessively long working hours or undue workplace stress. In return, employees are expected to co-operate with the health and safety activities of their employers and to act responsibly to ensure that they do not endanger themselves or others.

The Act covers non-employees who may be at a place of work, including contractors, suppliers, customers, and third parties.

In addition to its regulatory, inspection and, enforcement powers, the HSE issues a wide range of guidance documents, designed to help an organisation to improve its health and safety management practices. This guidance is topic and industry-based. Topics include:

- dealing with asbestos;
- workplace stress;
- working at height;
- completing risk assessments;
- preventing slips, trips and falls;
- occupational diseases; and
- dealing with noise, vibration, gas and electricity.

Industry specific guidance covers sectors like:

- nuclear power;
- fishing and farming;
- quarries;
- food;
- diving;
- tree work;
- cleaning; and
- the production and use of chemicals and explosives.

Stop and think 3.3

Choose an organisation within an industry sector that you are familiar with. Go to the HSE website and look at the guidance on offer. Identify the relevant guidance topics and industry sector guidance for your chosen organisation.

The HSE is responsible for enforcing three further pieces of UK legislation:

1. Control of Substances Hazardous to Health (COSHH) Regulations 2002
2. Reporting of Injuries, Diseases and Dangerous Occurrences Regulations (RIDDOR) 2013
3. Employers Liability (Compulsory Insurance) Act 1969

The COSHH regulations apply to substances that are deemed to be especially hazardous, such as acids, fumes, dusts and vapours, plus more modern developments such as nanotechnology and germs that are used in laboratories. Hazards such as asbestos and radiation are dealt with separately. Many organisations are affected by the COSHH regulations. For example, dangerous cleaning products like bleach are covered by the regulations, as is dust generated within agricultural processes and baking. Areas such as hairdressing and beauty are also covered by the regulations because of the chemical products, like peroxide, that may be used.

The RIDDOR regulations apply to all organisations in the UK. Here, organisations are required to report to the HSE any significant injuries, diseases or dangerous occurrences. Reportable incidents include:

- the death of any person on an organisation's premises;
- work-related accidents that result in serious injury (such as bone fractures, loss of limbs or serious burns);
- work-related accidents that incapacitate a worker for more than seven days (accidents that cause a worker to be incapacitated between three and seven days must be recorded in a register, but do not need to be reported to the HSE);
- non-fatal accidents to non-workers (such as a customer) that require them to be taken immediately (from the organisation's premises) to hospital for treatment;
- occupation-related diseases such as cancer or dermatitis or which arise due to contact with a biological agent;
- dangerous occurrences such as the collapse of a part of a building, a serious fire, equipment coming into contact with electrical cables and so on; and
- gas-related incidents, such as an accidental gas leak.

The premises of many organisations are subject to periodic inspections by trained HSE inspectors. The inspector will review health and safety management practices and examine how they are implemented. Areas of non-compliance with HSE regulations will be identified and an organisation will be issued enforcement notices that allow it a set time period to achieve compliance. The frequency of inspections is usually risk-based: the premises of an organisation that operates in a high-risk sector or one that reports high numbers of RIDDOR incidents will be inspected more frequently.

The Employers Liability (Compulsory Insurance) Act 1969 requires most organisations to maintain employers' liability insurance. This helps the employer to pay compensation if an employee is injured or becomes ill because of the work they do. The purpose of this insurance is to ensure that an employee will receive the funds that they are due if they make a successful liability claim against their employer for a health or safety related incident. If, for example, an organisation was to declare bankruptcy after a claim is awarded, then the employee might not receive the award. Compulsory insurance ensures that all legitimate claims are paid.

The Guernsey Health and Safety Executive

The Health and Safety Executive in Guernsey regulates workplace health and safety in Guernsey and Alderney. As part of this role, the Health and Safety Executive:

- provides advice;
- inspects workplace premises;
- investigates major accidents;

◆ ensures compliance with the relevant Guernsey law via enforcement notices and prosecutions; and

◆ licenses the use of hazardous materials.

The Guernsey Health and Safety Executive operates in a very similar way to the UK HSE. This includes the issuing of general ordinance (rules) on health and safety management in organisations, such as the duties of employers and employees. It also issues specific regulations for activities and substances that are deemed to be of high risk, such as petroleum and explosives. Organisations are required to purchase employers liability insurance.

The Jersey Health and Safety Inspectorate

The Jersey Health and Safety Inspectorate exists to enforce the health and safety laws of the States of Jersey, especially the Health and Safety at Work (Jersey) Law 1989. The Inspectorate provides advice and guidance and it also conducts health and safety inspections and investigates complaints and serious incidents.

As in the other jurisdictions of the British Isles, Jersey employers are legally required to provide their employees with:

◆ a safe place of work;

◆ proper health and safety training and information; and

◆ adequate welfare facilities on site, including access to water, first aid and heating.

Employees are expected to act responsibly and not endanger themselves or others while at work. They are also expected to use any safety equipment that is provided.

Jersey employers are expected to maintain employers liability insurance in accordance with the Employers Liability (Compulsory Insurance) (Jersey) Law 1973.

The Inspectorate has issued a range of regulations on specific activities and industries that are considered to be especially hazardous. This includes:

◆ asbestos;

◆ construction;

◆ cranes and lifting appliances;

◆ electricity at work;

◆ flammable liquids; and

◆ students on work experience.

Guidance in the form of 'codes of practice' have also been issued, in areas such as:

◆ working with ionising radiation;

◆ use of display screen equipment;

- diving safety;
- woodworking; and
- the safe use of machinery

Jersey-based employers are encouraged to use the resources provided by the UK HSE in areas such as the control of substances hazardous to health.

The Health and Safety at Work Inspectorate for the Isle of Man

The legal and regulatory framework for health and safety regulation in the Isle of Man rests on two key documents:

1. Health and Safety at Work etc. Act 1974; and
2. The Management of Health and Safety at Work Regulations 2003.

As in Jersey and Guernsey, this framework is very similar to that adopted in the UK. Organisations are required to carry out health and safety risk assessments and to ensure that effective controls are in place for any hazards that have been identified. Inspections of the premises of organisations operating in hazardous areas are carried out. Enforcement action is taken where serious breaches of the legislation are identified and organisations do not take appropriate steps to address these.

4.2 Irish Health and Safety Authority

The Irish Health and Safety Authority (IHSA) was established in 1989, under the Safety, Health and Welfare at Work Act 1989 (updated in 2005). The main roles of the Authority are to:

- protect employees from work related injury and ill-health via enforcing health and safety law, promoting accident prevention and providing information and advice to organisations across all industry sectors;
- oversee the operation of Irish and EU chemical regulations including the Registration, Evaluation, Authorisation and Restriction of Chemicals Regulation and the Seveso II Directive;
- to protect human health and the environment; and
- to conduct market surveillance to ensure that products bought and sold in the Republic of Ireland are compliant with the relevant health and safety regulations.

These roles mean that the work of the Authority is wider than many other health and safety authorities, given the focus on the environment and product safety as well as workplace safety.

The IHSA has issued a wide range of documents including regulations, codes of practice and guidance documents. These documents cover similar industries and topics to the UK HSE. The key piece of regulation for most organisations is the Safety, Health and Welfare at Work (General Application) Regulations 2007, most recently updated in 2016.

This regulation requires employers to identify hazards, assess the associated health and safety risks and to take steps to control these risks. This includes topics such as premises and machine safety, supply and use of protective equipment, manual handling, first aid, room temperatures and fire safety. Subsequent updates to the regulation cover specific activities and systems such as pressure systems, like boilers, woodworking and abrasive blasting.

4.3   Health and safety regulators in other countries

Most countries have health and safety laws, as well as a regulator tasked with managing the implementation and enforcement of these laws. Table 3.2 (see page 56 provides a list of these regulators and summarises their approaches.

Country profiles on national health and safety laws and regulators can be obtained via the International Labour Organisation's Occupational Safety and Health website.

5. Environmental regulation

Organisational activities can cause a range of environmental problems, including:

◆   pollution of the air, water or earth;

◆   resource shortages (such as excessive reduction of a local water table);

◆   the destruction of natural habitats;

◆   excessive noise;

◆   the generation of greenhouse gasses such as CO_2; and

◆   geological problems, such as subsidence or earthquakes.

These environmental problems can affect the health and safety of organisational stakeholders, as well as causing widespread environmental damage including global warming and the extinction of animal and plant species.

Environmental regulation exists because the free market cannot properly discipline organisations. One problem is asymmetric information, where stakeholders often do not have full information on the effects that organisational activities may have on the environment. This is a particular problem in relation to environmental pollution because it may take many years for effects to be realised, such as an increase in the rate of cancer.

Another problem is the issue of public goods. Pollution prevention is a public good because organisations and their stakeholders do not receive the full benefits of this prevention but incur all of the costs. As a result, there may be insufficient pollution prevention without regulation. This is especially the case where an environmental problem affects a large geographical area, as in the case of global warming.

Because of the public good nature of many environmental problems, international agreements and treaties exist to help mitigate the effects. One example of this is the Kyoto Protocol.

Country or region	Health and safety regulators	Approach
Africa	Kenya: Directorate of Occupational Safety and Health Services Nigeria: National Council for Occupational Safety and Health Ghana: Ministry of Employment and Labour Relations	Regulators are typically part of a government ministry and draw their powers from legal statutes. Regulators have the power to implement regulations, inspect premises, investigate major incidents, and take enforcement action. In most cases, laws exist to ensure that appropriate compensation is paid to injured workers where necessary – such as the Nigerian Employee Compensation Act 2010.
Caribbean	Regulation is usually provided by the government labour ministry, such as the Ministry of Labour and Social Security in Jamaica	Legal authority comes from specific health and safety acts as well as factory, construction and dock safety acts. Laws make clear the obligations of employers both in terms of health and safety and worker welfare. Government inspectors are often used to inspect premises and take enforcement action where necessary.
Mauritius	Ministry of Labour, Industrial Relations and Employment, assisted by an Advisory Council for Occupational Safety and Health	Employers are expected to implement an appropriate health and safety management system and safe systems of work. They are also expected to provide training and any necessary safety equipment. Regulations exist in relation to product safety. Various guidelines and codes of practice are available.
Russian Federation	Ministry of Labour and Social Security of the Russian Federation	The regulatory framework is complex and consists of a large number of decrees on specific activities such as construction and manufacturing, as well as topics such as smoking in the workplace and workplace hygiene. A social insurance fund is in place to provide compensation to workers in the event of injury.
United Arab Emirates	Ministry of Labour Ministry of Health	Health and safety regulation is based on the UAE federal law on labour (1980). In addition, Order No. 32 of 1982 on Protection from Hazards and Ministerial Decision No. 37/2 of 1982 are fundamental federal laws. Other regulations address specific hazards on a national level, such as Federal Law No. 1 of 2002 on use, monitoring and protection from radioactive material or the Determination of Retentive Methods and Measures for the Protection of Workers from the Risks Work (Ministerial Order no 32 –1982).

Table 3.2 Health and safety regulators

Case study 3.2

The Kyoto Protocol is an international treaty that extended an earlier UN convention on climate change in the 1990s. The purpose of the protocol is to limit global warming by controlling human-made carbon dioxide emissions. Higher limits on emissions are applied to countries that have been industrialised for the longest, on the grounds that they have contributed the most towards global warming.

The protocol is now in its second round of carbon dioxide emission limit commitments. The first round took place from 2008 to 2012 and the second round commenced in 2012.

Most of the world's countries have signed up to their second round commitments for limiting carbon dioxide. This includes the UK and Republic of Ireland. Other countries like Russia and Japan have not taken on new commitments in the second round of the protocol, though they did meet their first round commitments.

It is up to national governments and environmental regulators to implement these agreements and treaties. Many countries go beyond international agreements and treaties to better protect their local environment.

5.1   Environmental agencies in the British Isles

Within the UK, environmental laws and regulations are implemented and enforced by the Environment Agency (EA). The remit of the EA is very broad and encompasses the following:

◆   management of UK waterways;

◆   chemicals (land and air contamination, licensing and so on);

◆   meeting EU and international climate change agreement obligations, including regulating greenhouse gas emissions;

◆   promoting energy efficiency;

◆   environmental permits;

◆   managing and investigating environmental incidents;

◆   managing UK fisheries;

◆   flooding;

◆   industrial waste management;

◆   nuclear safety;

◆   oil storage and spills;

◆   protecting environmentally sensitive sites; and

◆   general wildlife and habitat conservation.

The EA is an executive non-departmental public body, sponsored by the Department for Environment, Food and Rural Affairs. This means that the EA is technically independent from government and has its own board of directors but it is responsible for implementing government policy. The EA has the power to take enforcement action against organisations and individuals where necessary. This can include prohibition orders to stop polluting activities and criminal prosecution resulting in fines and imprisonment for serious environmental offences.

Environmental regulation within the Crown Dependencies of Jersey, Guernsey and the Isle of Man is managed by the relevant government departments. These are:

◆   Isle of Man Department of Environment, Food and Agriculture

◆   Jersey Department of the Environment

◆   Guernsey Department of the Environment.

These departments have similar responsibilities to the UK EA, but local regulations can vary.

5.2   Irish Environmental Protection Agency

The Environmental Protection Agency (EPA) is responsible for environmental regulation in the Republic of Ireland. The EPA operates with the authority of the Department of Communications, Climate Action and Environment but is an independent agency with its own Advisory Committee.

The scope of the EPA's activities is very similar to the UK EA. The EPA is involved in environmental monitoring and assessment activities, licensing and permits, education and where necessary enforcement.

5.3   Environmental regulators in other countries

All countries have some form of environmental regulation and an environmental regulator. Table 3.3 lists some of these regulators and summarises their approaches.

Test yourself 3.4

Describe the regulatory powers of a typical environmental regulator.

Country or region	Environmental regulators	Approach
Africa	Kenya: National Environment Management Authority Nigeria: National Environmental Standards and Regulations Enforcement Agency Ghana: Ghana Environmental Protection Agency	Regulators typically report to a government ministry and draw their powers from legal statutes. Regulators have a wide remit covering issues such as land use, the extraction of natural resources, nature conservation and pollution. They are involved in implementing regulatory policy, training and education and enforcement.
Caribbean	Some states have a central environmental regulator, such as the National Environment and Planning Agency in Jamaica. Others rely on government ministries and departments.	Marine biodiversity and pollution are key issues in the Caribbean, as is the management of natural resources. Regulators have all the usual range of powers and draw their authority from national laws.
Mauritius	Ministry of Social Security, National Solidarity and Environment and Sustainable Development	The Department of the Environment within the Ministry has a broad scope and covers issues such as global warming, pollution and sustainable development. The Department monitors and enforces compliance with environmental laws and is also involved in local policy development and education.
Russian Federation	Ministry of Natural Resources and the Environment of the Russian Federation	The Ministry of Natural Resources and the Environment is responsible for the creation and enforcement of policies and regulations dealing with the environment, including conservation, regeneration, forestry and wildlife protection. It is also responsible for the exploration, management and conservation of the country's natural resources, including the management of the water supply, mineral deposit development, and the exploration of the country's territory and continental shelf. The Ministry regulates industrial and energy safety and monitors geological and earthquake activities.
United Arab Emirates	Federal Environmental Authority, which reports to the Federal Ministry of Climate Change and Environment.	The Federal Environmental Authority was created in 1993 to help co-ordinate environmental regulation and consolidate the diverse array of laws. The Authority is involved in a range of activities including pollution prevention, wildlife protection and the prevention of disease. The Authority also oversees compliance with the international treaties and agreements that the UAE has signed up to.

Table 3.3 Environmental regulators

Chapter summary

◆   Sector-specific risk management regulations exist in three main areas: financial services, health and safety, and environmental management.

◆   Financial services regulation in Europe is led by the EU. This helps maintain the stability of the European and global financial systems, which are highly interconnected.

◆   Financial services sector risk management regulation covers two areas: prudential regulation and conduct of business regulation. In some countries these areas are covered by separate regulators (UK and the Republic of Ireland). In others a single regulator is used, as in the case of Russia.

◆   Health and safety and environmental regulation combat asymmetric information and public good problems.

◆   Health and safety regulation is primarily focused on employees but often helps to also protect consumers (product safety) and third parties (contractors). This regulation seeks to protect stakeholders from injury and ill health, including mental ill health in some countries.

◆   Environmental regulation protects stakeholders and local, national and global eco-systems from environmental hazards such as pollution and global warming. Most countries have some form of environmental regulation and an environmental regulator.

Chapter four
Risk management frameworks and standards

Contents

1. Introduction

This chapter outlines the elements which comprise a typical risk management framework. It builds on the international standard for risk management, ISO 31000:2018, as well as a number of national standards and guides. The chapter provides a high-level, 'umbrella' view of what a risk management framework can look like. Further detail follows in subsequent chapters.

Risk management standards are not compulsory. There is no one single, best way to design a risk management framework. The role of risk management standards is to provide a benchmark for good practice but not every organisation will need to incorporate all of the good practice contained within a standard. When designing and implementing a risk management framework, it is up to the relevant actors in an organisation – the board, senior management and any risk management professionals – to decide what is appropriate for the organisation and its stakeholders.

2. The contents of a risk management framework

Risk management activity may be implicit or explicit. Consider your actions when you cross a road. Before you decide to cross the road, you look and listen to see if any vehicles are approaching and to assess their speed and distance. You may decide to walk to a safe place, such as a pedestrian crossing to further reduce the risk of an accident. You continue to look and listen for vehicles as you cross. All of these activities are risk management activities, even if you have not considered them to be such. Instead they are implicit activities that you engage in instinctively, often several times a day.

The risk management activities of organisations and the people that work within these organisations can be implicit and instinctive. Such an approach is unlikely to yield successful results on a long-term basis. Modern organisations face a wide range of risks and have a multitude of decision makers. Hundreds, if not thousands, of complex risk management decisions have to be made on a daily basis. To rely on intuition in this context is ineffective; it will lead to inconsistent and incorrect risk management decisions. An organisation needs a formal, explicit risk management framework to ensure that its risk management decisions support the achievement of its strategic objectives and that the risk preferences of its stakeholders are taken into account.

A recent conceptual perspective on risk management frameworks comes from ISO 31000:2018, as illustrated in Figure 4.1.

This ISO distinguishes between a risk management framework, principles and process. However, this does not imply that these elements are independent. Notice the direction of the arrows. The principle and process elements feed into the framework element. A risk management framework also includes risk management principles and the risk management process.

The ISO perspective is conceptual and so helps to avoid the confusion that can sometimes exist between these three elements. In practice, the term framework is used to refer to the variety of policies, procedures, processes and tools that comprise an organisation's risk management activities. The purpose of these policies, processes and tools is to provide a coherent structure to support the management of risk within the organisation. This framework should ensure that the level of risk taking within the organisation supports the achievement of its strategic objectives and is consistent with the risk preferences of its stakeholders. This will include taking potentially positive risks in order to exploit potential business opportunities, while at the same time attempting to prevent and mitigate more damaging risks, such as fraud, health and safety events, fires or pollution. The ultimate aim is to use the risk management framework to add value to an organisation, helping it to operate in a successful and sustainable way over the long term.

At a minimum, a risk management framework for a typical organisation will include mechanisms for:

◆ the identification of risks which could impact the organisation in either a positive or negative way;
◆ assessing the significance of identified risks, in order to help prioritise management attention and financial resources;
◆ monitoring to help detect any changes in the organisation's exposure to identified risks; and
◆ controlling the organisation's exposure to the risks that have been identified.

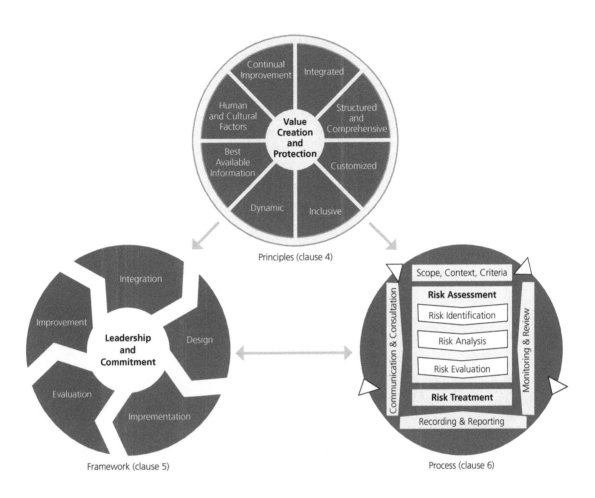

Figure 4.1 Principles, frameworks and risk management processes from ISO 31000 (Source: ISO)

These four activities: risk identification, risk assessment, risk monitoring and risk control are often known collectively as the risk management process (see Chapter 7).

Stop and think 4.1

How prescriptively do you think an organisation should use its risk management framework to control the risk management decisions of its employees and managers? Should the level of autonomy be limited or should decision makers be allowed some discretion?

Should every type of organisation implement equally prescriptive risk management frameworks? Consider, for example, a nuclear power plant versus an organisation that engages in research and development.

The four activities of the risk management process provide a solid foundation for any risk management framework but it is common for an organisation to add further elements. The 'A structured approach to Enterprise Risk Management (ERM) and the requirements of ISO 31000' report talks about three core elements: risk management architecture (committees, reporting structures and so on); risk management strategy (risk policies and risk appetite, for example) and risk management protocols (processes and procedures). In practice these elements will be contained within:

◆ a risk management policy or a series of policies for different categories of risk;

◆ risk management procedures;

◆ risk management information systems;

◆ risk reports;

◆ risk appetite statement;

◆ assessments of risk culture;

◆ training and awareness activities;

◆ risk governance and compliance arrangements;

◆ specialist staff and functions, including risk managers, auditors, compliance managers, company secretaries and other governance professionals; and

◆ risk or audit and risk committees.

Risk management policy

An organisation will usually have a risk management policy which outlines the following:

1. its aims and objectives for risk management, including how they support the wider strategic objectives of the organisation;

2. the processes, procedures, and activities that comprise its risk management framework, including any other risk or control policies (policies for health and safety management, information security or similar);

3. governance arrangements for risk management, such as the use of a risk committee; and

4. the allocation of roles and responsibilities for risk management.

A large or complex organisation may have multiple risk management policies. Different business units may maintain their own individual risk management policies or different policies may be drafted for different categories of risk. Such an organisation will often have an overarching risk management policy to ensure that any sub-policies are consistent with the overall objectives of the organisation, with each other, and with the risk preferences of its stakeholders.

2.1 Risk management procedures

An organisation will have procedures to specify how its employees and managers should perform specific tasks and activities. Many of these procedures will, in whole or in part, relate to the assessment and control of related risk. Examples include manual handling procedures for lifting and carrying objects as well as procedures for operating machinery. Financial procedures such as payroll procedures and procedures for making financial transactions are other examples.

Dedicated risk management procedures may be used to help control certain types of risk, such as managing incidents, escalating control weaknesses, building evacuations, critical systems recovery or reporting suspicious financial transactions.

2.2 Technology systems that support risk management

Organisations may use internet or internal network-based technology systems to support their risk assessment, monitoring and control activities. These are known as risk management information systems (RMIS). Systems may be built in-house, often using standard database applications, or they may be purchased from external specialists.

Risk management information systems can be expensive but they can help to improve an organisation's ability to co-ordinate its risk management activities. They can also reduce the time and effort required to produce risk management reports on the organisation's risk exposures or the effectiveness of its controls.

Risk reports

Most organisations will produce some form of risk report to help management understand the organisation's risk exposures and make effective risk management decisions. Different reports may be produced for different areas and levels of management, including reports for IT managers, human resource managers, senior managers, the board and the executive team.

The frequency of risk reporting will depend on how quickly risk exposures are changing or the materiality of the principal risks. Risk reporting can be real time in areas like information security or investment management. Alternatively, it may be monthly, quarterly, annually or any other required level of frequency.

2.3 Risk appetite statement

A risk appetite statement will usually outline the types and levels of risk that an organisation is willing to take in the pursuit of its objectives, as well as the risks that it is not willing to take or will only tolerate in specific circumstances. Stakeholder risk preferences should be taken into account when deciding what risks to take or avoid.

A risk appetite statement may be kept as a standalone document or included in the risk management policy. Larger organisations may choose to make some or all of their risk appetite statement public. Public limited companies often include information on their appetite for risk in their annual report.

Internally, an organisation may have more than one risk appetite statement. Statements may exist for specific categories of risk or for different business units. This is because an organisation may have a different appetite for different risks and business units. This will often reflect the strategy of the organisation, the risks it wishes to take to achieve its objectives and the risks it may want to reduce to avoid business disruption, unnecessary cost or operational inefficiency.

Stop and think 4.2

Access the annual reports for two quoted companies of your choice. Find the section on risk appetite and compare the statements made by these two companies. What might explain any similarities or differences?

Note that UK companies are required to include information on risk appetite but many companies in other countries include information on a voluntary basis or to comply with local governance codes.

2.4 Training and awareness

Risk management and risk awareness training courses help employees and managers to understand the types of risk relevant to them. They also help employees understand how to identify, assess, monitor and control these risks in an effective manner, ensuring that the organisation meets its strategic objectives and the risk preferences of its stakeholders.

Training courses may explain the importance of risk management for the organisation and its stakeholders, as well as the benefits and costs associated with taking specific risks. Courses may also reinforce the contents of policies and procedures or help employees and managers to operate the risk management process and use RMIS. Courses may be online or face-to-face.

2.5 Risk governance and compliance arrangements

Risk governance and compliance arrangements support the direction of the design and operation of risk management policies, processes and procedures, including risk reporting and incident management activities. Risk governance and compliance arrangements may be created to ensure compliance with internal policies and procedures, as well as laws and regulations imposed by external agencies or customers who have specific requirements to which the organisation has agreed (as part of contract terms, for example).

Risk governance and compliance arrangements exist to ensure compliance with the policies, processes and procedures that comprise a risk management framework and that any weaknesses in their design or application are identified and addressed promptly. The activities of external and internal auditors are part of these risk governance and compliance arrangements, as are compliance reviews and internal control assurance activities. Company secretaries and governance professionals often help to support the operation of risk governance and compliance arrangements.

2.6 Specialist staff

Medium to large organisations will often recruit risk management specialists to support the operation and ongoing improvement of their risk management framework. This may include health and safety professionals, information security processionals, business continuity managers and general risk managers.

A risk manager is a professional skilled at identifying, assessing, monitoring and controlling a wide range of risks. Other relevant specialists include auditors, compliance managers and governance professionals.

2.7 Risk committees

The purpose of a risk committee is to oversee and co-ordinate the design and operation of an organisation's risk management framework. This will include:

◆ ensuring that risks are managed in a consistent and objective-supporting way across the organisation;

◆ monitoring more significant risks

◆ balancing the sometimes-different risk preferences of stakeholders; and

◆ ensuring that adequate resources are devoted to risk management.

Generally, only large organisations will have a dedicated risk management committee. Small to medium-sized organisations may incorporate risk management oversight into their audit committee. Where this is the case, it may be called the audit and risk (or risk and audit) committee.

Merged audit and risk committees require careful management. The responsibilities of an audit committee can conflict with that of a risk committee. The focus of an audit committee is on accurate financial reporting and internal control to limit the risks which could threaten an organisation. In contrast, a risk committee should consider taking risk in a proactive manner to support the achievement of organisational strategy and objectives. Risk can be harmful and disruptive but it is also an essential part of generating social, environmental and financial returns. Where a committee is merged, the members should be reminded of this potential conflict to ensure that they apply the right risk mindset to each agenda item.

Stop and think 4.3

For an organisation that you know well, see how much you can find out about its risk management framework. Information may be provided in the annual report. Many public sector organisations and some charities publish their risk management policy or similar documents online. These policy documents are likely to contain information on risk management frameworks.

Test yourself 4.1

Should every organisation implement an identical risk management framework?

3. A detailed look at ISO 31000:2018

The practice of risk management took a major leap forward in 2009 with the publication of the ISO's ISO 31000. The original 2009 standard was updated in 2018 to reflect advances in practice and changes to certain risk exposures such as cyber risk and terrorism.

The objective for ISO 31000 is to provide a set of internationally recognised principles and guidance on the practice of risk management in organisations. These principles and guidance may be used to help improve the design and implementation of a risk management framework within an organisation.

As with any international standard, ISO 31000 provides a universal benchmark for risk management practice, helping an organisation to improve the effectiveness of its risk management framework and related activities, irrespective of its market sector or business model. The standard does not promote a uniform approach to the practice of risk management and encourages organisations to adapt the principles in order to design and implement a risk management framework that is consistent with the nature, scale and complexity of their activities.

ISO 31000 covers a wide range of topics, including:

◆ definitions for key terms such as risk, uncertainty, and risk management;
◆ the importance of managing both the opportunities and downsides that may come from exposure to risk;
◆ the basic principles for effective risk management, such as developing a risk aware culture, ensuring that it supports the organisation's strategic objectives and ensuring it is practised on a continuous basis to keep track of changing risks and exposures;
◆ how to design, implement, review and improve an effective risk management framework; and
◆ the key components of an effective risk management process for identifying, assessing, monitoring and controlling risk.

Copies of the standard may be purchased directly from ISO or its national members such as British Standards. In addition, guidance documents based on ISO 31000 may sometimes be obtained from recognised professional bodies (such as the Institute of Risk Management).

The 2018 update of the standard is more concise that the 2009 original. This is because a series of additional guidance documents are expected. Each will add further detail on the high-level content within the main ISO 31000 document.

The 2018 document is centred on three main topic areas:

1.   principles for risk management
2.   core elements of an effective risk management framework
3.   the risk management process.

The core principle in the revised standard is that risk management activity should help protect and create value in organisations. Value might be protected through the prevention of costly negative risk events. Value might be created by using risk management to satisfy the expectations of stakeholders or to help an organisation fulfil its strategic objectives.

Additional principles call for risk management frameworks to be structured, inclusive, customised, dynamic and responsive, and integrated. This last principle, along with several of the others, is aligned to the practice known as enterprise risk management (see Chapter 7).

In terms of designing an effective risk management framework, the standard highlights how the external and internal context of an organisation will influence the design, implementation and ongoing review and improvement of the framework. External context means factors such as regulation, technological development and market forces. The internal context relates to factors such as the culture and structure of the organisation.

The standard emphasises the importance of leadership in designing and implementing effective risk management frameworks. It argues that a tangible commitment to effective risk management is needed from an organisation's leaders, including its managers, senior managers and board or equivalent. Support for an organisation's risk management activities should be evidenced by what these leaders say and do. Leaders must communicate the importance of operating an effective risk management framework and support this operation through their own actions.

In terms of the risk management process, the guidance discusses three core elements:

◆ establishing the context
◆ risk assessment
◆ risk treatment.

These are supported by three activities:

◆ communication and consultation
◆ recording and reporting
◆ monitoring and review.

3.1 Establishing the context

Establishing the context includes understanding the internal and external drivers which may affect an organisation's exposure to risk, such as the physical environment, technology, organisational structures and processes. Context also means understanding the types of risk that may affect an organisation and the various assessment and control tools that are available for use. The aim is to ensure that the organisation understands the range and scope of its objectives and activities, and the risks that are associated with them.

3.2   Risk assessment

Risk assessment means that an organisation should identify, analyse and evaluate its exposure to all sources of risk to its objectives. Risk assessment may involve the use of statistical models or qualitative judgement.

3.3   Risk treatment

Risk treatment is another term for risk control. The aim is to ensure that the level of exposure is controlled: not too high or too low. The level of control will be influenced by the risk appetite of an organisation.

3.4   Communication and consultation

This is about communicating risk management information (such as risk management policies and procedures, or risk exposures) in a timely, accurate and factual way. Risk communication includes consulting with key stakeholders to ensure that they understand the risks that an organisation is taking and are satisfied that the organisation's approach to managing these risks is appropriate.

Communication seeks to promote awareness and understanding of risk and how to deal with it, whereas consultation involves obtaining feedback and information to support decision making.

3.5   Recording and reporting

Recording means ensuring that identified risks are documented properly. It also means documenting risk management processes and procedures to ensure that they are understood clearly and implemented coherently across the organisation.

Reporting means reporting on an organisation's risk exposures and the measures taken to control these exposures to relevant decision makers and stakeholders.

3.6   Monitoring and review

Monitoring and reviewing is about learning, improving and adapting.

The performance of an organisation's risk management framework can vary. If performance declines, changes may be required to maintain the efficiency and effectiveness of the framework. Performance monitoring and review might include activities such as audits, control effectiveness reviews and compliance reviews. ISO 31000 makes it clear that organisations should review and upgrade their risk management activities on a regular basis. Risk and an organisation's exposures to risk are never static.

As an organisation changes its strategic objectives or operational activities, it must ensure that its risk management framework and associated policies, processes, procedures and controls remain fit for purpose.

Why should an organisation follow the principles and guidance within ISO 31000?

4. National standards and guidelines

National standards and guidance documents on risk management are common. Many build on the work of the ISO to provide local context guidance for an organisation operating in a specific country.

4.1   National guidance on implementing ISO 31000

National guidance on implementing ISO 31000 has been issued in the UK and Republic of Ireland.

British Standard BS 31100

Published in 2011 by the British Standards Institute (BSI), BS 31100 provides advice and guidance on developing, implementing and maintaining proportionate and effective risk management that is aligned with ISO 31000:2009. It needs to be updated to accommodate ISO 31000:2018. The advice and guidance in BS 31100 is designed to be suitable for any organisation operating in the UK.

British Standard 31100 gives practical and specific recommendations on how to implement the risk management principles, framework, and process as outlined in ISO 31000. The guidance in BS 31100 includes:

◆ how to manage risk in a proactive rather than a reactive manner – for example, by preventing adverse risk events from occurring;

◆ the operation of effective risk management oversight via an organisation's governance and internal control functions;

◆ providing assurance to the board and senior management on the effectiveness of an organisation's risk management activities; and

◆ reporting to stakeholders, for example through disclosures in annual financial statements, corporate governance reports or corporate social responsibility reports.

National Standards Agency of Ireland

The National Standards Agency of Ireland (NSAI) provides additional guidance on ISO 31000 for Irish organisations in NWA 31000:2011. This guidance outlines various risk management methods and techniques that Irish organisations can use to implement an effective risk management framework.

The guidance covers topics such as:

◆   guidance on designing a risk management framework;

◆   how to draft a risk management policy;

◆   allocating accountability for risk management;

◆   establishing effective risk management communication mechanisms;

◆   risk assessment techniques;

◆   risk treatment options; and

◆   how to design an effective risk register (with an example).

4.2   The Orange Book

The Orange Book (HM Treasury, 2004) is published by the UK Government. The purpose of the document is to:

◆   provide an introduction to risk management for those new to the discipline;

◆   offer a set of principles against which risk management practices in organisations can be benchmarked;

◆   help senior leadership to understand their responsibilities for risk management;

◆   provide practical support for those tasked with day-to-day risk management responsibilities; and

◆   offer insights into more advanced concepts like risk appetite for those with more risk management experience.

The Orange Book is aimed at government organisations and departments, but it contains much that is of use to all other types of organisation. The document is a guide, rather than a standard or set of regulations. Government organisations are not required to comply with the contents or implement all of the practice that is contained within the Orange Book.

The Orange Book starts with what is termed a risk management 'model'. At the core of the model are four key tasks:

1.   identifying risks

2.   assessing risks

3.   addressing risks (another term for risk control)

4.   reviewing (monitoring) and reporting risks.

Government organisations are also asked to consider the 'extended enterprise', meaning they should consider the risk management needs of their stakeholders and their risk environment and context – such as laws, economy and applicable corporate governance rules.

Running through all aspects of the risk management model is the notion of continuous improvement via effective risk management communication and learning to ensure that an organisation's risk management framework is kept up to date.

The Orange Book offers guidance on how to design and execute the four tasks of the risk management model to help build an effective risk management framework. The guidance explains the concept of risk appetite, including how to implement the concept in a government organisation.

The Orange Book is supported by the Green Book (HM Treasury, 2011). The Green book offers guidance on the conduct of appraisals and evaluations, particularly in relation to the development of new policies, work programmes and funded projects.

Test yourself 4.3

What type of organisation is the Orange Book aimed at?

4.3 The Institute of Risk Management Standard

The Institute of Risk Management (IRM) Standard (IRM, 2002) adopts a very similar approach to ISO 31000. Its major advantage over the international standard is that it is free to download in 14 languages and it is shorter. A disadvantage is that the IRM standard has not been updated as recently as ISO 31000.

The IRM Standard was developed by a team of risk management professionals working for professional associations and consulting organisations. Input from other experts was obtained during a consultation process.

The Standard is not intended to be prescriptive. It provides a best practice benchmark that organisations can use to help design and implement effective risk management frameworks.

The Standard takes the view that risk management is an essential activity in all organisations and that it complements both strategic and operational management. Within the Standard, risks are considered to have an upside as well as a downside. Good risk management should help an organisation to exploit risky opportunities and at the same time mitigate the costs that may be associated with the adverse effects of risk exposures.

The Standard explains that the risks that may affect an organisation can result from factors that may be external or internal to the organisation, or a combination of the two. These factors are further categorised into financial, strategic, operational and hazard risks. External risk factors, termed drivers, include:

◆ financial risks such as interest rates and foreign exchange risks;

◆ strategic risks such as research and development;

◆ operational risks such as regulatory changes; and

◆ hazard risks such as environmental threats and the weather.

Internal risk factors include:

◆ financial risks such as volatile cash flows;

◆ strategic risks such as the threat of competition and changes in consumer demand;

◆ operational risks such as systems failures and employee misconduct; and

◆ hazard risks such as health and safety risks.

The Standard emphasises that the management of internal and external risks can help to protect and create value in organisations. Value might be protected by helping to preserve the reputation or tangible assets of an organisation by preventing risk events or mitigating their impacts. Value could be created by using risk management techniques to help exploit the opportunities associated with these risks or via improving operational efficiency.

The standard includes a detailed discussion of what the IRM sees as an effective risk management process (see Figure 4.2).

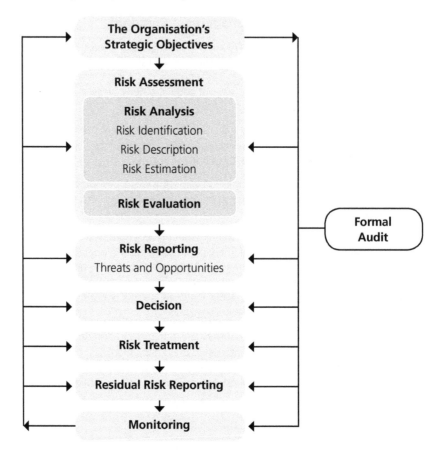

Figure 4.2 Principles, frameworks and risk management processes from ISO 31000 (Source: ISO)

Figure 4.2 includes the basic process elements of risk treatment – risk identification, assessment, monitoring and control – but breaks these elements down into sub-tasks such as risk reporting and risk evaluation. Risk evaluation relates to evaluating whether or not to treat a risk, such as by considering whether the level of risk exposure is within or outside appetite.

Residual risk reporting relates to the reporting of risk exposure levels that remain after risk controls have been used to reduce the level of risk.

The Standard indicates that an organisation's risk management process should be audited periodically to determine whether it remains fit for purpose and to ensure it is operating effectively.

The IRM Risk Management Standard discusses two further important components of a risk management framework: the contents of a risk management policy and the documentation of roles and responsibilities for risk management.

4.4   COSO Enterprise Risk Management Framework

The COSO 2004 Enterprise Risk Management (ERM) Framework underwent a major revision in 2017. Along with the revision of ISO 31000, the COSO ERM Framework represents the latest thinking in terms of the design and implementation of risk management frameworks in organisations.

Copies of the full COSO ERM Framework can be purchased from the COSO website. The executive summary can be downloaded for free, as can a number of ERM thought papers which build on the COSO ERM Framework.

The 2017 COSO ERM Framework emphasises that, although risk management is an important part of effective corporate governance and internal control, this does not preclude using risk management to help improve the strategic and operational performance of an organisation.

The COSO ERM Framework explains that the adverse consequences of an ineffective risk management framework are significant in the 21st century, especially as the world becomes more complex and interconnected and as stakeholders exercise increased scrutiny over organisational activities. Risk is an element in every organisational decision. Effective risk management should help organisations to make better decisions that exploit the available opportunities and mitigate the potential downsides. Risk management is not only about limiting risk, rather it is a tool that allows an organisation to exploit risk in order to increase its performance.

The COSO ERM Framework is intended for organisations of all sizes and sectors and provides insight into how an organisation can better integrate risk management into its strategy, operations, and decision making. The framework is different in approach to most conventional risk management frameworks but this helps emphasise the performance-enhancing focus for risk management that COSO believes is important. The framework is presented as a set of principles organised into five inter-related components:

1.   governance and culture;
2.   strategy and objective setting;

3.   performance;
4.   review and revision; and
5.   information, communication and reporting.

Governance and culture

The first element of the COSO ERM Framework is about ensuring that employees and other relevant stakeholders (such as suppliers and contractors) behave in a manner that is consistent with the organisation's values and codes of conduct, as well as undertaking activities that support the organisation's strategic, operational and risk management objectives.

This includes overseeing management decisions to ensure that opportunities are exploited and any downsides are mitigated. It also includes managing risk management attitudes and perceptions to ensure that there is a good understanding of risk, its consequences and the benefits of effective risk management.

Strategy and objective setting

Strategy and risk management complement each other closely in the COSO ERM Framework, each playing their part in enhancing organisational performance. Key to this is the concept of risk appetite, which helps to direct strategic and risk management decisions across the organisation.

By determining its appetite for different types of risk, an organisation can plan a strategy that is less likely to result in any associated risk exposures that exceed this level of risk appetite. Where there is the potential for risk exposures to exceed appetite, risk management can be used to help reduce this potential or ensure that the organisation is resilient enough to withstand the effects of these exposures.

Performance

This activity is concerned with identifying and assessing risks that may affect the achievement of an organisation's objectives. An organisation's objectives are usually determined as part of the annual planning and budgeting process, and are often aligned with its broader strategic goals or mission.

Risks that are believed to be a threat to objectives are compared against the organisation's appetite for risk. Where the level of risk exposure is considered too high actions are taken to control these exposures.

By focusing management attention on the risks which represent a major threat to an organisation's objectives, resources can be used in an efficient way, ensuring the maximum benefit for the costs that are incurred in managing risk. Stakeholder value can be protected and possibly enhanced by reporting on these risk exposures and control activities – an action that should provide stakeholders with the assurance they need that the organisation is meeting their expectations by fulfilling its stated objectives.

Review and revision

This COSO component has multiple objectives (especially when compared to the ISO 31000 standard):

◆ the organisation should identify and assess substantial internal and external changes that may affect strategy or the achievement of its objectives;

◆ the organisation should evaluate its performance and the achievement of its objectives in light of the chosen strategy and risk response; and

◆ based on the outcomes of the previous activities, the organisation should evaluate the continued appropriateness of its risk management arrangements and revise them accordingly.

Information, communication and reporting

Within the COSO ERM Framework, organisations are involved in a continuous process of collecting and sharing information. Information may be collected from internal and external sources. Sharing is up, down and across the organisation to ensure that all decision makers have the information that they need to manage risk in an effective way.

Not all risk management frameworks involve the continuous processing and sharing of information. Some rely on periodic – monthly, quarterly or annual – risk reports, along with incident and issues reporting of risk events and identified control failures. The COSO ERM Framework considers this to be ineffective because an organisation, its external operating context and things like regulation, politics and the environment change constantly. Periodic reports can go out of date very quickly.

Stop and think 4.4

◆ **Identify five risks that affect an organisation with which you are familiar.**

◆ **Consider how exposure to these risks may threaten the achievement of the organisation's objectives.**

◆ **Determine the effect that these threats to the organisation's objectives may have on its performance. This might be in terms of its ability to generate a profit or surplus, for example.**

◆ **Reflect on how changeable these risks might be – do they require continuous monitoring?**

Tip: select an organisation that publishes an annual report. Many organisations today discuss the risks that may affect their objectives in their annual report. This is especially the case for UK public limited companies, which are required to report on their most significant risks to stakeholders as part of the Corporate Governance Code.

Test yourself 4.4

Explain how exposure to risk may prevent an organisation from achieving its objectives.

4.5   The COBIT framework for IT governance

The guideline Control Objectives for Information and Related Technologies (COBIT), published by the Information Systems Audit and Control Association (ISACA), provides a good practice framework for the control of IT-related risks. COBIT is currently in its fifth iteration (COBIT 5).

The COBIT framework is business-oriented and links IT goals to business goals, providing example metrics and benchmark maturity models to help an organisation assess and enhance the effectiveness of its IT risk management activities. The COBIT 5 framework incorporates the following elements:

◆   core governance principles;

◆   generic process descriptions for the governance of IT risks;

◆   control objectives;

◆   management guidelines; and

◆   process maturity models.

Core governance principles
COBIT 5 is based on five governance principles.

1.   *Meeting stakeholder needs*: providing a financial return or protecting them from risk.

2.   *Covering an enterprise end-to-end*: effective IT risk management must cover the entire operational processes and supply chains of an organisation.

3.   *Applying a single integrated framework*: to ensure that IT risks are managed in a way that is consistent with the organisation's objectives.

4.   *Enabling a holistic approach*: one that covers the whole of the organisation – all departments, activities and functions.

5.   *Separating governance from management*: this ensures that those responsible for overseeing the operating of an organisation's IT risk management activities are not involved in the day-to-day running of the organisation. This should, in theory, mean that they maintain a degree of impartiality allowing them to challenge management practices where necessary.

Generic process descriptions
Building on the principles discussed above, COBIT 5 presents a process reference model for the effective management of the organisation's IT arrangements.

This model consists of one overarching governance domain – 'evaluate, direct and monitor' – and four management domains: 'plan, build, run, and monitor'. Together, the activities grouped in these domains help organisations create optimal value from their IT investments by maintaining a balance between realising benefits and optimising risk levels and resource use.

The domains are further explained in Table 4.1. Each of these five domains is broken down into a total of 37 IT management processes, summarised in the third column.

Domain	Description	Management objectives
Governance domain: evaluate, direct and monitor	These governance processes are concerned with meeting the needs of stakeholders and include practices and activities aimed at evaluating strategic options, providing direction to IT risk management activities and monitoring outcomes	• Ensure governance framework setting and management • Ensure benefits delivery • Ensure risk optimisation • Ensure resource optimisation • Ensure stakeholder transparency
Management domain 1: align, plan and organise	This group of management processes covers the design of an organisation's IT arrangements. It is focused on developing IT systems and related risk management processes that support the achievement of the organisation's objectives.	• Manage IT management framework • Manage strategy • Manage enterprise architecture • Manage innovation • Manage portfolio • Manage budget and costs • Manage human resources • Manage relationships • Manage service agreements • Manage suppliers • Manage quality • Manage risk • Manage security
Management domain 2: build, acquire and implement	Organisations use a wide range of IT systems. This process is about selecting and implementing IT systems that support the organisation's objectives (they must work effectively and be secure). Changes in and maintenance of existing systems are also covered by this process group, to ensure that they continue to meet the organisation's objectives.	• Manage programme and projects • Manage requirements definition • Manage solutions identification and build • Manage availability and capacity • Manage organisational change enablement • Manage IT changes • Manage organisational change acceptance and transitioning • Manage knowledge • Manage assets • Manage configuration

Management domain 3: deliver, service and support	This is concerned with making IT systems usable for the end user and includes the final delivery and support of required services (such as service delivery, management of security and continuity, service support for users, and management of data and operational facilities).	• Manage operations • Manage service requests and incidents • Manage problems • Manage continuity • Manage security services • Manage business process controls
Management domain 4: monitor, evaluate and assess	All IT processes need to be assessed on a regular basis to ensure that they continue to provide the level of usability, reliability and security required by the organisation and its stakeholders.	• Monitor, evaluate and assess performance and conformance • Monitor, evaluate and assess the system of internal control • Monitor, evaluate and assess compliance with external requirements

Table 4.1 COBIT generic processes

Control objectives

The COBIT 5 framework provides a list of control objectives that are linked to the IT management objectives in the third column of Table 4.1. For example, the management objective of 'manage human resources' is assigned the control objective of 'control over the process of managing human resources'.

Management guidelines

The COBIT 5 management guidelines cover topics such as the assignment of roles and responsibilities for IT risk management and performance measurement. In relation to performance measurement the framework provides examples of key performance indicators (KPIs) for each control objective.

In the case of 'control over the process of managing human resources', suggested KPIs include:

◆ time lag between changes in the IT strategic plan and the IT human resources management plan;

◆ percentage of IT personnel with completed professional development plans; and

◆ the percentage of training time per person.

Process maturity models

Maturity models are provided for each control objective. These models help organisations to review their control arrangements, conduct gap analyses to identify areas for improvement and record the actions taken to address these gaps.

Each of the models is based on six maturity levels:

1. non-existent
2. initial/ad hoc
3. repeatable but intuitive
4. defined process
5. managed and measurable
6. optimised

Stop and think 4.5

To what extent is it possible to use the COBIT 5 Framework for non-IT risks? Does the framework provide useful insights for developing risk management frameworks more generally? Can you find examples of the use of the COBIT 5 Framework for non-IT risks on the internet?

Test yourself 4.5

Why are governance processes included as part of the COBIT 5 IT risk management framework?

Chapter summary

◆ Risk management is an activity that all decision makers engage in, often intuitively.

◆ In an organisation it is necessary to formalise risk management activity by creating a tangible risk management framework.

◆ An organisation needs a formal risk management framework to ensure that risks are managed in a consistent manner by all decision makers, in accordance with the interests of the organisation and its stakeholders.

◆ An organisation's risk management framework consists of various policies, procedures, processes and activities. The purpose of these policies, processes and activities is to provide a coherent structure for risk management activities and decisions.

◆ A key element of any risk management framework is the risk management process. This is concerned with the identification, assessment, monitoring and control of risk.

◆ The practice of risk management took a major leap forward in 2009 with the publication of ISO 31000. The international standard for risk management provides a set of internationally recognised principles and guidance on the practice of risk management in organisations. The standard serves as a universal benchmark for risk management practice, helping organisations, irrespective of their market sector or business model, to improve the effectiveness of their risk management practices.

◆   ISO 31000 was updated in 2018. The revised guidance reflects changes in risk exposure and risk management practice.

◆   National standards and guidance documents on risk management are common. Many build on ISO 31000 to provide local context-specific guidance for organisations operating in specific countries.

◆   The COSO ERM framework was updated in 2017 and is a complementary resource to ISO 31000. The 2017 COSO ERM Framework emphasises that. although risk management is an important part of effective corporate governance and internal control, this does not preclude using risk management to help improve the strategic and operational performance of an organisation.

◆   COBIT 5 provides a risk management framework for IT risks. The framework is business-oriented and links IT goals to business goals, providing example metrics and benchmark maturity models to help an organisation review and improve the effectiveness of its IT risk management activities.

Chapter five
Key risk management concepts

Contents

1. Introduction

Before establishing a risk management framework, an organisation needs to understand what kind of risks it currently faces or is willing to face. It also needs to group these risks into categories based on the cause of risk.

A well designed risk categorisation framework is crucial to this task. By focusing on key risks that are relevant to an organisation, its decision makers can be more effective. Organisations also need to be mindful of the fact that risks are often interconnected, while risk estimation and interpretation is prone to subjectivity.

This chapter provides an overview of common definitions and approaches to categorising risk, as well as how different perception biases may affect risk taking decisions within an organisation.

2. Defining risk

The term risk has many different meanings, depending on the context. Dictionaries often define risk in terms of exposure to danger or a threat. In the business world, risk is usually associated with the volatility of unexpected outcomes (uncertainty) that could lead to a loss of value.

Traditionally, risk has been viewed as negative (destroying value) with a focus on estimating and managing threats. More recently, risk has also been seen as an opportunity to create value, with upside potential in addition to threats.

Interestingly, the term risk has always been composed of two symbols in Mandarin Chinese: one signifying danger and another one opportunity.

In an organisational setting, risks arise whenever a single decision or an action could result in more than one potential outcome. Figure 5.1 illustrates this in the simplest possible terms.

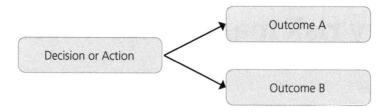

Figure 5.1 Risk in its simplest form

In reality, decisions or actions usually result in a much larger number of outcomes, with each outcome having a different probability of actually materialising. Some of these outcomes will be positive and others negative. The degree of positivity or negativity will also vary.

Furthermore, some actions can take a form of inaction – a decision to not do anything. An example of this would be when an organisation is choosing not to respond to threats or opportunities presented by blockchain technologies.

Stop and think 5.1

Identify two common decisions and/or actions that can be made within an organisation. Write down the different outcomes, positive and/ or negative, that may arise as a result of these decisions or actions. Examples of decisions or actions may include:

◆ **decisions to develop new products or enter new markets;**

◆ **decisions to change work processes or IT systems;**

◆ **production activities, such as manufacturing;**

◆ **the delivery of a service, for example, consulting or social services;**

◆ **managing a supply chain;**

◆ **hiring new staff;**

◆ **advertising;**

◆ **providing credit to customers or receiving credit from a lender; and**

◆ **maintaining office space or factory space.**

Reflect on whether a decision or an action within an organisation can ever be risk free. Is there such a thing as 100% certainty when managing an organisation?

2.1 Risk versus uncertainty

The terms risk and uncertainty are often used interchangeably, but there is a practical difference between the two. In the 1920s, the influential economist Frank Knight formalised a clear distinction between risk and uncertainty, creating what is now known as the Knightian uncertainty concept.

For Knight, uncertainty is something that is unquantifiable due to the unpredictability of future event constraints. It is therefore impossible to calculate, whereas risk is something that can be estimated with a certain degree of confidence using statistical methods.

For example, playing roulette at a casino is a risky activity because it is possible to calculate the odds of winning or losing with a high level of precision. In contrast, though global warming is widely believed to be a human-made problem, its effects remain difficult to predict with any accuracy, resulting in a significant degree of uncertainty about the exact timing and the eventual impact.

In an organisational setting, it is rare for any risk to be calculated with 100% accuracy. Most decisions or actions will contain some element of uncertainty. The degree of uncertainty will often depend on:

◆ the chosen risk model and underlying assumptions;

◆ the availability and quality of data;

◆ the chosen model parameters such as time horizon or frequency of data inputs; and

◆ the chosen confidence level, amongst other factors.

It is worth noting that each of these steps in itself is also prone to some additional risks. For example, choosing an incorrect model and assumptions is known to result in model risk (risk that the model fails or performs inadequately).

Examples of uncertainty in an organisation include, but are not limited to:

◆ the research and development of a new product, for example whether there is a market for new products;

◆ organisational change initiatives, changes to reporting structures or an attempt to change the culture of an organisation may have unintended and unpredictable consequences;

◆ emerging risks such as cyber-attacks;

◆ how financial markets may react to unfamiliar scenarios such as a natural disaster or a major economic downturn;

◆ the effects of political or regulatory change; or

◆ the effects of negative news media coverage.

A common factor in these examples is the human element. Human behaviour can be very unpredictable, making it hard to determine how people will react to specific decisions, activities, or outcomes.

The concept of confidence intervals can be used to measure the level of uncertainty of a particular risk. A confidence interval is expressed in percentage terms from zero to 100. A higher confidence interval means that there is greater confidence in the degree of accuracy that can be assigned to any statistical estimates of the risk in question.

For example, it is possible to estimate the range of possible outcomes of a fair game of casino roulette with 100% confidence, along with the expected 'return' from playing. In the case of global warming, there is a high level of confidence in the fact that it is a man-made problem (most studies suggest over 90%), but a much lower degree of confidence in the ultimate effects. In financial organisations, the most common confidence levels used are 95% and 99%.

Not all organisations use statistical concepts like confidence intervals, although it is common to do so in sectors such as banking and insurance when dealing with financial risks such as stock market movements or movements in interest rates. Even if the organisations that you know do not use statistical concepts, it is important to remember that risks can rarely be estimated with 100% accuracy. In reality, unexpected outcomes can and do occur. Expected outcomes can be more or less positive or negative than initially anticipated, or they may occur more or less frequently.

Test yourself 5.1

How are risk and uncertainty linked?

2.2   Risk events

A risk event is any outcome that arises from a single decision or an action that could result in more than one potential outcome. Every outcome in an organisation is technically a risk event.

In many organisations risk events may be defined as accidents. This means that only negative events, such as financial losses or injury, are considered to be risk events. A more accurate term in this context is a **loss event**. Risk events may also be thought of as events which result in outcomes that are significantly more positive or negative than expected.

Risk events are often categorised into a specific type of event, such as business or operational, to aid management and reporting (see section 3).

2.3   Probability, impact and exposure

The outcomes that result from a single decision or an action can be expressed in terms of probability and severity. This allows organisations to understand the likelihood and potential impact of an outcome.

The concept of probability is concerned with estimating the likelihood of a single outcome or a range of outcomes. In terms of a single outcome, probability can be expressed as a percentage or a decimal fraction. For example,

loss event
A risk event that results in some form of loss for an organisation. This may be a financial loss, such as asset damage or a regulatory fine, or a non-financial loss, such as a loss of customer goodwill or reputation. Loss events may also involve the death or injury of employees, customers and third parties.

a 10% or 0.1 probability means that the likelihood this specific outcome will occur is one in ten.

Probability can also be expressed as a qualitative metric. For example, a 'highly unlikely' probability means that it is highly unlikely this specific outcome will occur. The qualitative route is often used to estimate probabilities of intangible risks such as culture or reputation.

Impact relates to the scale of a particular positive or negative outcome. Impact is commonly estimated in relation to how the specific objectives are affected. This can be in either financial (monetary) terms, criticality terms or both. For example, an organisation that is heavily dependent on attracting high quality employees may estimate the impact of losing their largest client at £100,000, while seeing the impact from losing their reputation as critical and even catastrophic.

Exposure, specifically risk exposure, is the measure of probable future outcome resulting from a single decision or an action. Risk management often focuses on the downside exposure by estimating potential loss arising from the outcome.

Another important factor to consider when analysing risks is the time horizon over which probabilities are estimated. The time horizon that is used varies depending on the specific decision, objective, action or risk. In roulette, the time horizon will last for the total time it takes to complete one spin of the wheel (a few seconds). In an organisational setting, it is common to link time horizon to the speed at which a specific risk changes.

For certain financial risks, much shorter time horizons can be used. For example, traders can use a one-day time horizon to estimate the risks of their currency trading positions. In contrast, the probabilities for environmental risks are usually estimated over a one-year (or longer) time horizon. Time horizons are most commonly expressed in days. Therefore, it is important to use the appropriate time horizon over which probabilities of a specific outcome are estimated. For example, a day trader using a one-year time horizon to capture the probability of a particular trading position losing its value during the course of a day will most likely over or underestimate potential risks.

Some risk models can be designed to assign higher weights to most recent data. For example, when a three-year time horizon is used, it is possible to calculate probability as 20% based on the first two years and 80% based on the last year. In its simplest form, exposure in risk context can be estimated using the following equation:

Probability × impact = exposure

If we assume that the probability of an outcome is 0.2 (20%) and the impact of that outcome is a financial loss of £100 million, then an organisation's exposure to that outcome is:

0.2 × £100 million = £20 million

The cost of the organisation's exposure to the outcome in question is £20 million. Exposure to positive outcomes can be calculated in the same way.

Exposure can also be estimated for multiple events with multiple outcomes. This requires more complicated equations and statistical methods.

The concept of exposure helps organisations compare different types of risks across a common category. This can help organisations make better decisions by choosing between mutually exclusive options based on risk exposure analysis.

2.4   Pure and speculative risks

pure risk
Risks that may only have neutral or negative outcomes, such as fire risk, risk of a physical injury or risk of illness.

Most dictionary definitions of risk are based on the concept of a pure risk. **Pure risks** are risks that may only have neutral or negative outcomes, such as fire risk, risk of a physical injury or risk of illness.

Speculative risks are risks that may have three outcomes: positive, neutral or negative. Gains are usually financial but they can also be non-financial human welfare or social gains such as improved health, happiness or environmental benefits.

speculative risk
Risks that may have three outcomes: positive, neutral or negative. Gains are usually financial but they can also be non-financial human welfare or social gains such as improved health, happiness or environmental benefits.

In an organisational setting, risk in its rawest and uncategorised form is generally speculative. Organisations exist to fulfil specific missions and objectives. The decisions they make and actions they take are all aimed at fulfilling these missions and objectives. These decisions and actions will result in positive, neutral or negative outcomes, depending on a number of factors such as the wider economy, specific business decisions or simple luck. The presence of uncertainty means that the outcomes that occur may be more or less positive than expected.

Risks should always be approached neutrally. This is because 'good' or 'bad' risk categorisation is very much dependent on a specific objective, making risk as much a part of the success of an organisation as its failure.

Test yourself 5.2

Provide three examples of pure risk and three examples of speculative risk in organisations.

2.5   Inherent and residual risks

inherent risk
The level of risk exposure with no controls applied. Also known as gross risk.

Some organisations distinguish between inherent risk and residual risk. **Inherent risk** means the level of risk – more specifically exposure – that is present in the absence of any controls or mitigating actions to manage the risk in question. **Residual risk** describes the level of exposure that remains once controls have been applied to manage the risk in question.

residual risk
The level of risk exposure with controls in place. Also known as net risk.

In practice, inherent risk tends to assume the existence of controls at their current level rather than a scenario with no controls whatsoever. Residual risk then accounts for the remaining risk exposure. For example, when driving a car, the risk of having an accident is inherent risk. The driver can decrease their inherent risk by wearing a seatbelt or buying insurance. However, a certain residual risk will still remain.

The distinction between inherent risk and residual risk is most common for risks that are framed as pure risks, such as operational risks like health and safety or environmental risks. In this context, the level of inherent risk exposure is usually greater than the residual exposure.

2.6 Principal and emerging risks

To make the oversight of organisational risks more effective, boards typically focus on large impact risks.

A principal risk, also referred to as a significant or key risk, is a risk that is considered material and can affect the viability of the business. In finance, principal risk is also defined as the risk of losing an entire investment. Talent and data security are two examples of principal risk. It is worth noting that principal risks are different for different organisations.

Emerging risk, also known as disruptive risk, refers to the risk that does not yet affect an organisation but may develop to become a principal risk in future. Changes in consumer tastes and preferences, use of data automation techniques or a shift towards a digital advertising model are the examples of emerging risks. These risks are also different for different organisations. Boards are responsible for making sure that emerging risks are properly assessed and responded to accordingly.

Risk profile represents a combination of all principal and emerging risks that an organisation faces.

Principal risks are reported as a part of the strategic annual report. There is an expectation that board members understand what these risks are, why they are considered material, how they may affect an organisation and its future performance and how they are managed or mitigated.

emerging risk
A risk that does not yet affect an organisation but may develop to become a principal risk in future. Also known as disruptive risk.

risk profile
An organisation's risk profile refers to the number and types of risks to which it is exposed, as well as the size of these exposures.

2.7 Other useful concepts and definitions

There are a number of other concepts and definitions that it can be useful to understand when dealing with risk management.

Tail risk, also referred to as unknown unknowns or a 'black swan' event, is the risk arising from a highly improbable and difficult to predict event, or an event that has a very small probability of occurring and has widespread ramifications (high impact). The 9/11 attacks and the Lehman Brothers bankruptcy filing are examples of such an event.

Black swan events are typically random and hard to predict. They are therefore difficult to plan for and manage. The black swan term was popularised by financial services professional and academic Nassim Taleb, in his 2007 book *The Black Swan: The Impact of the Highly Improbable*.

Cliff risk, also known as cliff edge risk or cliff effect, refers to the risk arising from an event that is probable and has widespread ramifications (high impact). A credit rating downgrade or the UK leaving the EU without a deal in place are examples of cliff risk events. Technically, cliff risk can be planned for and risk managed. In reality, fully managing this risk can become a very expensive exercise. Organisations usually opt for some sort of a tactical plan while closely monitoring for any changes in the status of this risk.

Wrong way risk occurs when the risk exposure to a counterparty is adversely correlated to the credit quality of that counterparty. Wrong way risk is mostly used in relation to poorly collateralised transactions. An example of this is a bank lending money to a company against that company's own equity shares as collateral, with the bank now exposed to the wrong way risk. This exposure will grow further should the company be suddenly downgraded or worse, default.

Risk taxonomy is a set of all risk categories used within an organisation. Very often, there will be a difference in how risks are categorised from one organisation to another. Things get even more challenging when different departments categorise the same risks differently within the same organisation. This is known as a fragmented taxonomy. This can cause a lot of confusion, so an increasing number of organisations have been working towards unifying organisational risk taxonomy.

3. Categorising risk

It is common for organisations to group their risks in categories. Risk grouping helps decision makers to narrow down key risk categories that are relevant to their organisations. Risk grouping also helps to establish a common risk taxonomy within an organisation, which in its turn improves the quality of communication and increases the effectiveness of decision-making processes. Categorisation also supports the management of risk because different types of risk may require different management approaches.

There are many different approaches to categorising risk. An organisation may use its own approach. It may rely on an established approach provided by a risk management standard such as ISO 31000:2018, a professional body such as the Institute of Operational Risk (IOR) or a regulator.

Whatever approach is taken, it is important that the choice of specific risk categories is appropriate for an organisation. These categories form the foundation upon which the organisational risk management framework will be built.

3.1   A common approach to risk categorisation

A common approach is to group organisational risks into the following six categories:

1. business risk
2. credit risk
3. market risk
4. liquidity risk
5. operational risk
6. reputation risk.

Business risk

Business risk is a type of non-financial risk that relates to the positive and negative outcomes that are inherent in an organisation's operating environment, such as specific actions of its competitors and changes in economic or political conditions. Business risk is willingly assumed by organisations in order to gain a competitive advantage.

Changes in consumer demand or supply chains (such as selling products and services online) fall under business risk, as do changes in government or regulatory policy as they can have an effect on consumer demand or the cost of running a business. For example, an increase in a minimum wage rate or a reduction of maximum leverage the UK spread betting industry can extend to retail clients, limiting the extent of their activities and corresponding fee income.

Business risks can be grouped as external or internal. For example, a mining company may identify a natural disaster as one (external) risk, and a premature or a complete failure of its key production equipment due to inadequate maintenance as another (internal) risk.

Stop and think 5.2

Identify five business risks for an organisation of your choice. Remember that government enterprises, charities and not-for-profit organisations may still be exposed to business risks as their activities are often business-like.

Business risks are generally intangible risks, which are quite hard to quantify. Organisations manage these risks by conducting an assessment to identify key business risks. Each risk is then assessed in terms of severity and the likelihood of occurrence.

Organisations will then usually try to reduce high impact, high probability business risks to an acceptable level, either by means of changes within the business itself, by purchasing a relevant insurance policy or a combination of both. In some cases, there may be a legal requirement to take out insurance.

Risks that cannot be effectively reduced or eliminated are monitored through a designated risk management framework (in this context, effectively means at a reasonable cost given the benefit).

Case study 5.1 shows an example of an organisation what was too slow to address emerging threats to its business model.

Case study 5.1

Blockbuster, also known as Blockbuster Video, was a US-based provider of home movie and video game rental services, mainly offered through rental shops and postal deliveries. Originally established in the late 1980s in Dallas, Texas, the company rapidly expanded its national and international presence in the 1990s, turbo-charged by consumer demand for a subscription-type rental service. At its peak, Blockbuster was generating over $6 billion in annual revenues while employing almost 85,000 people worldwide. In 2000, Blockbuster declined an offer to buy a start-up called Netflix for $50 million.

Blockbuster went bankrupt in 2010. Why? Because Blockbuster's business model was based on owning physical DVD copies of movies that the company had to rent enough times to recoup its initial purchase costs. Furthermore, 70% of the company's income was generated through late fees whenever customers failed to return the movie on time.

As the internet grew to be more accessible, competitors such as the aforementioned Netflix, Apple and Amazon started offering various streaming and video on demand services, which significantly reduced a number of people looking to rent a physical DVD. This eventually reached the point where Blockbuster's business model became unviable. By failing to change its business model in line with changes in consumer demand, Blockbuster quickly lost its competitiveness and the ability to survive. As of 2018, Netflix's value was close to $150 billion.

Credit risk

Credit risk is the risk that a borrower or counterparty will suffer a real or perceived deterioration in its credit rating, or an outright default that will make that borrower or counterparty unable to meet its outstanding obligations. Credit risk is a financial risk.

Credit risk is relevant to many types of financial instruments, including loans, securities, derivatives and financial guarantees. A borrower or counterparty's cash generation capacity, its level of indebtedness and the availability of easy-to-sell assets are all significant factors in estimating credit risk exposure.

In credit risk, exposure is measured as the amount of loss that would be realised if a borrower or counterparty actually defaults. This loss is expressed in terms of expected and unexpected losses. As the name suggests, the expected loss is the expected loss from a credit exposure, whereas the unexpected loss is the loss in excess of expectations. Regulators typically require banks to hold capital against unexpected losses.

Credit risk and default risk terms are used interchangeably. Typically, credit risk terms are used in relation to lending activities which either take the shape of a direct loan (a bank extends a cash loan to a corporation) or an indirect loan through debt securities purchases (a bank holds debt securities issued by a corporation). However, credit risk can also take a number of other forms.

Concentration risk is the risk of any single exposure or a group of (possibly connected) single exposures that has a potential to result in losses that can threaten the ability of an organisation to maintain its core business activities. For example, if an organisation relies on one client to generate 80% of its revenues, it has a concentration risk to this client. Similarly, if an organisation relies on a group of three suppliers all based in a country associated with an unstable political environment to deliver a new product, it has a concentration risk to this group.

Credit risk which is specifically attributable to trading activities is called Counterparty credit risk (CCR) is concerned with default on trading obligations such as derivative contracts. It is unique in several important ways. Counterparty exposures can be netted. For example, if a bank sold and bought euros from the same counterparty via multiple derivatives contracts, the net counterparty exposure will be calculated as a sum of all these transactions – either net euros sold, net euros purchased or net flat outcome. In addition, collateral arrangements are often in place to reduce the extent of counterparty risk.

Settlement risk is concerned with the risk of a trading transaction not settling as per pre-agreed terms and conditions in the first place, such as when a counterparty fails to deliver securities against the payment (see Case study 5.2).

It is also worth highlighting sovereign risk. By definition, sovereigns cannot declare bankruptcy but they can default on their debt obligations (as Argentina did in 2001). Therefore, sovereign risk arises from actions taken by sovereign governments that can negatively affect the value of sovereign obligations.

Case study 5.2

Herstatt was a privately owned medium-sized bank based in Cologne, Germany. The bank was very active in the foreign exchange markets and by 1973 it had racked up a large currency position betting that the US dollar would depreciate against the German mark.

During 1973/1974, the US dollar significantly appreciated against the German currency. By June 1974, Herstatt's capital was standing at a fraction of accumulated losses, putting the bank's solvency at risk and attracting the attention of regulators.

On 26 June 1974, in the middle of the day, German regulators officially forced the troubled Herstatt bank into liquidation. Due to the time differences between Germany and the US, the news of the bank's insolvency arrived after some of Herstatt's counterparties in New York irrevocably paid large amounts of German marks to the bank but before receiving any US dollars back, thus making these counterparties exposed to Herstatt to the full value of those transactions.

Even today, counterparties continue bearing 'Herstatt' risk when settling transactions across different time zones. Use of centralised settlement platforms such as Continuous Linked Settlement (CLS) helps to reduce this type of risk.

Depending on the type of exposure, credit risk is managed through a combination of:

◆ statistical models
◆ stress testing and scenario analysis
◆ risk appetite and limits (including concentration limits)
◆ credit underwriting and diversification standards
◆ qualitative assessments.

All of these form part of the overall risk monitoring and reporting framework within an organisation.

Market risk
Market risk measures the extent of change in the value of an investment due to changes in factors that affect the overall performance of the financial markets. Market risk is often referred to as systematic risk: the risk inherent to the entire market or market segment, not just a particular investment. Market risk is another example of financial risk.

In its simplest form, market risk is taken by individuals or organisations looking to make a return from an investment. There are four major categories of market risk:

◆ equity risk
◆ interest rate risk
◆ foreign exchange risk
◆ commodity price risk.

Market risk can be relevant to both trading and non-trading exposures. Trading market risk is the risk of loss from a trading position. For example, trading market risk may originate during securities underwriting. Fully underwritten securities issuance is a process when a bank commits to buying 100% of new debt or equities issuance from a client for a fee. From the moment these securities are purchased from the client (into the bank's trading book), the bank takes market risk that the value of these securities can materially depreciate (or appreciate) from the initial purchase price. Trading market risk and market risk terms are often used interchangeably. Non-trading market risk usually arises from off-balance sheet exposures such as equity compensation and pension scheme risk, as well as structural interest rate or foreign exchange risk.

Volatility (implied volatility, to be precise) is the key driver of market risk. It represents the degree of dispersion of returns for a given investment: the higher the volatility, the higher the potential for an extreme loss or a gain. In statistical terms, volatility is estimated using standard deviation.

Market risk is predominantly measured by using the value at risk (VaR) method. VaR quantifies the potential loss of an investment as well as the probability of taking this loss at a defined confidence interval. For example, if an investment has a one-day 1% VaR of £100, there is a 1% probability that this investment will lose £100 over a one-day time horizon (the confidence interval is set at 99%).

Examples of market risk exposures that an organisation may face include:

◆ financial institutions may have to manage market risk arising from a particular service sold to a client;

◆ large charities and organisations with large investment portfolios may be exposed to market risk through their holdings;

◆ organisations that produce commodities such as oil and electricity may be exposed to a degree of market risk when they sell some of their products in advance; and

◆ airliners and shipping companies may have exposure to market risk by trying to actively manage the cost of fuel through derivatives contracts.

Depending on the type of exposure, market risk is managed through a combination of:

◆ statistical models;

◆ stress testing and scenario analysis;

◆ risk appetite and limits;

◆ diversification and hedging strategies; and

◆ qualitative assessments.

All of these form part of the overall risk monitoring and reporting framework within an organisation.

Liquidity risk

Liquidity risk is another example of financial risk. There are two types of liquidity risk: asset liquidity risk and funding liquidity risk.

Asset liquidity risk is an asset's degree of illiquidity – the inability to easily sell this asset. For example, a US Treasury Bond is much easier to sell than a real estate property. Funding liquidity risk is the risk that an organisation is unable to fulfil its payment obligations in a timely manner in normal or stressed market conditions. Funding liquidity comes either in a form of cash or high-quality government securities that are held in lieu of cash.

Liquidity risk management came into focus during the financial crisis of 2007–08, when a large number of banks were locked out of the financial market and either had to be bailed out by governments or rely on central banks to remain solvent. As a result, there is a much higher expectation for organisations to proactively manage their liquidity risk. At a minimum, organisations keep a minimum amount of cash and other liquid assets to cover day-to-day liquidity needs and fund long-term assets with long-term loans.

Depending on the type of exposure, liquidity risk is managed through a combination of a comprehensive assets and liabilities management (ALM) framework, statistical models, stress testing and scenario analysis, risk appetite and limits, funding diversification and qualitative assessments, all of which form a part of the overall risk monitoring and reporting framework within an organisation.

Funding strategy and ALM management is often executed by a designated treasury function. Case study 5.3 shows how an organisation that funds its long-term assets with short-term loans can easily suffer a liquidity squeeze during stock market turbulence.

Case study 5.3

Northern Rock was a British bank listed on the London Stock Exchange. Between 2000 and 2006, Northern Rock expanded aggressively into residential mortgages (long-term lending) which the bank extensively funded by short-term borrowings amongst other funding sources.

As the global financial crisis unfolded in 2007–2008 and banks stopped lending to each other, Northern Rock was essentially locked out of the overnight borrowing market. Spooked by this news, the bank's retail depositors rushed to withdraw their savings. This triggered the eventual insolvency and nationalisation of the bank by the UK government.

Operational risk
Operational risk is often defined as the 'risk of loss resulting from inadequate or failed internal processes, people and systems or from external events'. Operational risks are generally pure risks that can only result in losses. These risks arise within the business as usual operations and are closely linked to factors such as organisational culture, the internal controls environment, contingency planning and crisis management.

An organisation's day-to-day operations can encompass a wide array of risks. Examples include:

◆   fraud by staff members, customers or third parties. This includes fat finger error – human error caused by pressing the wrong keyboard key when using a computer to input data, such as accidentally instructing a payment of £100 million instead of £10;

◆   loss due to inadequate performance of a risk model;

◆   damage to physical assets, such as due to fire or flood;

◆   business disruption events including power cuts, system failures and employees going on strike;

◆   health and safety incidents;

◆   customer service problems; and

◆   security breaches such as cyber-attacks that compromise the integrity of organisational data and result in a prolonged operational disruption. For example, a WannaCry cyber incident in 2017 disrupted NHS services in the UK for one week.

Operational risk typically includes legal, regulatory compliance and data quality risks. Legal risk is the risk that an organisation will be unable to meet its obligations as required by law. Examples of legal risk are regulatory fines or losses due to a legal action taken by private parties (such as an organisation being sued and losing a case for breach of contract).

Regulatory compliance risk arises when an organisation may be in violation of applicable laws and regulations. As a result, it may face severe consequences and penalties such as fines, higher capital requirements (for banks) or negative media publicity.

Data quality risk is the risk that data used to calculate internal or regulatory risk exposures is incomplete or incorrect. For example, the consequences for banks regularly submitting wrong regulatory risk exposures can be higher capital and liquidity requirements, and increased regulatory scrutiny.

Case study 5.4 shows how an operational risk event can be a cause of a material financial loss.

Case study 5.4

Allied Irish Bank (AIB) is a one of the 'Big Four' banks in Ireland that offers a wide range of personal and commercial banking services. It is listed on the Euronext exchange.

In 2002, AIB became embroiled in an operational fraud scandal when one of its employees was exposed for entering a large number of unauthorised trades that ultimately resulted in around $700 million losses.

This incident exposed weak operational controls within AIB. It attracted a lot of negative publicity as well as regulatory attention.

Reputation risk
Reputation risk, also referred to as reputational risk, is an example of strategic risk. It refers to a risk of loss resulting from damages to the reputation of an organisation, the value of its brand and perceived goodwill.

The Reputation Institute define reputation as 'the level of trust, admiration, good feeling, and overall esteem a stakeholder has for that organisation'. Reputation risk can be defined as an event that will negatively affect the relationship between an organisation and its stakeholders.

Although reputation is an intangible asset, it can be very valuable. A good reputation gives an organisation a competitive advantage. It helps to attract more customers and high-quality employees. It also contributes to lower overall marketing and financing costs. Charities and not-for-profit organisations rely on good reputation to attract donations and volunteers.

It takes an organisation years to build a good reputation and only minutes to ruin it. Damage to a reputation often corresponds with negative publicity, increased regulatory scrutiny, litigation costs and loss of customers and key employees. Very often, loss of reputation directly translates into the loss of the CEO, the chair of the board or both (for example, the 2018 Danske bank money laundering scandal cost both the CEO and the chair their jobs). One signal of a reputation loss in a quoted company is a sudden drop in its share price.

Reputation losses are often associated with some kind of a risk event, most commonly a large-scale operational incident or a substantial liquidity loss. This is because the management of operational and liquidity risks is embedded within the overall organisational governance framework. Any large-scale failure suggests a material deficiency in internal control. Examples of such risk events include the VW emissions scandal and the BP Deepwater Horizon incident. In both cases, the extent of VW's and BP's share price decline following reputational damage was more severe than the actual costs from these events. The difference was due to investors repricing VW and BP on the expectation that both companies would lose a portion of their future profits due to loss of reputation.

Reputation losses may also be caused by employees' actions (employee risk), such as ethical lapses or a criminal offence. Organisational culture has a significant influence on the risk of employees engaging in unethical activities. To reduce this risk, organisations are encouraged to develop and enforce comprehensive employee ethics and conduct training programmes.

Organisations manage reputation risk by examining their strategies, principal and emerging risks and other vulnerabilities to identify key drivers of reputational risk. A designated risk management framework can then be created to flag reputation threats. For example, if an organisation conducts some of its critical business activities in a country prone to bribes and other unethical behaviours, a special risk committee can be established to oversee and evaluate any such activities for reputational risk. Another popular measure is tracking social media sentiment around an organisation itself and a group of its key competitors. Large organisations also tend to appoint a designated reputation risk manager.

With an increasing number of communication channels, which includes the growing power of social media, bad news now travels at the speed of light. A timely and effective response by an organisation should there be a threat to its reputation is critical.

A range of contingency and crisis planning, training and testing activities needs to happen in the background. This is to ensure that contingency and crisis management teams are ready to respond to any reputational threat at any time. Preparation and response activities should be carried out by designated individuals who have the knowledge, skills, authority, agility and courage to rapidly respond to the unexpected.

Case study 5.5 remains one of the best and purest examples of reputation risk. Reputational loss was entirely driven by statements made by the CEO: no other event, such as a fire, fraud or internal control failure pre-empted this loss.

Case study 5.5

The Ratner Group was a successful jewellery business in the 1980s. The jewellery sold by the Group was regarded as cheap and tacky and the media reported on this frequently. Sales grew despite this perception, with Ratner Group eventually becoming the UK market leader, as people believed it to be good value.

On 23 April 1991, CEO Gerald Ratner, made the following statement at a high-profile Institute of Directors dinner at the Albert Hall: 'We also do cut-glass sherry decanters complete with six glasses on a silver-plated tray that your butler can serve you drinks on, all for £4.95. People say, "How can you sell this for such a low price?", I say, "because it's total crap"'.

Ratner went on to remark that one set of earrings he sold was 'cheaper than a Marks and Spencer's prawn sandwich but probably wouldn't last as long'.

The speech at the Institute of Directors dinner and his unfortunate remarks were pre-meditated and made against the advice of some of those close to him. His immediate reaction was that the speech had 'gone well'.

Ratner's comments have become textbook examples of why CEOs must choose their words carefully. As a result of the media storm that ensued, customers chose to stay away from Ratner Group shops. After the speech, the value of the Ratner Group plummeted by around £500 million, which very nearly resulted in the Group's collapse.

Ratner initially hired a chairman in an attempt to stabilise the situation. This did not help to save his job and in 1992 Ratner was fired. The Group was re-launched under a different name in 1993.

After several years contemplating the reasons for his failure, Ratner rediscovered his zest for business and entrepreneurial flair as he went to set up a health business, followed by an online jewellery business. Gerald Ratner went on to document his experiences in 2007 in a book *The Rise and Fall…. and Rise again*.

'Doing a Ratner' has become UK business shorthand to describe how one can destroy a business in 10 seconds and how not to behave as a business leader.

3.2 An alternative approach to risk categorisation

Kaplan and Mikes (2012) developed an alternative risk categorisation framework that segregates all organisational risks into three categories:

◆ preventable risks
◆ strategy risks
◆ external risks.

Kaplan and Mikes used this approach to highlight some important aspects of risk management in organisations:

◆ Organisations are in the business of taking risk – in a world full of risk, organisations cannot achieve their objective without taking certain risks;
◆ not all risks are within the direct control of organisations; and
◆ weaknesses in risk governance and control are the central cause of human-made risk events in organisations.

Kamensky (2012) suggested that the new framework would enable organisations to determine the way in which risks should be managed.

Preventable risks are defined as internal risks faced by organisations that are controllable. Ideally, organisations should look to eliminate or avoid such risks whatsoever. In reality, organisations may choose to have tolerance levels for risks that cannot be managed at a 100% elimination rate as the high cost may outweigh the incremental benefit. Employee risk (discussed earlier) would fall in the category of preventable risks. Preventable risks are best managed through active prevention: monitoring risky activities and guiding human behaviours within an organisation.

Strategy risks are assumed by organisations willingly in order to gain a competitive advantage and to achieve their objectives. Examples of strategy risks include:

◆ credit risk;
◆ research and development risks;
◆ risks associated with merging two organisations; and
◆ undertaking a major change project, such as implementing a new IT system.

Strategy risks are different from preventable risks because they are not explicitly undesirable and cannot be managed via a rules-based control model. Strategy risks are best managed through a framework that is designed to minimise the actual materialisation of risks and to enhance the overall organisational ability to contain and respond to such risks should they occur.

External risks are risks external to an organisation and are beyond its influence or control. Major political changes, wars and natural disasters are examples of external risks.

External risks are best managed through identification and mitigation actions. An organisation may manage the impact of external risk events through effective business continuity and contingency planning programmes. An organisation may also alter its physical presence to reduce the impact of political change. For example, an international company originally based in the UK may relocate some of its operations to mainland Europe to reduce any adverse effect from Brexit.

3.3 Risk of internal control failure

Internal control risks are related to the governance and internal control activities of an organisation. Any organisation with employees and managers (including directors) may find that they do not always act in the best interests of the organisation and its stakeholders. This may be because they make an innocent mistake, a deliberate (possibly criminal) act or a negligent omission.

Internal control risks may arise from the processes, systems and controls that an organisation has in place to manage its employees and managers. Poorly designed processes, systems and controls may increase the potential for innocent mistakes and can facilitate less innocent activities. Weaknesses in policies, procedures and staff training can increase the risk of internal control failures where employees and managers are unclear about their roles and responsibilities.

Internal control risks are within the control of an organisation. It is the responsibility of an organisation's board and senior management to ensure that internal control risks are mitigated appropriately.

Case study 5.6

The London Interbank Offer Rate (LIBOR) scandal stemmed from the illegal fixing of interest rates for the provision of credit from one bank to another. Banks frequently borrow and lend money between each other to help manage their liquidity. The rates at which banks lend to each other are agreed on a case-by-case basis and the agreed price is reported to facilitate the calculation of LIBOR. The interest rate at which a bank can borrow money is a key indicator of its financial health.

Staff within Barclay's investment banking operation decided to manipulate the interest rates reported to LIBOR during and after the financial crisis of 2007–08. The purpose of this was to make Barclays appear to be stronger financially than it actually was. This misreporting had the effect of increasing the LIBOR rate, which is a key factor in the determination of credit interest rates on mortgages and other loans.

The independent inquiry into the Barclay's LIBOR scandal (Salz, 2013) found that failures in the risk sub-culture of Barclays investment banking division was the primary cause, coupled with weaknesses in relation to the management of this culture by Barclay's senior management and board.

In terms of the sub-culture, the investment bank had a management and recruitment policy that focused on winners and winning at any cost. The

traders involved in fixing the LIBOR rate did not see anything wrong with what they did at the time, because it helped Barclays to 'win'. Employees in the retail banking and credit card businesses were not found to exhibit the same cultural trait.

In terms of the broader risk culture, Barclay's senior management and board were criticised for not making clear the codes of behaviour that all staff should adhere to while at work. Since the scandal Barclays has made major changes to its employee code of conduct and to the enforcement of this code.

Barclays received a large fine of £290 million from UK regulators and $100 million from US regulators. The CEO and chair resigned. Since the scandal, Barclays has made significant changes to its internal control environment, including the implementation and enforcement of a new code of conduct for employees.

3.4   Deciding on appropriate risk categorisation

The approach chosen by an organisation to help categorise its risks will depend on the nature of its activities. Small and less complex organisations may not require detailed risk typologies. The three categories proposed by Kaplan and Mikes will probably be sufficient. Larger organisations, especially in complex sectors like financial services, can have very detailed typologies.

The issue is not just the way in which risks are categorised, but the number of sub-categories. Organisations have to decide how detailed to make these sub-categories. Too many categories can make it difficult to categorise risks; too few and important differences between risk types may be missed.

Test yourself 5.3

What is the purpose of classifying risks using the common categorisation approach?

3.5   The role of the board

The board is ultimately responsible for overseeing the effectiveness of risk management practices within an organisation, as well as compliance with all relevant regulations.

The board is encouraged to exercise this oversight by defining the process for ongoing monitoring and review of risks, including the scope and frequency of reporting and assurance. Typically, key risks are regularly communicated to the board through a dedicated risk dashboard.

4. Risk interconnectivity

With the rise of globalisation, innovation and technological advances, there has been a growing recognition that risks are becoming much more complex, impactful and interconnected.

Traditionally, risk management practices would rely heavily on pre-existing knowledge and experience within a specific area, failing to identify potential interconnections with other areas. In fact, the whole concept of interconnectedness was seen as unimportant.

As a result, there has been a noticeable increase in unexpected low-probability, high-impact risk (black swan) events that were not adequately captured by traditional risk management frameworks. The financial crisis of 2007–08 is a good example of such an event.

In statistics, interconnectedness is expressed by correlation which measures the extent to which different variables move together. Positive correlation between two variables means that both variables will increase or decrease together.

For example, there was an increased correlation between the growth of the household debt, the growth in residential mortgages and the growth of house prices prior to the 2007–08 crisis, indicating that more buyers were able to purchase homes on credit and more credit was needed to keep up with rising house prices. What this correlation also shows is that: mortgage credit was more accessible; home buyers were over-extending themselves by buying potentially overvalued homes; and home buyers were hoping that future increases in house prices would help them to pay for their mortgages. As house prices started to decline from their peak in 2006, many mortgage borrowers found themselves in either delinquency or default, an event that triggered the unfolding of the financial crisis.

Another way to appreciate the interconnectedness of risks is by looking at how one risk can trigger the occurrence of another. For example, a 'fat finger' error placing an accidental order to buy a large number of highly risky securities may lead to a sudden deterioration of liquidity, as well as an increase in market and credit risks, making all these risks interconnected.

Since the financial crisis of 2007–08, there has been an increase in use of 'what if?' scenarios within the financial services industry to analyse how a systemic shock can affect the overall financial system and its players. Such scenarios help to identify risk connections and organisation-specific vulnerabilities.

From the non-financial industry perspective, interconnected risk management is often focused on strengthening operational resilience and emergence response.

Chapter 15 looks at the issues surrounding complex risks in detail.

5. Risk perception

There is considerable debate within academic literature on whether risk can or should only be expressed in objective terms. While primarily theoretical, this debate has practical considerations for an organisation.

In an objective sense, risk is a statistical concept that can be quantified using probability, impact and exposure. Therefore, any organisation should be able to estimate its risk exposures objectively. A number of challenges arise with this view.

◆ The choice of a specific statistical model, underlying assumptions, model parameters and a confidence interval is a subjective action.

◆ The output is only as good as the input and thus, patchy or erroneous data can skew the results. The choice of how to clean patchy data is also a subjective action.

◆ Many risk models use historical data to predict future risk events and rely on supporting subjective judgements around any forward-looking modelling enhancements or qualitative statements.

◆ Not every risk can be quantified using conventional statistical methods.

◆ Even where risks can be quantified, decision makers and those involved in the process of quantifying these risks may not interpret their findings in an objective manner. In other words, different people would make different estimates and conclusions about the same risk.

5.1 Subjective judgements and actions

The choice of a risk model, underlying assumptions and other model parameters usually sits with an organisation, although some regulatory risk models may come with a set of pre-defined assumptions. At this stage, subjective choices or omissions through human judgement (or negligence) can have a far-reaching impact on the accuracy or the relevance of produced estimates.

Another important subjective parameter of a risk model is the confidence level. An organisation may apply a specific confidence interval to reflect the accuracy of calculated estimates. For example, a 95% confidence interval means that the estimates produced by the risk model are expected to be correct 95% of the time and wrong 5% of the time. Application of the confidence level is very common in financial institutions like banks and insurance companies.

In order to estimate probability and impact, an organisation needs large amounts of data, either generated internally or sourced through approved external data providers. An organisation uses risk models to convert this data into estimated probabilities and impacts. Subjectivity around the data choice comes in many shapes.

◆ Should an organisation use an internal or an external data source?

◆ If an organisation must use an internal data source because of cost considerations, is this data independent or generated by interested and potentially conflicted parties? For example, are there issues when traders supply data to risk managers, who then use this data to estimate the extent of risk taken by these traders?

◆ What specific data series should a risk model use?

◆ If the data frequency is chosen to be daily and a selected data series has gaps (a significant number of daily data inputs is missing), what statistical approach should be used to clean this data?

◆ If no specific data series is available, is there a proxy series that can be used instead (can a risk manager opt to use index data series to approximate the risk of a constituent of this index)?

◆ If multiple similar data series alternatives are available, which one should be chosen for the model? It is worth noting that, while data series may look similar, there may be structural differences in underlying calculation methodologies. One data series may be calculated by using a simple average of all daily data inputs as submitted by authorised data providers, whereas another might be based on a more complex approach aimed at removing any extreme and potentially erroneous data submissions.

A significant number of risk models use historical data to predict risk events that may occur in future. This practice makes the whole exercise somewhat backward-looking, as there is no guarantee that past outcomes are a reliable indicator of future ones. This can be a significant issue in volatile environments where risk exposures are increasing or decreasing at an exponential rate.

Historical models are often enhanced with overlays to correct for this deficiency. The most common overlay is some sort of a stress scenario. For example, a common stress scenario overlay used by the financial services industry is the financial crisis of 2007–08. It is also fair to say that as a prudent measure, risk modes tend to be over-conservative.

All of the above subjective judgements and actions make it extremely difficult to conduct a like-for-like comparison of similar risks across a group of organisations that share similar characteristics and interests. In the financial services industry, an output from a more standardised regulatory model can be used as an alternative benchmarking option.

5.2 Unquantifiable risk

Unquantifiable risk is the risk that cannot be measured using conventional statistical methods. Lack of relevant or quantifiable data is often the primary reason. Reputational risk, compliance risk or corporate culture health are good examples of unquantifiable risks.

Organisations use a combination of quantitative and qualitative solutions to manage such risks. For example, one way to measure an organisational culture is to build a framework that would combine quantitative inputs – for example, a number of whistleblower complaints per year or employee retention rates – with qualitative inputs such as employee satisfaction surveys and exit interviews.

5.3 Subjectivity of risk perception

Studies show that most people do not think of risk in statistical terms. Even when they are presented with objective data about risk exposures, they may not respond to this data in a statistically rational way by making the decisions that yield the best possible outcomes. Instead, people usually base their decisions on subjective factors that influence how they perceive risk.

People react to risk using a complex array of perceptions that cause them to interpret the statistical data that is presented to them in different ways. Common perception issues are outlined in Table 5.1.

Risk perception	Description
Choice	A person's perception of risk is reduced if they take risks they choose. This is because they focus on rewards while being confident in their personal ability to control risks. This means that organisational decision makers may underestimate the risks associated with decisions that they choose to make, such as strategic decisions to exploit profitable opportunities.
Control	People are more willing to accept risks they believe they can control. Risks that are out of a person's control are of greater concern because they cannot influence their outcome. Most people overestimate their ability to control risk, thinking they are better than average – which, of course, everyone cannot be. Organisational decision makers will tend to underestimate the risks associated with activities they believe they can control.
Familiarity	Familiarity with risks can affect risk perception. People get used to living with certain risks, such as the risk of having an accident while driving, and therefore perception of the real risk can diminish with time and experience. Spotting new and unfamiliar risks can be a particularly difficult task for people influenced by a familiarity bias.
Distant risks	If the effect of a certain risk is far into the future, people may be more willing to accept that risk now. A typical example is a smoker willing to accept known risks spelt out on the packet for the transient pleasure a cigarette may bring. In an organisational context, this means that the long-term effects of environmental hazards, for example cancer, will tend to be underestimated.
Media	The media has a huge impact on shaping people's perceptions of risk. Risks ignored by the media are not seen as important as those that receive media attention. Rightly or wrongly, people think a risk must be important if the media has chosen to cover it. The media, including social networks and the internet, are one of the main influences on peoples' perception of risk.
Randomness	Natural 'Act of God' or fate risk versus human-made risks are perceived differently. Naturally occurring events are more accepted, as they are believed to be a random bad luck, whereas people assume that something can be done to control or reduce human-made risks. As analytical and technological advancements improve organisational defence mechanisms, people are less willing to accept that certain risks are simply a result of bad luck. For example, an organisation that operates a bridge is expected to evaluate the structure of the bridge against a number of probable natural disaster scenarios such as prolonged periods of heavy rain or the temperature raising or falling below observable levels in the past.

Table 5.1 Common risk perceptions

Stop and think 5.3

Which of the perceptual biases in Table 5.1 may have affected your risk management or risk-taking decisions when at work?

In addition to common risk perceptions, behavioural economists have also identified a series of **cognitive biases** that may influence the decision making process, especially when it comes to estimating the impact from emerging risks. A cognitive bias is an influencing factor that causes someone's judgement to deviate from a norm or rationality. Cognitive biases are directly connected to how people perceive and process information. Common cognitive biases include:

cognitive bias
An influencing factor that causes someone's judgement to deviate from a norm or rationality. Cognitive biases are directly connected to how people perceive and process information.

◆ *Group-think bias* happens when individual decision makers strive for group consensus over alternative viewpoints;

◆ *Authority bias* arises when a senior member's viewpoint overrules the viewpoints of other contributors;

◆ *Status quo bias* favours preservation of the current state; and

◆ Myopia bias leads to an increased focus on smaller and less impactful risks at an expense of more strategic and more impactful risks.

People who perceive risk in these ways are not stupid or irrational. They are simply responding to risk in a human manner. Risk perceptions are deeply seated in the human psyche and may also be influenced by past experiences, education, training, social interaction, and organisational and national cultures. When weighing up risk management or risk-taking decision options, an organisation should consider the availability of objective data as well as psychological biases that may influence the results.

Test yourself 5.4

What risk perception factors may cause decision makers to underestimate the level of risk?

6. Other practical challenges

There are several other common practical challenges and trends surrounding risk models, including (but not limited to) the following.

◆ Risk models have become increasingly complex due to the availability of advanced analytical tools and techniques.

◆ Balancing multiple outputs from different risk models that are meant to estimate the same type of risk is becoming more of an art than a science.

◆ Risks are interconnected, whereas many risk models are often designed to address an individual component of risk at a loss of a bigger picture.

◆ In the financial services industry, the number of required regulatory risk models has been growing exponentially due to increased regulation since the financial crisis of 2007–08.

◆ The link between risk model assumptions and long-term strategic objectives needs to be stronger. The FRC encourages organisations to develop viability statements to connect long-term organisational strategy with principal risks.

6.1 Remediation techniques

A number of remedies are available for organisations striving for objective risk management solution in the light of numerous judgemental and psychological barriers that they face.

Taking charge of an organisational data infrastructure is a major remedy. In fact, instituting an appropriate enterprise data management strategy is now seen as a necessity rather than optional.

Fully utilising the potential of the board is another. The expectation that boards will oversee organisational risk taking and risk management practices has increased since the financial crisis of 2007–08. This includes the oversight of risk culture. Strong boards will question key risk assumptions and challenge risk mitigation strategies, while helping the management to keep an eye on principal and emerging risks.

Chapter summary

◆ In an organisational setting, risks arise whenever a single decision or an action could result in more than one potential outcome.

◆ Uncertainty can arise where it is not possible to calculate the probability and impact of the outcomes associated with a risk. Given that it is rarely possible to calculate probability and impact with complete accuracy, a degree of uncertainty almost always exists.

◆ In an objective sense, risk is a statistical concept that is quantified using probability, impact and exposure. Exposure is a function of probability and impact. The greater the exposure, the greater the risk.

◆ It is common for risks to be categorised. This helps an organisation to understand the range of risks to which it may be exposed. Categorisation also supports the management of risk because different types of risk may require different management approaches.

◆ There are many different approaches to categorising risk. An organisation may develop its own approach or use an established approach provided by a risk management standard or regulator.

◆ There has been a growing recognition that traditional risk management approaches do not adequately capture interconnected risks. The use of 'what if?' scenarios can help organisations to identify and manage such risks.

◆ Decision makers in organisations do not always perceive risk in an objective sense. Risk perceptions may affect how they view risk and may cause them to over or under-estimate the level of risk.

Chapter six
Risk management as a foundation of organisational success

Contents

1. Introduction

Modern risk management is a fully integrated part of an organisational decision-making process. It is used to anticipate and quickly respond to different risk events that can otherwise negatively impact the value of an organisation. Connecting risk to strategy allows organisations to directly link their long-term objectives with risk-taking opportunities.

This chapter explains how the risk management discipline has evolved during the twentieth century and how different risk management practices can be deployed to make an organisation more valuable. It ends with a short summary of how regulators view risk.

2. The evolution of risk management

Risk management as it is understood today is a discipline that evolved during the twentieth century. It is a formal approach to anticipating and dealing with risk and uncertainty in setting and achieving certain objectives.

People have always been interested in foretelling the future. Our decisions as to what to do today are influenced by what we want to achieve and what we think will happen in that regard in the future. It is only very recently that this was considered to be within human control.

The concept of measuring risk dates from the middle of the seventeenth century, when two mathematicians, Pascal and Fermat, first proposed theories of probability. Gamblers knew long before this that the chance of throwing a particular number with a fair dice was the same for each number on the dice, but they had no mathematical means of expressing this. Most people believed a particular number came up because of 'fate' or some decision of the 'gods'. You cannot manage an event that is decided by the gods.

A significant development came in 1662 with the publication of an analysis of birth and death records in London. This was compiled by a businessman called John Graunt with help from William Petty, a professor of anatomy and music and author of a pioneering book on 'political arithmetic', a precursor to modern economics. Graunt summarised the available data and drew from it a variety of conclusions, including a forecast of life expectancy. He established the value of analysing past data as a reasonable guide to what might happen in the future. From then on, mathematicians became obsessed with collecting measurements to provide reliable past data for analysis.

By the twentieth century, attention had moved on from essentially mathematical developments and the study of distributions of naturally occurring phenomena. People were interested in the human element of decision making and risk taking, such as:

◆ how people decide which risks to take;

◆ why people with the same facts make different decisions; and

◆ why people gamble when they know the mathematical odds are unfavourable.

It was not until the 1950s that risk management theory developed into a form that would be recognised today. Traditional insurance products were becoming costly and incomplete, and some types of risk were uninsurable. During the 1960s, attention turned to contingency planning, self-protection and self-insurance schemes, and protection against work-related illness and accidents. Hazard prevention and safety management became fashionable.

The 1970s saw large fluctuations in interest rates, stock market returns, exchange rates and commodities. To manage these risks, financial instruments like derivatives were used for the first time. By the 1980s, large companies were introducing financial risk management and financial institutions were increasing their market and credit risk management activities. Operational risk and liquidity risk management became popular in the 1990s due in part to some high-profile organisation failures, such as Barings Bank, and because organisations realised the benefits of more efficient cash flow and operations management. Regulation increased at this time in an attempt to better protect organisational stakeholders.

Computers became affordable in the 1990s: with them, new opportunities were created for the assessment and reporting of risk. Computers also brought with them a complex array of new risks that needed to be managed, and cyber risk management was born.

A parallel force during the 1970s, 1980s and 1990s was globalisation. Economies and markets became more interconnected, making risk management more challenging. It also made it harder for stakeholders to monitor the risk management activities of organisations. A series of corporate governance scandals from the 1980s led to increasing governance regulation. Areas such as environmental management and health and safety became more regulated.

A major regulatory milestone was in 2002 in the USA, with the introduction of stringent governance and financial reporting regulations via the Sarbanes-Oxley legislation. This covered all companies listed on the New York stock exchange, which includes many international organisations. The US corporate governance requirements emphasised risk management controls and recommended risk management standards to be followed. These developments were echoed in the UK with particular attention paid to the role, responsibilities and actions of directors, chief executives and senior management of organisations, who were to be held accountable for their long-term decisions.

In the 21st century, risk events are no longer accepted as fate in most countries of the world. People look for the causes and try to allocate responsibility. Expectations regarding the professionalism of risk management activities have increased, due in large part to the development of international standards like ISO 31000. The financial implications of risk events are argued by lawyers; social media means that there are few hiding places for organisations accused of management failings. While events such as lightning strikes are still attributed to 'Acts of God', authorities are expected to recognise the probability of other natural disasters occurring in their region and legislate to mitigate their effects.

3. The role of risk management in organisations

Risk management is a profession that supports decision making in organisations. Risk is an inevitable and sometimes desirable part of organisational activity. It should still be identified, assessed, monitored and controlled, however. Effective decisions require information on their potential outcomes as well as implementation approaches that maximise the potential for positive outcomes while reducing the potential for negative ones.

3.1 Reducing uncertainty

Uncertainty, in terms of the absence of a clear understanding of the probability and impact associated with the range of possible outcomes that may result from a decision or activity, is rarely if ever desirable.

In the face of uncertainty, risk management can be used as an information-gathering tool. This might include collecting data on past risk events to build a clearer picture of what can occur. Trend analysis and risk modelling may be used, as can scenario analysis, which involves asking 'what if' questions and imagining worst case scenarios.

It is rarely possible to collect a 100% accurate picture of probability and impact. With sufficient information gathering, probability and impact can often be estimated with a relatively high degree of confidence.

3.2 Anticipation and resilience

Risk management is a tool that can be applied in two main contexts:

◆ as a means to anticipate and predict risk events so that the probability of negative events can be reduced and positive ones increased;

◆ as a means to help organisations respond effectively to, and recover quickly from, risk events that have not been anticipated. This context is often known as resilience.

Risk management and anticipation

The anticipation of risk is an important part of the risk management process. Risks are identified, assessed and monitored before they are controlled. Identification is used to highlight the range of risks that an organisation is exposed to, and assessment and monitoring is used to help prioritise scarce control resources. Controls are used to manipulate probability and impact to achieve more favourable outcomes and reduce an organisation's exposure to negative outcomes.

A major problem with this approach is that not all risks can be anticipated. Risks may be unknown. Even where they have been identified, it may be impossible to calculate probability and impact with sufficient accuracy (there may be a high degree of uncertainty). Risks such as those associated with global warming and the use of the internet are examples of risks that are known. However, the probability and impact of their associated outcomes are difficult to estimate because of insufficient information.

Risk management and resilience

From time to time, organisations will encounter risk events that they did not foresee. This failure of foresight may be because a risk event was unknown or because the event was known but it was impossible to estimate probability and impact.

One example of this is the so-called 'black swan' event (Taleb, 2007). Black swan events are risk events that occur which were previously thought to be impossible or highly improbable based on the information that was available.

By definition, black swan events are hard to predict and cannot be quantified using statistical methods. That does not mean that they are uncommon, as illustrated by the range of major risk events that have occurred in recent years. These include the 2007–08 financial crisis, terrorist attacks, the grounding of aircraft for several days due to volcanic activity, and category five hurricanes and cyclones larger than almost all seen before. Growing global populations, increasing reliance on technology, and interconnected economies and markets all mean that black swan events occur on a regular basis.

Stop and think 6.1

Identify five black swan events that have occurred since 2001.

In the face of high levels of uncertainty, organisations may find that they need to invest in resilience. This means:

◆ responding quickly to mitigate the immediate effects of unanticipated events as they unfold (effective crisis management);

◆ recovering quickly from the aftermath of an unanticipated event to ensure that the organisation is able to maintain its operations and achieve its objectives (business continuity management); and

◆ reviewing past unanticipated events in order to improve future resilience (organisational learning).

Test yourself 6.1

What is a black swan event?

3.3 Supporting the internal control environment

Risk events due to a breakdown in internal control arrangements (see Case study 5.6 on page 101) can be very costly, damage the reputation of an organisation, and divert attention from strategic and operational priorities. In most organisations, ensuring effective internal control is an important part of risk management. This is emphasised by many types of regulation, such as the US Sarbanes–Oxley Act and the UK Corporate Governance Code.

Risk management can help to strengthen internal control by providing a means to identify, assess, monitor and control internal control risks. This can be done as part of an organisation's regular risk management activities as well as through the use of specialist internal control management tools, such as:

◆ risk-based compliance reviews

◆ internal audits

◆ external audits.

Risk-based compliance reviews
Many organisations assess whether their employees and managers are complying with applicable laws and regulations, such as health and safety or environmental regulations.

Compliance reviews are often risk-based, meaning that more detailed and more frequent reviews are conducted in areas where the consequences of non-compliance are high, or risk assessment and monitoring activities suggest that there is a higher risk of non-compliance. It would be very difficult to organise a risk-based compliance review without effective risk management.

Internal audit

Most organisations conduct internal audits to ensure that their policies and procedures are designed and implemented in an effective way and to check that operational processes are working efficiently. Internal audits may incorporate compliance reviews to investigate the degree of compliance with applicable laws and regulations.

Internal audits often identify issues that relate to risk management practices in organisations, typically failures in the design or application of risk controls. Effective risk management in advance of an audit should help to reduce the number of control failures identified in internal audits. Failures can be identified much sooner, reducing the possibility of an adverse risk event.

Risk management can be used to support the practice of risk-based auditing, where more detailed and more frequent internal audits are conducted in organisational functions, activities and processes that are assessed as high risk. For example, functions or activities that involve a significant degree of manual handling may have more frequent safety management audits.

External audit

External auditors review on an annual basis whether the financial reporting controls within an organisation are adequate. This is to ensure that the annual report and accounts are accurate and free from material financial misstatements, and also directs the workplan of the auditor.

Many external audits go beyond the more immediate financial reporting controls within an organisation to review the broader governance and internal control environment of an organisation. The accuracy of an organisation's financial statements are not solely dependent on financial controls. A broader review of controls will help the external auditor provide a more accurate opinion on whether the organisation is likely to continue as a going concern.

Case study 6.1

The VW emissions scandal is an example of how ineffective risk management can destroy value and affect an organisation's ability to create value in the future.

In September 2015 the US Environmental Protection Agency (EPA) found that a software device (known as the defeat device) had been installed on certain models of diesel car to provide false readings in emissions tests.

Subsequent investigations revealed that there were problems with the emissions testing of millions of vehicles worldwide. The scandal forced VW to recall millions of its vehicles and led to it reporting its first

quarterly loss in 15 years in October 2015 (of $2.5bn). The value of VWs shares also dropped by 23%.

As at 2017, costs have totalled around $25 billion (in fines, recall costs and so on and VW is facing a major class action legal challenge from a group of customers which could cost billions more.

The scandal is a painful lesson in the value that can be destroyed by risk events, especially where deliberate wrongdoing has been identified. Managing the scandal will also have cost significant amounts and diverted resources from developing new products or process improvements. The company may have sold more cars had the scandal not emerged.

Effective risk management by the external auditor should minimise the risk of not detecting material financial misstatements and minimise wrong opinions. This will ensure that external auditors can provide reasonable assurance regarding the validity of the organisation's financial information.

4. Linking risk to strategy

There has been a growing demand for more effective risk management practices to cope with the rapidly changing business environment, especially since the financial crisis of 2007–08. Many of these changes involve regulatory or industry standard-related compliance that put organisations under great public and regulatory scrutiny, such as:

- anti-money laundering
- anti-terrorism financing
- climate change disclosures
- corporate governance reporting
- environmental compliance
- contingency planning
- data protection regulations
- Basel financial regulations.

As a result, many organisations are already incorporating the management of strategic risks within their overall risk management framework. However, the scope of strategic risk management practices is often too narrow.

Many organisations focus on assessing and managing risks that arise from a chosen strategy or different components of a strategy. For example, a strategic risk management framework often does not capture the preliminary step of assessing and categorising alternative strategies, nor does it capture the execution of a strategy risk or the assessment on how a chosen strategy supports organisational expertise, corporate mission and long-term objectives.

Expertise and mission alignment is particularly relevant when an organisation is pursuing a sizeable business acquisition. For example, one of the key reasons why Interserve plc (a UK based construction company with over £3 billion of annual revenues and 75,000 employees worldwide) faced a collapse in its share price throughout 2017–18 and a real risk of bankruptcy in 2019 is because of its ill-conceived strategic decision to expand into the energy-from-waste sector where it had no expertise (including risk management expertise).

There remains a further need to strengthen the strategic risk framework to better connect different decision-making steps, including:

◆   the initiation of a strategic review;

◆   the assessment of alternative strategies (including their overall fitness);

◆   the execution of a strategy; and

◆   monitoring and managing risks that arise from a chosen strategy.

4.1   The role of the board

Boards have undergone a considerable evolution in relation to their oversight of both risk and strategy, often including the appointment of senior executives responsible for managing these areas.

Boards are already responsible for formally approving the aggregate level of risk an organisation can take in pursuing its strategy, (the risk appetite statement). They also set the strategy that must be reflective of the organisational values and behaviours (corporate culture).

As organisational strategies evolve, and business threats become more complex and frequent, bringing risk closer to strategy is the next logical step in order for boards to remain effective in their oversight of an organisation. However, many organisations still struggle when it comes to articulation of their aggregate risks and how they link to their strategy.

A more comprehensive understanding of non-financial risks that emanate from strategy is also an area that is still evolving. Many boards employ third-party experts to help them independently review different aspects of external threats and understand how these threats may translate into actual losses for an organisation.

The advantages of linking risk to strategy are that it allows for a clearer assessment of aggregate risks related to a particular strategy, as well as enabling board level discussions on whether alternative strategies present a more attractive risk/return choice for an organisation.

Overall, boards have been taking a more significant role in linking organisational risks to the strategy, by incorporating new processes and behaviours.

◆   Challenging management on key risk appetite assumptions and definitions. Boards are expected to have a comprehensive understanding of the different risks that form the risk appetite statement and treat risk as part of the decision-making process.

◆ Seeking more comprehensive assurances from management on how the non-financial risks are monitored and mitigated versus a simple 'yes or no' approach. Boards are expected to ask management to quantify such risks in terms of their impact on the value of an organisation.

◆ Encouraging management to discuss risks in relation to the strategy.

◆ Hiring independent external advisors to evaluate risks of acquiring a sizable business or an asset.

◆ Connecting the internal audit function to strategic planning and strategic risk management processes, as well as calibrating the output from the internal audit reports within the context of strategy.

As stewards of an organisation, boards have an opportunity to expand their role beyond traditional risk oversight by providing strategic advisory guidance to management and helping them see the bigger picture.

5. Creating value through risk

Ultimately, the main objective of an effective risk management is to make an organisation more valuable.

Traditionally, the focus of risk management has been on protecting the value of an organisation by reducing the likelihood and the impact of negative outcomes, in context of its tangible assets such as buildings, machinery or cash as well as its intangible assets such as reputation. For example, a number of tobacco companies diversified their operations by entering the faster-growing e-cigarettes niche in order to protect their overall value within the cigarettes sector.

More recently, by increasing the probability and the impact of positive outcomes, risk taking has been seen as a way of generating additional rewards for the organisation. Organisations identify risk-taking opportunities by understanding key drivers of revenue growth, operational efficiency, asset and investment efficiency, balance sheet optimisation and stakeholder expectations, amongst other things.

5.1 Exploiting risk as a part of day-to-day operations

Exploitation of day-to-day risks usually refers to optimisation opportunities found within the existing risk management framework, based on the current strategy.

For example, an organisation may decide to roll out secure remote business communication tools to allow its employees to carry out their duties in a flexible and operationally efficient manner, while managing the downside risk of data loss or disruption.

5.2 Strategic risk taking

Strategic risk taking refers to the willingness by an organisation to make strategic business decisions that may lead to an increase in its total value. Strategic risk taking activity often requires a recalibration of the existing risk management framework so it remains fit for purpose.

For example, Facebook took a strategic risk by buying a photo-sharing app Instagram for $1 billion in 2012, which only had 30 million users and zero revenue. By June 2018, Instagram counted over 800 million users and its estimated US ad revenue stood at over $5 billion (according to eMarketer), with users now spending as much time on Instagram as they are on Facebook. This puts the standalone valuation of Instagram at $100 billion. By intentionally exposing itself to the risk of acquiring a non-revenue generating business and successfully integrating it within its more mature revenue generating infrastructure, Facebook managed to achieve additional awards valued at $99 billion.

On the other hand, there is also evidence that strategic risk taking can sometimes hurt organisations. A good example is Hewlett-Packard making a strategic purchase of the UK information management software vendor Autonomy Corporation plc at almost $12 billion in 2011, only to take a write down of $9 billion in 2012, $5.5 billion of which was due to accounting misrepresentations which inflated the original value of the acquired company.

Strategic risk taking is considered to be a more risky alternative versus exploiting day-to-day risks. The most common barriers that hold organisations back include the following.

◆ *Corporate culture*: management does not support strategic risk taking initiatives.

◆ *Lack of risk prioritisation*: organisations place higher priority on managing day-to-day risks at an expense of missing the bigger picture.

◆ *Failure to perform adequate due diligence*: organisations fail to properly conduct risk/benefit analysis that would make management and boards comfortable about taking strategic risks.

◆ *Lack of a designated risk manager* to stay on the top of emerging trends and navigate different strategic risk taking ideas throughout the organisation.

5.3 Adverse risk taking

In some instances, excessive risk taking may sometimes lead to an organisation assuming greater and less justifiable risks that can erode or completely destroy its value.

Excessive risk taking is often linked to the corporate culture of an organisation through its organisational **risk attitude**. Risk attitude is defined as a chosen state of mind or a response to a single decision or an action that could result in more than one potential positive or negative outcome (risk event). An organisation promotes a particular risk attitude through an adaptation of a range of allowable behaviours in response to a risk event, with any differing behaviours leading to consequences. These consequences are usually formally enforced through the compliance framework.

risk attitude
A chosen state of mind or a response to a single decision or an action that could result in more than one potential positive or negative outcome (risk event).

Organisations that promote excessively high risk-taking behaviours and/or have inadequate compliance monitoring and training procedures are at risk of having their value significantly eroded or destroyed, often by the hands of a very few people that put their own personal interests above of the interests of an organisation.

Enron's bankruptcy is a prominent reminder of how a corporate culture that encourages arrogance and excessive risk taking can lead to the demise of an organisation. Despite having a 64-page code of ethics in place, Enron failed to adequately monitor and prevent behaviours that were not aligned with its code. Enron's corporate culture was described as a culture of arrogance that made people believe that they could take excessive risks without any consequences. Upon its bankruptcy filing, numerous Enron executives were charged with criminal offences, such as fraud, insider trading and money laundering.

5.4   The role of the board

Because board members have the depth and breadth of knowledge and experience, boards that assume an active role in assessing value creative risk-taking opportunities can be powerful allies to the management team.

Boards should understand different value creation initiatives available to an organisation and be comfortable with chosen risk-taking initiatives that are presented to them by management. To ensure boards can provide effective oversight, management should present information in a receptive manner and seek timely advice and guidance from the board members.

Whenever boards have a knowledge gap in evaluating a specific risk-taking opportunity, boards should actively explore different avenues on how this gap can be addressed. Boards may wish to utilise organisational resources or hire an independent third party subject matter expert.

6. The regulatory view of risk

Globally, the banking sector faces the most prescriptive regulatory risk framework. This was developed by the Basel Committee on Banking Supervision (BCBS) to strengthen regulation, supervision and risk management practices in banks.

In Basel III, credit, market and operational risks are closely linked to the amount of economic capital held by banks. Regulators require a riskier bank to hold more capital to compensate for potential losses. Banks are allowed to either use an internal approach which takes into account their own estimated risk parameters (subject to regulatory approval) or a standardised approach to calculate their minimum risk-based capital requirements.

Liquidity regulatory requirements are a fairly recent development. The importance of sound liquidity risk management practices was reinforced by the financial crisis of 2007–08, when many banks faced a liquidity squeeze as they (unsuccessfully) tried to roll their overnight borrowings to fund illiquid long-term assets. As a result, banks have now to comply with additional requirements, chiefly:

◆ the liquidity coverage ratio (LCR) that covers short-term liquidity requirements (up to 30 days); and

◆ the net stable funding ratio (NSFR) that focuses on the longer-term funding profile of a bank (one year).

Regulatory stress tests are another regulatory requirement introduced after the financial crisis of 2007–08. Regulatory stress tests measure banks' resilience to severe macroeconomic shocks, such as a sharp economic slowdown or a severe interest rate shock. They are comprised of different scenarios meant to capture different types of risks, including credit risk. Banks that fail to pass regulatory stress tests may face the whole range of restrictions such as inability to buy back their shares, for example. The comprehensive capital analysis and review (CCAR) overseen by the US Federal Reserve is an example of a regulatory stress test.

Regulators have also recently introduced two other types of tests. The first type is meant to test vulnerabilities in the organisational business model by making banks come up with scenarios that would make their operations unviable. These include the PRA's annual reverse stress test (RST). The second type focuses on the ability of banks to wind down their businesses (also referred to as 'living wills'), such as the PRA's solvent wind down (SWD) test or the Federal Reserve's annual resolution plan. These assessments capture a wide range of different risks, including credit risk. Banks are required to adhere to all relevant regulatory requirements or face a regulatory compliance risk.

There are no explicit regulatory requirements on how organisations should manage their business and reputation risks. However, organisations are encouraged to have an appropriate risk management framework in place and report key risks as a part of their strategic annual report.

Chapter summary

◆ Risk management as it is understood today is a discipline that evolved during the twentieth century as a formal approach to anticipating and dealing with risk and uncertainty. A key premise of risk management is that risks can be assessed and controlled for the benefit of an organisation and its stakeholders.

◆ Risk management is a discipline that supports decision making and the achievement of objectives. Effective decisions require information on their potential outcomes to maximise the potential for positive outcomes while reducing the potential for negative outcomes.

◆ Linking risk to strategy allows for a clearer assessment of aggregate risks related to a particular strategy. It also enables board level discussions on whether alternative strategies present a more attractive risk/return choice for an organisation.

◆ More recently, risk taking has been seen as a way of generating additional rewards for the organisation.

◆ The banking sector has to deal with the most prescriptive regulatory risk framework.

Chapter seven

Risk management processes, perspectives, and responsibilities

Contents

1. Introduction
2. The standard risk management process
3. Enterprise risk management
4. Roles and responsibilities for risk management

1. Introduction

All organisations are exposed to risk. Consciously or not, they will go through some kind of process to support the management of these risks. In most organisations the risk management process is formalised to facilitate successful and consistent decisions regarding risk taking and control. However, this does not mean that all organisations operate exactly the same process. Differences in approach are common.

This chapter outlines the various activities that comprise a typical risk management process. It will begin by describing the standard risk management process, as well as exploring the concept of enterprise risk management (ERM). It will also look at the roles and responsibilities of those individuals or functions which are involved in designing and operating the risk management process.

2. The standard risk management process

Formal risk management activities in organisations are organised into a process: more specifically, a series of sub-processes and related activities. For simplicity, the core elements of any risk management process will be labelled the standard risk management process to differentiate them from more complicated risk management processes (notably ERM), which build on these core elements.

While these core elements are present in the risk management processes of most organisations, differences can occur depending on the nature, scale, and complexity of an organisation. Even where the basic process is similar, different terminology may be used. Do not be alarmed if the risk management processes you encounter in organisations are organised a little differently to the process outlined below or if different terminology is used.

2.1 Process overview

At its most basic, the standard risk management process consists of four elements, as illustrated in Figure 6.1.

Figure 6.1 The core elements of the standard risk management process

There are two key characteristics of this standard risk management process.

1. The process is performed sequentially, meaning that one element of the process precedes the next element.
2. This is a circular process in continuous use in most organisations. There is no clear distinction between where the process starts and ends. It is commonly assumed that the process starts with risk identification and ends with risk control, but that is an over-simplification. For example, a failure in a control or a change in the way that a risk is controlled could lead to the identification of a new risk. This could include the installation of a sprinkler system: although reducing the risk of fire in certain circumstances, it creates a new risk of water-related damage, especially if the system is unnecessarily triggered or poorly maintained.

Risk management is used for much more than board or senior management reporting. Although board or senior management risk reporting may take place monthly, quarterly, semi-annually or annually, this does not mean that each report involves a single iteration of the process. Managers and other staff across the organisation will be constantly and sometimes instinctively using the standard process to manage a range of risks.

Stop and think 7.1

Reflect on how a board of directors may use the risk management process to identify, assess, monitor and control the risks which may affect the strategic objectives of their organisation. How frequently might the board be expected to use the process?

Now reflect on how a factory operations manager may use the standard risk management process to manage the risks that may affect the efficiency and continuity of a production line. How frequently might the manager use the process? Will they always start by identifying risk?

2.2   Risk identification

Risk identification involves identifying the risks to which an organisation is exposed, for better or for worse. Organisations operate in a world of wide-ranging, changing risks and opportunities. They also have to make strategic and operational decisions on a regular, if not constant, basis to maintain their activities and achieve their objectives. This combination of wide-ranging, changing risks and constant decision making means that maintaining an accurate and up-to-date picture of the risks that an organisation is exposed to can be very difficult.

Imagine that you are a senior manager in an organisation. You and your fellow senior managers are developing a new online delivery channel for the organisation, but you face a range of questions that you must answer.

◆ What technology will you use to develop this delivery channel?

◆ How will you ensure the channel is secure?

◆ How will you fund this new venture?

◆ What will you do if the implementation of this new channel fails?

Questions such as these are hard to answer and the decisions that you make in answering them will carry a range of risks, potentially leading to outcomes that you had not expected. The more you know about the risks that you may encounter when designing and implementing this new online delivery channel, the greater the likelihood that the project will be a success. The same is the case for any other decision or set of decisions that you might make in the course of running an organisation.

There are a wide variety of tools and techniques that can be used to identify risk. Some are relatively simple, such as checklists, where a list of common risks within an organisation is provided to management to help them identify the risks associated with a particular activity or decision. Others are much more complicated, such as root cause analysis and the Delphi technique.

2.3 Risk assessment

Risk assessment usually occurs once a risk or a set of risks have been identified. The purpose of risk assessment is to determine the potential significance of the risk or risks in question. This allows these risks to be placed in rank order to help establish their priority. Higher priority risks will usually require greater management attention in terms of risk monitoring focus and risk control.

Much of the risk assessment activity that is conducted by organisations is concerned with assessing an organisation's exposure to specific risk events, where exposure is defined as:

Figure 6.2 Risk exposure equation

In some organisations you may encounter different terms to those in Figure 6.2. For example, likelihood may be used instead of probability and severity instead of impact. Some organisations may even use the term severity instead of exposure. However, the basic meaning is the same, whatever terms are used.

It should also be noted that the above equation assumes a very simple, binary outcome. Either a risk event occurs, with a given probability and impact, or it does not. In the real world it is much more likely that a range of risk outcomes are possible; sometimes an infinite range of probability and impact combinations. Organisations may – given limited time, resources and information – ignore this reality. Others attempt, with varying degrees of success, to estimate multiple probability and impact combinations using quantitative risk assessment techniques such as statistical modelling.

2.4 Risk monitoring

The risk monitoring element of the risk management process incorporates all of the activities that an organisation uses to monitor and report on potential changes in its exposure to risk or the effectiveness of its risk controls and risk management activities in general. The purpose of risk monitoring is to provide a comprehensive picture of an organisation's current risk profile in relation to the objectives it pursues and to provide an indication of how this risk profile may change.

Risk monitoring looks at both the risks that an organisation is exposed to, the effectiveness of the various controls and other risk management activities that are used to understand and manage these exposures. Risk monitoring involves the collection and dissemination of a wide range of data from different sources.

This may include:

◆ loss data, on risk events that have occurred in the past;

◆ a range of other risk, control and performance indicators, such as customer complaint data, identified internal audit issues, staff turnover statistics or financial ratios and accounting data;

◆ the production of risk reports for board directors, senior management and operational/department managers; and

◆ external risk reports for stakeholders such as shareholders and regulators.

2.5 Risk control

Risk control involves the application of tools and techniques to influence the probability and impacts of a risk event, or to mitigate any secondary business disruption and reputation effects which may follow the initial risk event.

A wide variety of tools and techniques are available ranging from physical devices, such as door locks, to financial tools, such as derivatives. There are also tools to transfer risk, such as insurance and outsourcing, as well as tools to help detect potential risk events, like smoke alarms.

Stop and think 7.2

Choose either the organisation that you work for or an organisation you are familiar with and review its risk management process. Investigate whether formal mechanisms are in place to identify, assess, monitor and control risk. Explore how these mechanisms work and see if you can find out why they were chosen. Was the choice due to cost, for example, or effectiveness?

If you are reviewing your own organisation, look for the risk management policy and any associate procedures. Normally these are not confidential and are often provided on the internal staff intranet, if you have one. If not, ask your risk function or risk manager for a copy. If you are reviewing another organisation take a look on the internet for information. Many non-commercial organisations will make public their risk management policies and procedures. A commercial organisation may provide information in its annual report.

Test yourself 7.1

Provide one sentence explanations of the following:

◆ **risk identification**

◆ **risk assessment**

◆ **risk monitoring**

◆ **risk control.**

3. Enterprise risk management

Many risk management standards and guides (see Chapter 4) promote the concept of ERM and view it as good practice.

The concept of ERM extends the standard risk management process. Many organisations are updating their risk management processes to incorporate the concept. However, this does not mean that ERM is right for every organisation. There are many benefits to ERM, but the effectiveness of ERM can depend on how it is implemented within an organisation. Poorly implemented ERM processes can do more harm than good and are often inferior to a properly implemented standard risk management process.

ERM is a hard concept to define and there is no perfect definition. The American Committee of Sponsoring Organisations of the Treadway Commission provides a definition that is in common use:

'Enterprise risk management is a process, effected by an entity's board of directors, management and other personnel, applied in strategy setting and across the enterprise, designed to identify potential events that may affect the entity, and manage risk to be within its risk appetite, to provide reasonable assurance regarding the achievement of entity objectives.'

There is one key point that you should note here: 'enterprise risk management is a process'. ERM may be a more complicated and sophisticated risk management process but at its heart it remains focused on the identification, assessment, monitoring and control of risk. The tools used within ERM to undertake these activities are often the same as those which might be used by organisations using the standard process. What changes is the philosophy that underpins the process of risk identification, assessment, monitoring and control.

3.1   The essential characteristics of ERM

There are three essential characteristics that distinguish ERM from the standard risk management process:

◆   a holistic focus;

◆   an emphasis on value added risk management; and

◆   the blending of formal and informal risk management tools and activities.

Holistic

ERM should be applied across an organisation. Enterprise risk management embraces all types of risk in every part of an organisation, recognising that different risks, functions, business lines and processes are all interconnected.

When organisations began using the standard risk management process in the twentieth century, they adopted what is now called a silo approach to risk management. This meant that different categories of risk were managed individually, often by different people or functions across the organisation. The problem with such an approach is that gaps and overlaps between risk categories may be ignored. In terms of gaps, important risks may go undetected and unmanaged because they do not fall within the responsibilities of the different individuals or functions tasked with managing specific categories of risk. New risks, as in the case of reputation risk during the latter part of the twentieth century and cyber risks in the early part of the 21st century, may be ignored because no individual or function has been assigned responsibility for their management. In terms of overlaps, correlations between risk types may be ignored. For example, in order to help manage business risk the sales and marketing function may decide to launch a new product. However, this could in turn create new operational risks, which the sales and marketing function might ignore as they do not fall within its area of responsibility.

Case study 7.1

A classic case study of the problems of a silo approach to risk management is the Perrier benzene scandal. In 1990, high levels of the toxic substance benzene were discovered in bottles of Perrier. The company took steps to recall the product and within a week Perrier withdrew 160 million bottles worldwide.

When the media first found out about the problem, Perrier did not know how to respond. For a brand whose whole identity was based around the idea of 'natural purity', the benzene incident was a major disaster. Perrier's failure to recognise and manage the growing reputation risk, as well as how it had managed the recall, led to an information vacuum which provoked much more consumer anxiety than there should have been.

The Perrier brand survived the scandal. However, Groupe Perrier was taken over by Nestlé in 1992, and the brand has never regained its pre-1990 sales volume.

One way in which the holistic characteristic of ERM can be implemented is through the creation of an integrated risk function, often under the control of a chief risk officer (CRO). The role of the integrated risk function is to look at all risks across all levels of the organisation to build a comprehensive picture of where risk lies within the organisation – particularly risks which may affect the strategic objectives and value of an organisation. Risks which can affect the strategic objectives and value of an organisation may come from anywhere, not just from top level decision making and activities. One example is IT-related risks: although IT risks may be viewed as the responsibility of IT professionals they can have far reaching implications, particularly if systems are disrupted for a prolonged period or sensitive data is lost.

A common misconception relating to the holistic nature of ERM is that the application of ERM does not mean that all risks should be identified, assessed, monitored or controlled using the same tools. For example, operational risks require different assessment and control tools than financial risks such as credit or market risk. Equally, organisations will typically use different tools in the alternative risk categorisation approach proposed in Chapter 5.

Value added

Conceptually, risk management can be viewed as an activity that is inconsistent with objectives such as profit or shareholder value maximisation. The rationale is that risk management activity is at best concerned with operational matters such as the prevention of **downside risks**, like health and safety risks, and that at times risk management may even hinder strategic success via the implementation of costly bureaucratic processes and procedures.

From an ERM perspective risk management should, if applied correctly, create and protect value to an organisation. This value is created through effective strategic level risk management decision making and operations that function smoothly without costly interruption.

The link between value creation and effective risk management is reflected in the COSO definition of ERM. Here we can see that ERM is something that should be applied to strategy setting, as well as a tool for providing assurance that an organisation is on track in meeting its objectives.

Strategic level decisions such as business expansion decisions, the creation of a major new project, cost cutting or process and product innovations, come with a variety of risks that may affect the success or failure of these decisions. To make effective strategic decisions, boards and senior managers need to understand what these risks might be, as well as how significant they are. They also need to know that these risks are being managed in an appropriate manner, so that they can be assured that their organisation is on track in implementing their strategic level decisions.

From an organisational objective perspective, boards and senior managers need to understand the risks that may threaten or support these objectives, as well as whether these risks come from their own strategic level decision making, external factors or the day-to-day operations of the organisation. They also need assurance that these risks are being managed appropriately so that risk events do not prevent the achievement of these objectives.

downside risks
Risks which have no upside and can only impact negatively on an organisation.

Formal and informal factors

This characteristic relates to the management of the formal and informal factors within organisations that can influence exposure to risk.

Formal factors relate to the tangible systems, processes, procedures, policies, committees and forums that exist within organisations, as well as organisation structures, hierarchies and such like. The design and implementation of these formal factors will affect many aspects of an organisation, including how risks are perceived and managed.

The standard risk management process is generally focused on formal factors, such as risk management policies and procedures, risk registers, risk reports and documented systems of controls. All of these formal factors have an important role to play in risk management; however, they are only part of the solution from an ERM perspective, where informal factors also have a role to play.

Informal factors relate to things like organisational culture, social networks and how risk and risk management are perceived. For example, whether risk is viewed as a threat or an opportunity, or whether risk management is perceived to be costly red-tape or value adding.

Within ERM, using these informal factors to help manage risk is just as important as using the formal ones.

3.2 The benefits of ERM

ERM creates benefits for organisations on an organisation-wide level, as well as for local business units, departments and functions. The organisation-wide benefits are presented in Table 7.1 and the local business unit, department or function benefits are presented in Table 7.2.

Benefit	Explanation
Improved reporting to support strategic decision making	Boards and senior managers should be able to make better strategic decisions by having a holistic understanding of the risks that may affect the organisation. In particular, they should be able to achieve a better balance between risk and return, taking risks only when this is justified by the potential returns. For example, an organisation that is looking to grow will need to balance this against the associated risks. ERM should allow the organisation to do this.
Avoidance of silos	Enterprise risk management should ensure that gaps and unrecognised overlaps in an organisation's risk profile are avoided.
Improved operational efficiency and cost effectiveness	Effective ERM should help to reduce the costs of risk management activity by better co-ordinating this activity across the organisation. It should also help to reduce the duplication of controls and help the organisation to learn from its risk management mistakes. With effective ERM, mistakes made in one area can be communicated rapidly across the organisation.
Improved profitability and equity value	In the case of for-profit organisations, ERM may help to reduce the costs that can be associated with more strategically significant risk exposures, thus improving profits and the value of any shareholder equity that may be invested in the organisation. This reduction is generally achieved by insulating organisation-wide cash flows from unnecessary volatility, where volatile cash flows can lead to increased financing costs. In not-for-profit organisations, a reduction in costly risk events may help to prevent operating deficits and protect surpluses. See Chapter 1 for more on the value of risk management in general.
Improved ability to achieve other business objectives	For-profit and not-for-profit organisations may benefit from ERM where it helps them to achieve non-commercial objectives, such as corporate social responsibility (CSR) and sustainability objectives. Risk events that have an organisation-wide effect can be highly disruptive and may divert management attention and funding from other objectives. Risk events such as pollution events may directly interfere with CSR and sustainability objectives.

Table 7.1 Organisation-wide benefits of ERM

Benefit	Explanation
Consistent decision making	Without a clear and consistent ERM framework, managers in different business units, functions or departments may make inconsistent decisions – for example one area may increase a particular risk and at the same time another is working to reduce their exposure to this same risk. The idea is to ensure that all decision makers achieve an appropriate balance between risk and return that is consistent with the organisation's appetite for risk and its strategy and objectives. Risk appetite will be explored in more detail in Chapter 10.
Effective resource allocation for risk management	ERM should ensure that funds are allocated on a risk exposure basis – where inherently high-risk areas receive more resources and central support to ensure that these risks are managed appropriately.
Spreading risk ownership, allowing risks to be managed by the local experts	Operational risks and internal control risks are hard to manage via a central risk function. They are very diverse and often require local insight, especially in relation to the informal aspects of these risks. ERM should allow local managers to manage these risks within an organisational framework that provides appropriate boundaries for discretion, as well as escalation procedures should a risk event occur.

Table 7.2 Local benefits of ERM

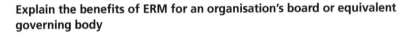

Test yourself 7.2

Explain the benefits of ERM for an organisation's board or equivalent governing body

3.3 The elements of an effective ERM process

ERM processes that are implemented poorly can be costly and may result in ineffective decision making at an organisation-wide and local level.

An organisation that uses ERM should go beyond the core elements of the standard risk management process if they are to have an effective approach. The additional factors that need to be considered when implementing an effective ERM process are:

◆ ERM policies and procedures;
◆ risk appetite;
◆ enterprise risk reporting;
◆ risk and audit committees;
◆ escalation and whistleblowing; and
◆ business continuity management.

ERM policy and procedures

Any formalised risk management process requires a documented policy and an associated set of procedures to ensure that it is used correctly. An ERM policy should include the following items.

◆ The organisation's overarching approach to risk, which is usually set out in terms of a set of guiding principles for risk taking, risk management and associated compliance requirements. Where an organisation has a mission, vision and values and strategic objectives, these should be aligned to its risk management principles to show how strategic and risk management objectives are connected.

◆ Specific risk management and associated governance, internal control and compliance objectives. Some of these objectives may be generic/non time-specific: others may vary year-by-year to reflect current priorities.

◆ How the organisation balances risk and opportunity – most opportunities involve a degree of risk therefore the organisation must be clear on the level of risk that is appropriate. Usually this is expressed in terms of risk appetite and it is common to include a statement of risk appetite within an ERM policy.

◆ A high-level overview of the ERM process used by the organisation.

◆ A statement regarding the organisation's risk culture. This will often discuss the risk culture that the organisation believes exists or would like to exist, as well as the mechanisms used to assess and manage risk culture where appropriate.

◆ Roles and responsibilities for ERM, including the role of the board and senior managers, local business-units, functions and departments, the risk function and CRO and internal audit, as well as other relevant areas.

◆ The reporting structure for ERM, including reporting lines into the CRO and any organisation-wide risk committee, where appropriate.

Enterprise risk management procedures relate to organisation-wide procedures for risk identification, assessment, monitoring and control. Depending on the scale and complexity of an organisation, these procedures may be included within the policy or in separate procedure documents.

The IRM report A Structured Approach to Enterprise Risk Management and the Requirements of ISO 31000 provides further insights on the contents of an ERM policy document.

Stop and think 7.3

On the Internet you will find examples of risk management policies, especially from government and civil service institutions, universities and charities. Look at three different policies to explore their similarities and differences. Do any of these policies contain all or some of the above elements of an ERM policy?

Test yourself 7.3

Explain the purpose of drafting an ERM policy

Risk appetite
In the 2004 COSO definition of ERM there is an explicit reference to the concept of risk appetite. This recognises the close relationship between the two concepts. An effective ERM process is as much about taking risk as it is reducing it. This is because an organisation has to take risks to achieve its objectives. The key is to understand what risks may help to create valuable opportunities for an organisation and the risks likely to have a negative effect.

For example, developing a new product or implementing a new IT system are risky activities but a new product should help to increase revenues. A new IT system may help to reduce costs and increase worker efficiency. In contrast, risks such as fraud or a compliance breach are downside risks that will only reduce revenues or increase costs. Even here, the organisation may need to weigh up the benefits versus the control costs of reducing such risks.

Risk reporting
All forms of risk management involve an element of risk reporting. The key is to develop reports that provide a holistic, organisation-wide picture, without drowning boards and senior managers in large amounts of detail. Equally, the reporting approach should provide the level of granularity needed for local business unit, function or department managers.

Risk and audit committees
Almost all organisations should have an audit committee, though not all will have a risk committee. They may be combined into one committee in some organisations; in others they are separated.

From an ERM perspective there are two key considerations.

1. Wherever risk is considered, the relevant committee should consider risk and opportunity. Audit committees are understandably focused on internal control and risk reduction. This means that where risk and audit is combined it can be hard to get into a more risk-positive opportunity mindset. This is one reason why risk and audit committees may be separated by organisations using ERM – to avoid any conflict of interest between internal control and opportunity-taking goals.

2. The risk committee must consider all categories of risk across the whole organisation. This does not mean that it has to view every single risk to which the organisation is exposed. Rather, the committee need only consider those risks which, on their own or in combination with other risks, may have a significant effect on the strategy and business objectives of the organisation.

Escalation and whistleblowing

Escalation and whistleblowing arrangements are an important part of risk monitoring. From an ERM perspective, concerns regarding control failures or other unauthorised breaches of policies and procedures including criminal acts must be reported in a consistent manner across the organisation to a single point of contact. This might be to the CRO or their delegate. In a smaller organisation it may be someone else with an organisation-wide perspective, possibly the company secretary or another governance professional.

Whistleblowing procedures should only ever be organisation-wide, given the potential seriousness of the information provided. However, distinctions may be made in terms of local versus organisation-wide escalation procedures. For risk events or control failures that are not of organisation-wide significance, local management escalation processes may be required. Where a distinction is made, escalation procedures should include rules and guidance on how to assess significance so that risk events or control failures are escalated to the appropriate level of management.

Business continuity management

Much of the focus of ERM is on anticipating potential risk events and taking steps to ensure that the probability of these events occurring is reduced. However, no organisation will ever be able to fully eliminate or control risk, especially since a degree of risk taking is needed in order to achieve its objectives. When major risk events such as a fire, flood or hacking attack occur, they may disrupt the operations of an organisation, potentially for months or even years after the initial event.

Given the impossibility of eliminating all risk, an effective ERM process must include mechanisms to ensure that the initial impacts of risk events, and their longer-term effects on the continuity of the organisation's operations, are properly managed and mitigated where it is cost effective to do so. This should ensure that the disruptive effects of risk events on the finances and operational effectiveness of the organisation are reduced, ensuring that the organisation can continue to achieve its objectives.

4. Roles and responsibilities for risk management

Risk management involves a variety of individuals, functions and committees. As with areas like health and safety, it is tempting to conclude that risk management is everyone's responsibility. To a large extent, this is true. However, this is an overly simplistic view as different individuals, functions and committees will have different types and degrees of responsibility.

4.1   The board of directors and executive management

Most of the regulations and standards for risk management indicate that an organisation's board of directors or equivalent governing body have primary responsibility for risk management. The term 'board' shall be used to mean the board of directors or equivalent governing body.

This does not mean that the board has responsibility for performing an organisation's risk management process. Rather, the board has an oversight responsibility and must ensure that it receives appropriate assurance from management that the organisation has an appropriate risk management process in place and that this process is used correctly.

In addition, boards have a key role in determining an organisation's risk appetite, as well as periodically monitoring the organisation's risk profile to ensure that the organisation remains within the agreed appetite for risk. This does not mean that the board needs information on every risk to which an organisation is exposed. The board only needs information on those risks which may cause the organisation to breach its risk appetite, since these are the risks which may affect the strategy of an organisation and its ability to achieve its objectives.

4.2 Risk committees

Some organisations will have a combined risk and audit committee; others will have a stand-alone risk committee. An organisation's size and structural complexity are factors in this decision, as is whether it has put in place ERM processes.

Risk or risk and audit committees are usually board delegated committees. This means that the committee reports directly to the board and will usually be comprised of two or more board members.

In some organisations, especially larger organisations and those with multiple business units or subsidiaries, a hierarchy of risk committees may be established (see Figure 6.3). This may consist of risk committees for specific risk categories, such as an operational risk committee, credit risk committee and a market risk committee. The latter is also called a treasury committee or asset and liability committee (ALCO). This hierarchy may include risk committees for individual subsidiaries. Where a range of risk committees are used, it is usual for these committees to report up to an organisation-wide risk committee which has visibility over any risks that may affect the whole organisation.

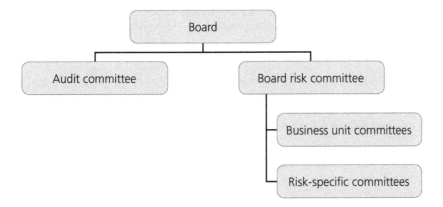

Figure 6.3 Risk committee example hierarchy

Risk committees exist to take a more detailed look at the risk management process, risk profile and risk appetite of an organisation than the board can. The role of risk committees, especially organisation-wide committees, is similar to that of the board – assurance and ensuring that the organisational risk profile does not exceed appetite. Risk-specific or subsidiary-specific committees may get into the management of specific risks and risk events, and have a more operational-level role. In all cases, risk committees will have a central role to play in the approval of risk management policies and procedures. Organisation-wide risk management policies will usually be reviewed by the board delegated risk committee, but will then be sent to the full board for final approval.

4.3   The chief risk officer

Not all organisations will have a CRO, especially small to medium-sized organisations, but the number of CROs in organisations is increasing. The first CROs appeared in financial institutions during the early 2000s and the role has now spread to other industry sectors. The role of the CRO is as follows.

◆   To support the board and organisation-wide risk committee, where appropriate, in the fulfilment of their responsibilities. This includes raising any concerns that the CRO may have regarding the risks associated with strategic decisions, major risk exposures and internal control failures that may affect the organisation's ability to meet its objectives or regulatory obligations.

◆   To direct the work of the organisation's risk function.

◆   To oversee the risk management activities of the whole organisation and ensure that risks are managed in a manner consistent with the organisation's appetite for risk, as well as its risk management policies and procedures.

◆   To work with the compliance and internal audit functions to ensure that regulatory-compliant risk management governance arrangements are in place across the organisation.

Chief risk officers may be recruited as executive directors or as senior managers, which report to the board via the CEO or finance director. Chief risk officers are especially common in organisations which have implemented ERM processes.

4.4   The risk manager and risk function

Most organisations will have either a dedicated risk manager or an individual with responsibility for risk management within their role. In larger organisations, it is common to have multiple risk managers and support staff as part of one or more specialist risk functions.

Organisations which have implemented ERM will typically have a central risk function that looks at all types of risk across the organisation. Organisations that have not yet fully implemented ERM may have separate risk functions for different types of risk. Specific risk categories, especially operational risk, may be split further into separate functions such as health and safety, fraud or IT security. Organisations with multiple business units or subsidiaries may have local risk functions, which are co-ordinated via a group risk function.

The role of the risk manager and wider risk function is to oversee, co-ordinate and facilitate risk management activity across an organisation. The risk manager may get involved in managing specific risks in some small organisations but, as an organisation grows, it is impossible for any single manager or function to manage risks on a day-to-day basis. This will be the responsibility of other managers and functions across the organisation.

Risk managers and functions also have a key role to play in risk monitoring and reporting. They will often collect risk exposure and risk management information from across the organisation in order to provide risk reports for a variety of internal stakeholders, including the board, CRO, risk committee and business unit management.

As part of their co-ordination and facilitation roles, risk managers and functions may help with risk identification and assessment exercises, such as the completion of risk registers. They may also provide advice about how to effectively control specific risks and training on the organisation's risk management policies and procedures.

Finally, the risk manager or function has a key role to play in supporting the design and implementation of risk management processes. They will often also draft risk management policies and procedures on an organisation-wide basis, or locally in the case of business unit or subsidiary specific risk functions.

Stop and think 7.4

Consider the range of risks that a multi-product, multinational organisation will have to manage. Is it practical for such an organisation to use a single risk manager or risk function to manage all of its risks? What might be a more effective approach?

4.5 The compliance manager and compliance function

Most organisations will have a full or part-time compliance manager, or a compliance function of multiple compliance managers and associated support staff.

The role of the compliance manager or function in relation to risk management is to ensure that the design and ongoing operation of an organisation's risk management processes are compliant with all applicable rules and guidance. This will include ensuring that health and safety risks and environmental risks are managed appropriately. Specific types of organisations, such as charities, government bodies and financial institutions, may be subject to additional risk management regulations concerning the conduct of their staff or their financial management.

It is important that the compliance manager or function works closely with the risk manager or function. The compliance manager or function can help to ensure that risk management processes are designed in a compliant manner. They may also support oversight of the risk management policy and processes to ensure that the compliance relevant elements of this policy or processes are implemented appropriately across the organisation. This might include conducting compliance audits in specific business units, functions or departments to ensure that compliance sensitive risk management activities are carried out correctly.

Finally, the compliance manager or function may act as an intermediary between the organisation and risk management-related regulatory and supervisory bodies. This might include commenting on regulatory consultation papers, answering questions about the organisation's risk management activities, managing supervisory inspections and providing risk management information to regulators and supervisors in accordance with regulatory reporting requirements. Usually, any risk management related information will come via the risk manager or function, although the compliance manager or function should normally check that this information is correct before passing it on.

4.6   Internal audit and risk management

Where an organisation has an internal audit function provided internally or via a third party service provider, it has a role to play in providing assurance that an organisation's risk management process is effective in terms of its design and implementation.

The internal audit function may conduct audits of the risk function and of the process that has been developed to support the management of risk. This might include benchmarking this process against industry standards or audits to determine whether managers across the organisation are using the process correctly. Routine business unit or function audits, as well as thematic internal audits, may also identify risk management-related issues in terms of how the process is used and in terms of specific control failures or new risk exposures. In addition, where an organisation has determined its appetite for risk, the internal audit function may provide an opinion on whether the organisation as a whole, as well as specific business units and functions, are keeping the organisation's risk profile within risk appetite.

The risk and audit functions will usually work closely together, supporting each other's activities. Such a close working relationship should not interfere with the independence of the internal audit function.

4.7   The company secretary or governance professional

The role of a company secretary or governance professional in risk management can vary. In very small organisations it is not uncommon for a company secretary or governance professional to be given the responsibilities of a risk manager; however, this is rare in larger organisations. Company secretaries and governance professionals may also have compliance related responsibilities.

An area where company secretaries and governance professionals may have direct risk management responsibilities is in the purchase of insurance, given the legal aspects of insurance contracts and insurance claims.

Where a company secretary or governance professional is not responsible directly for any risk or compliance management activities, the governance role that they play in supporting the activities of the board means that they must be ready to advise board members of their responsibilities for risk management and ensure that board agendas devote sufficient time to risk management. A company secretary or governance professional will need to work closely with the risk and compliance managers or functions, as well as the CRO if one is in place, to ensure that the board receives the risk reports and risk management assurance it needs to fulfil its obligations.

The company secretary or governance professional may lead on assessments of board member skills and experience. This should include assessing their skills and experience in risk management.

Test yourself 7.4

Compare the role of the company secretary or governance professional with the compliance and internal audit functions in relation to risk management

4.8 Other key functions

Other functions with responsibilities for risk management include:

- finance;
- health and safety;
- human resource management;
- information security;
- marketing and public relations;
- operations; and
- all other functional areas

Finance

The finance director and function are a key source of financial information, much of which is relevant from a risk management perspective. For example, information relevant to the financial solvency and cash flows of an organisation will come from the finance function. This information is important because, should a risk event cause a significant financial loss, an organisation may suffer liquidity problems and even become insolvent.

The finance function is a key source of risk. This includes risks relating to the accuracy of financial statements and the annual report and accounts. It may also include risks relating to the funding of the organisation's activities, such as interest rate risks and credit risks, as well as fraud. As a result, it is imperative that the finance function complies with the organisation's risk management policies and procedures to ensure that these risks are managed appropriately.

In organisations without a CRO it is common for the risk manager or function to report to the finance director.

Health and safety

Responsibility for overseeing health and safety-related matters may be assigned to the risk manager or function, as with any other area of risk. Where a separate health and safety manager or function is in place it is important that the two individuals or functions work together. In particular, the work of the health and safety manager or function must be compliant with any relevant regulations, as well as an organisation's risk management policy and procedures. The health and safety manager or function will need to report information about health and safety risks and incidents to the risk manager or function to ensure they have a comprehensive picture of an organisation's exposure to risk.

Human resource management

The human resources (HR) manager or function has a role to play wherever risk exposures may be influenced by the actions or inactions of staff. The HR manager or function may support the completion of risk assessments that have a people dimension. They also have a responsibility for ensuring that HR-related risk controls are operating effectively across the organisation, such as recruitment and disciplinary controls, escalating any concerns where appropriate. They may also supply the risk function with risk monitoring-related information, such as staff turnover statistics or absence rates.

The HR manager or function may have a role to play in supporting the assessment and management of risk culture and in behavioural risk management (see Chapters 10 and 14).

Information security

Although the risk manager or function will often have responsibility for overseeing information security risk management activities across the organisation, the day-to-day management of information security risks will usually be conducted by information security professionals working within the IT function. It is important that these professionals manage information security risk in a manner that is consistent with the organisation's risk management policy, process, and appetite for risk. It may also be necessary for these professionals to supply information to the risk manager or function to support their risk monitoring and reporting activities.

Marketing and public relations

Marketing and PR activities are a significant source of risk and they must comply with all relevant risk management policies and procedures.

The PR function can be an important source of information regarding any negative press reporting about the organisation and will have a role to play in helping to prevent such adverse reporting in the first instance.

Operations

Many of an organisation's risks will come from its day-to-day operations. Operations managers must ensure that these risks are managed in accordance with the relevant risk management policies and procedures. They must escalate any significant increases in risk exposure, which may cause a breach of risk appetite, as well as information on any significant risk events that occur.

All other functional areas

All organisational functions are a potential source of risk. It is important that every function manages these risks in accordance with the relevant risk management policy and procedures. They must ensure that risk exposures are kept within the agreed risk appetite and that any significant risk events or increases in risk exposure are escalated appropriately.

Test yourself 7.5

Contrast the role of the risk function and the finance function in relation to risk management.

Chapter summary

◆ Formal risk management activities are usually organised into a process and associated sub-processes.

◆ The standard risk management process consists of four activities: risk identification, risk assessment, risk monitoring and risk control.

◆ The process of risk identification, assessment, monitoring and control is continuous. Organisations will use this process to manage a wide range of risks on a day-to-day basis.

◆ The standard risk management process can be extended through the adoption of enterprise risk management (ERM).

◆ ERM is a process, but it adds further dimensions to the standard process. In particular ERM is concerned with the management of organisation-wide risks that may affect the strategic decisions of organisations and their ability to meet their objectives.

◆ There are various benefits associated with implementing ERM processes. These include ensuring that gaps and overlaps between risk categories are not missed and enhancing risk governance by providing clear and consistent rules for risk management decision making.

◆ To obtain the benefits of ERM, there are several important considerations. This includes having an organisation-wide risk management policy and risk appetite.

◆ A wide range of individuals and functions have different responsibilities for risk management. It is important that these responsibilities are fulfilled to ensure that the risk management process operates effectively.

Chapter eight
Frameworks for governance, risk and compliance

Contents

1. Introduction
2. Role of governance and compliance within a risk management context
3. Components of an effective compliance management framework
4. Governance structures for risk management
5. ISO 19600:2014 – compliance management systems
6. Combining governance, risk, and compliance

1. Introduction

This chapter outlines the governance and compliance frameworks that an organisation will use to ensure that its risk management framework and associated processes and procedures are implemented effectively. An organisation's risk management framework must be implemented effectively to ensure compliance with relevant laws and regulations and to meet the risk management needs of stakeholders – keeping them and their assets safe and providing a stable level of return over the long run.

Governance and compliance frameworks are a necessary component of effective risk management. Without governance and compliance frameworks for risk management, organisations will be vulnerable to bad behaviour on the part of their employees, including negligence or criminal activity. Numerous scandals, such as the VW emissions scandal, highlight the potentially severe consequences of bad behaviour.

In addition, effective governance and compliance frameworks for risk management help all employees to understand the 'rules' regarding risk management, including the risks that can be taken to support the achievement of objectives and those that are out of bounds. However, while governance and compliance frameworks are necessary, they are not sufficient on their own. Equally important is culture and risk culture, particularly the tone from the top in relation to risk taking and control (see Chapter 10).

Risk management, governance and compliance are, therefore, inseparable. It would be impossible to have effective risk management without appropriate governance and compliance frameworks. Equally, effective governance and compliance relies on risk management processes, tools and techniques.

2. Role of governance and compliance within a risk management context

An organisation's risks are managed by its employees. Employees at all levels are involved in risk taking and control. If they are competent in their role and comply with all relevant policies, procedures and codes of conduct then they should take those risks that may add value to the organisation – primarily strategic risks that have a significant upside – and control those that may have significant downsides, generally external risks and internal control risks.

Problems arise when employees are not competent in their role or, for whatever reason, do not comply with the relevant policies, procedures and codes. This can lead to inappropriate risk taking and significant control weaknesses. Cases such as the VW emissions scandal and the Barclays LIBOR scandal are examples of the serious consequences associated with weak controls and inappropriate risk taking.

Cases like the VW or Barclays scandals are rare and extreme, but less severe risk management related governance and compliance issues are common. Examples include:

◆ not following health and safety procedures (neglecting to wear safety equipment or not performing a display screen risk assessment for an at risk employee);

◆ taking excessive amounts of financial risk, such as investing too much money in high risk commodities or stocks and shares;

◆ non-compliance with expenses policies (claiming more that the allotted amount for meals or travel);

◆ fraud and the theft of company assets;

◆ diversity and discrimination issues;

◆ breaching financial mandates (such as budget approval limits or investment limits);

◆ not reporting serious risk events to senior management;

◆ hiding control weaknesses;

◆ sharing personal access passwords;

◆ taking data outside the organisation, including leaking sensitive data;

◆ not declaring any conflicts of interest; and

◆ accepting a bribe.

All of these examples may have financial consequences for an organisation and could lead to regulatory enforcement action or adverse media reporting. They will also divert management attention from strategic and operational priorities. Effective governance and compliance should prevent these adverse outcomes and increase the chance that an organisation will achieve its objectives and meet the needs of its stakeholders.

Test yourself 8.1

How are governance, risk and compliance activities complementary?

2.1   Implementing effective risk management policies and procedures

Policies and procedures are the cornerstone of effective governance and compliance. From a risk governance and compliance perspective, this means implementing risk management policies and procedures that comply with relevant governance codes, laws and regulations, and which are in the interests of stakeholders. Effective risk management policies and procedures should also ensure that the risk taking and control decisions and actions of all employees support the effective setting and achieving of an organisation's objectives.

The primary role of risk management policies and procedures is to ensure that the risk management decisions and activities of all employees are consistent and appropriate in terms of an organisation's objectives, as well as legal and regulatory obligations. These policies and procedures should make clear the principles and rules that guide risk taking and the identification, assessment, monitoring and control of risk.

Without effective policies and procedures, employees, including contractors and outsource service providers, would not know how to act and could make decisions that are not in the interest of the organisation or its stakeholders. This could lead to chaos within an organisation, with inconsistent actions and decisions leading to serious governance and compliance breaches.

Stop and think 8.1

What policies and procedures guide your actions and decisions when at work? How many of these policies and procedures are linked to your organisation's risk management activities?

If you do not currently work for an organisation, think about one you worked for previously or a school or university that you attended.

To support effective governance and compliance, the implementation of risk management policies and procedures require the following:

◆   an explanation of why they are needed;

◆   the organisation's risk management principles in a risk management policy;

◆ clear and unambiguous roles and responsibilities;

◆ board and senior management support;

◆ sanctions for non-compliance;

◆ communication and training; and

◆ regular reviews and updates.

Explanation of why the policy or procedure is needed

Employees must understand that a policy or procedure is needed to ensure regulatory compliance, to protect stakeholders, and to help the organisation set and achieve its objectives.

Employees that understand why a policy or procedure is needed are more likely to accept and comply with its contents.

Risk management principles

This relates to the principles that underpin an organisation's risk management activities. For example, one principle might be to protect the environment or to protect stakeholders from physical harm. Other principles include regulatory compliance, providing excellent customer service or treating co-workers with fairness, integrity and respect. Where an organisation has values these will often be integrated with its risk management principles.

Roles and responsibilities

The people to whom a policy or procedure applies should understand their roles and responsibilities in relation to the execution of the policy or procedure (for example, how they are expected to make decisions or perform certain activities). This will generally mean employees but policies and procedures may apply to contractors, on-site third parties and customers. For example, health and safety policies and procedures will apply to a customer in relation to their safety and personal conduct while they are on the premises of an organisation.

Board and senior management support

Employees are unlikely to comply with the contents of a policy or procedure if they see that those higher up the organisational hierarchy are not complying with it or do not see it as important.

Boards and senior managers should make clear in their words and deeds that every risk management policy and procedure is important. They should take steps to comply with all policies and procedures and remind others to do the same.

Sanctions for non-compliance

Non-compliance with a policy or procedure can have serious consequences for an organisation. Using line management structures, employees should be reminded of the importance of compliance and of the sanctions for non-compliance. This might include verbal or written warnings, poor performance reviews, the withholding of bonuses or promotion, suspension, and, ultimately, dismissal.

Communication and training

Employees need to be informed when a policy or procedure is introduced or updated. They also need access to the policy or procedure, for example via an intranet portal.

Training on how to comply with a policy or procedure can help to increase compliance rates. If employees do not understand the contents of a policy or procedure, they may accidentally make decisions or take actions that are non-compliant.

Regular reviews and updates

Regulations, working practices, and organisational structures change. To cope with these and other changes, policies and procedures should be reviewed at least annually to ensure that they remain up to date and fit for purpose. As required, policies and procedures should be updated.

2.2 Determining and implementing an effective risk appetite framework

From a governance and compliance perspective employees should understand:

◆ the risks that may be taken and any limits to the level of risk exposure that may be taken – for example, an organisation may wish to take investment risks, business risks such as launching a new product or financial risks such as providing credit;

◆ the risks that should not be taken where practicable, for example health and safety or pollution risks; and

◆ the management roles and committees that have the authority to waive limits or take risks normally considered outside of appetite where this supports organisational objectives.

The risks that may or should not be taken will usually be communicated via a written risk appetite statement. This statement should be made available to all employees, though commercially sensitive information may be redacted.

To accompany the statement an organisation may develop and monitor a set of risk metrics – for example the number of reported policy breaches or health and safety incidents – against agreed limits and thresholds. This allows management to determine whether an organisation is within or outside its appetite for risk and to take action to address any issues.

Risk acceptance processes may be a part of the risk appetite framework. The board or risk committee may be given the power to waive, on a temporary basis, normal risk limits or to take risks considered outside of appetite, where keeping the risk within limits or avoiding the risk may prevent the achievement of important organisational objectives. This might be to facilitate a major organisational change, the development of a new product or because the cost of additional controls is prohibitive.

Where an organisation has an internal audit function, it is common during internal audits to assess whether the activity, process, or function being audited is controlled in accordance with its appetite for risk. Where controls are weak and this causes an organisation to exceed its appetite for risk, immediate action will be required to rectify the situation, or the board or risk committee may need to go through the agreed risk acceptance process to accept a degree of control weakness for a brief period of time.

Risk appetite is covered in detail in Chapter 10.

3. Components of an effective compliance management framework

Compliance management frameworks are necessary to ensure:

◆ compliance with an organisation's internal policies and procedures;

◆ compliance with applicable laws and regulations (such as health and safety or environmental regulations)

◆ compliance with and standards, guidelines and codes of conduct that the organisation has chosen to comply with, such as ISO 31000.

Non-compliance with any of the above may create a range of compliance risks. For example, without an appropriate compliance management framework, an organisation's employees and managers may deliberately or accidentally take actions or make decisions that are unethical, contrary to internal policies, or fail to comply with applicable laws and regulations. This could lead to criminal sanction or other enforcement action such as fines or the loss of a licence to operate. Non-compliance with internal policies and procedures or external standards and guidelines may lead to otherwise avoidable losses or reputation damage, and disrupt the efficiency of day-to-day operations. Extreme compliance-related events, such as the Barclays LIBOR scandal or VW emissions scandal, can have long lasting financial and reputational consequences. In the case of a public limited company, they can reduce the value of shareholder equity.

3.1 Establishing compliance standards

An organisation's compliance standards are a combination of:

◆ compliance standards that are imposed on the organisation via laws and regulation; and

◆ compliance standards determined by the organisation to meet its objectives and stakeholder needs.

Imposed standards of compliance
The degree of compliance required for health and safety, environmental laws or sector regulation can vary by jurisdiction. In some jurisdictions, there may be little discretion in terms of what constitutes compliance or non-compliance; in others there may be more discretion.

An example of discretion comes from UK health and safety law, which, like some other regimes, is based on the principle of 'as low as reasonably practical' (ALARP).

The key term here is 'reasonably practical' which allows an organisation to weigh up hazards against the time and money required to control them. This means that organisations have to decide for themselves what is 'reasonably practical' and what is not.

Discretion can be useful when it prevents an organisation from taking costly compliance related actions that are grossly disproportionate to the benefits of compliance. However, it can lead to problems where the organisation and its regulator disagree on the standards for compliance. Inflexible rules that require specific actions, irrespective of the costs involved, remove this problem but can result in excessive compliance costs.

Where an organisation has discretion in determining the nature of their compliance with laws and regulations, it is important that they decide in advance the standards they will expect for compliance. It is recommended that an organisation discusses these standards with the relevant regulatory or supervisory agency to avoid any subsequent disagreements.

Voluntary standards

An organisation will have much more discretion over the degree of compliance expected from its employees when it comes to compliance standards for internal policies and procedures, or voluntary external guidance, standards or codes of conduct.

An organisation may decide that compliance should be absolute. Alternatively, it may decide to tolerate a degree of non-compliance providing that this is reported and accepted with a clear rationale provided. This rationale will usually be on cost-benefit grounds. Where the costs of compliance exceed the benefits, a degree of non-compliance may be accepted.

Extreme care should be taken when a degree of non-compliance is allowed. All such cases should be reported to the audit committee or board so that an organisation's directors or trustees are kept informed.

Test yourself 8.2

Why are compliance standards needed? When might a degree of compliance of less than 100% be acceptable?

3.2 Developing compliance processes and controls

To ensure that the agreed compliance standards are enforced within an organisation, three processes and controls are required:

◆ compliance management policies and procedures
◆ compliance reporting and escalation processes
◆ compliance training and communication.

Compliance management policies and procedures

An organisation may have a dedicated compliance management policy. This policy should contain:

◆ the compliance standards and principles that are expected;

◆ links to key compliance management procedures;

◆ reporting and escalation arrangements; and

◆ roles and responsibilities for the board, senior management, other managers and employees, and the risk, audit, governance and compliance functions if present.

In terms of compliance management principles, common principles include:

◆ an expectation that all employees will act honestly and with integrity;

◆ to manage compliance risks in order to preserve the reputation and financial resources of an organisation;

◆ that all decision makers own the compliance risks that are associated with the decisions that they make, even though the board is ultimately responsible for effective compliance; and

◆ that compliance-related risks must be monitored adequately and all cases of non-compliance escalated to the appropriate level of management.

Compliance management procedures can be varied. Compliance-related elements may be present in operational procedures, such as procedures for operating machinery, recruiting staff or making cash transfers.

In terms of specific procedures, there may be procedures for reporting and escalation, as well as procedures for testing compliance related controls to ensure that they are operating effectively. Other procedures include:

◆ how to deal with enquiries from regulators, such as who should speak with them;

◆ how to investigate cases of unauthorised non-compliance;

◆ disciplinary procedures for unauthorised non-compliance; and

◆ procedures for temporarily allowing non-compliance on cost-benefit grounds.

An organisation may permit a degree of non-compliance where the costs of compliance far exceed the benefits. Extreme care is needed when making such decisions. Before such a decision is made it is recommended that an organisation should discuss it with the relevant regulatory authority.

Compliance reporting and escalation processes

The managers and directors of an organisation will require regular assurance that it is complying with relevant laws and regulations and that any associated compliance risks are managed effectively. This assurance may come in the form of compliance reports.

One common form of reporting is a periodical review of compliance. This review is normally prepared by a company secretary or governance professional and reported to the board of directors or trustees. The review will remind the board of the various laws and regulations that must be complied with and outline the various processes and controls that are in place to ensure compliance. Evidence on the effectiveness of these processes and controls may be provided, such as the results of compliance reviews and internal audits.

Compliance monitoring and reporting to management and senior management will occur much more regularly. This might include daily control effectiveness checks to ensure that compliance with financial crime regulations are adhered to, such as the prevention of money laundering. Regular food hygiene checks and checks on health and safety equipment may be required, for example. Management need to know that these checks have been performed and the results of these checks, especially where non-compliance is detected.

Escalation processes come into play when ineffective controls are detected or where employees or managers are not behaving in an appropriate manner. Escalation may occur as a result of an audit finding, regular compliance control checks, or whistleblowing. Escalation should be to the appropriate level of management. Where non-compliance threatens the whole organisation, it should be escalated to the most senior level possible, usually the board. Non-compliance that is considered to be less serious, such as a minor breach of health and safety rules, should be escalated to the appropriate line manager for action.

Compliance training and communication

Employees may require training to understand the importance of complying with all applicable laws and regulations and to help them operate the relevant compliance controls effectively.

This training may be provided in-house or by an external training agency. For example, health and safety training can be purchased from external providers, such as training on how to perform risk assessments, safe manual handling, fire or food safety training.

Regular compliance-oriented communication can supplement formal training. This might include emails or memos reminding staff of specific compliance responsibilities, poster campaigns, discussions in staff meetings, away days or awareness weeks.

Stop and think 8.2

External training companies provide health and safety-related training courses. Search the internet to find examples. How many different types of training course can you find?

3.3   Linking compliance management with internal control

Compliance management and internal control are closely related. In some organisations, the two terms may be used interchangeably, or compliance management may be viewed as part of internal control and vice-versa.

Whichever way an organisation looks at the two areas, ensuring that employees are complying with laws and regulations, internal policies and procedures, external standards, guidance and codes are an important part of internal control.

In larger organisations, where compliance and internal control may be organised into separate functions, action may be needed to co-ordinate the activities of these functions. Busy line-managers and employees will not want two separate functions asking them to perform very similar activities.

3.4   Risk-based compliance

Risk-based compliance is organised on the principle that activities or decisions that have a higher degree of compliance risk should receive more compliance management resources.

Areas of higher compliance risk will include laws and regulations that could result in criminal sanction or enforcement action that might affect the achievement of an organisation's objectives. For example, incurring a large fine or losing an operating licence due to a breach of financial crime regulation or pollution laws.

Risk-based compliance management will require an assessment of compliance risk. This involves identifying and evaluating the probability and impact of a variety of adverse compliance scenarios, such as a breach of specific health and safety requirements. Greater compliance management resources will be devoted to the areas of greater risks. This may include more frequent control effectiveness monitoring and compliance reviews and internal audits.

3.5   Roles and responsibilities

Roles and responsibilities for compliance management will vary according to an organisation's sector, scale and structure. Common roles and responsibilities include:

- the compliance function;
- boards and risk and audit committees;
- company secretary and governance professionals; and
- other business areas.

The compliance function

A small organisation may not have a dedicated compliance function. This role may be performed by a nominated manager (such as the company secretary) or be outsourced to an external compliance services provider.

Where a compliance function exists it will normally be responsible for:

◆ keeping up to date with legal and regulatory changes, including informing management about new laws and regulations or changes to existing laws and regulations;

◆ communicating with legal, regulatory and supervisory agencies, such as the HSE;

◆ monitoring the effectiveness of compliance procedures and controls;

◆ compliance monitoring reporting to management and the board of directors or trustees;

◆ working with all other managers and business functions to ensure that that any non-compliance is rectified as quickly as possible; and

◆ co-ordinating compliance related training and communication activities.

Boards and risk and audit committees

An organisation's board is accountable for the effectiveness of its compliance management activities and any cases of non-compliance. In some cases, boards and individual board members may be held criminally accountable, for example via corporate manslaughter charges.

Compliance management reviews and exception reports on any serious cases of non-compliance can provide a board with the assurance that it needs and to take action where necessary.

Where present, risk and audit committees will support the work of the board on compliance management. Their work will include looking into the detail of compliance reviews and relevant internal audits. These committees may oversee any actions taken to address identified compliance weaknesses or areas of non-compliance.

An organisation's compliance management policy should be reviewed and approved on a periodic basis by the board or the risk and/or audit committee if present.

Company secretary and governance professionals

The company secretary or governance professional should work with the compliance function to ensure that an organisation's board has the assurance information that it needs to determine whether its compliance arrangements are appropriate.

In the case of a smaller organisation the company secretary or governance professional may have direct responsibility for compliance management.

Other business areas

All employees and contractors have a personal responsibility to comply with relevant laws and regulations. In addition, an organisation's managers and senior managers have a responsibility to ensure that their employees are compliant. This might include:

◆ monitoring the effectiveness of local compliance procedures and controls;

◆ taking steps to address non-compliance on the part of employees; and

◆ escalating concerns to more senior management and the compliance function.

Test yourself 8.3

Assess whether compliance management is the equal responsibility of all employees within an organisation.

---

4. Governance structures for risk management

Organisations that have a formal risk management framework will usually have governance arrangements to ensure that this framework is implemented in an effective way, as well as reviewed and updated on a periodic basis.

There is no one right way to implement a governance structure for risk management. Structures vary according to industry sector and the scale and complexity of an organisation's structure and operations.

In a smaller, simpler organisation, governance of the risk management framework may be left to the board of directors or trustees or an appropriate senior manager. Often the company secretary or governance professional will support this work. For an organisation with an audit committee or audit and risk committee, governance may be delegated to this committee.

More formal governance structures for risk management are common in larger organisations or in more complex sectors such as financial services. This includes the 'three lines of defence approach' and the 'five lines of assurance'.

4.1 The three lines of defence

The three lines of defence approach to risk management governance began in the financial services sector, especially banks. Most financial services organisations employ the three lines of defence approach following the 2007–08 financial crisis, with strong support for the approach from regulators. Organisations outside the financial services sector are also beginning the make use of the approach to help organise their risk management governance arrangements.

The three lines of defence are illustrated in Figure 8.1.

The three lines of defence separates three complementary roles in the governance and operation of a risk management framework:

1. Day-to-day risk taking, assessment and control.
2. Oversight of how risks are taken, assessed and controlled.

3.   Assurance that risk taking, assessment and control activities are operating effectively and that the decisions made are consistent with the organisation's objectives.

1st Line: Operational Management	2nd Line: Risk Management	3rd Line: Internal Audit
Front line decision makers who take and control risk	Responsible for the design and implementation of the risk management framework and for risk reporting to senior management and board	Provide assurance to senior management and board that the risk management framework is operating effectively
Must ensure that the decisions they make are consistent with organisation's strategic and risk management objectives	Must ensure that business managers follow the framework and make risk management decisions that are consistent with the organisation's objectives	Must ensure that any weaknesses in the design or implementation of the risk management framework are detected and corrected, including any control failures or inappropriate risk taking

Figure 8.1 The three lines of defence

segregation of duties
An internal control designed to prevent error and fraud by ensuring that at least two individuals are responsible for the separate parts of any task or activity. Segregation of duties involves breaking down tasks that might reasonably be completed by a single individual into multiple tasks so that no one person is solely in control.

This approach is based on a classic governance control – **segregation of duties**. Different employees with different responsibilities and objectives and separate reporting lines are assigned one of the above roles only. This ensures that there are no conflicts of interest. For example, if a manager was assigned roles one and two, they might ignore elements of the framework or perform tasks such as risk assessment ineffectively in their eagerness to pursue a profitable opportunity. Equally, a manager tasked with roles two and three may not be sufficiently critical of their organisation's risk management framework if they were also involved in its design and implementation.

One caveat is that the segregation of the three roles does not mean that the individuals performing each of the roles should be physically segregated. These individuals need to communicate on a regular basis and will at times need to work together. Trust must be built up between these individuals to ensure that they are open and honest with each other. This can only be achieved if they understand each other and the value of all three roles.

4.2 The five lines of assurance

The five lines of assurance approach is a relatively new concept, originally proposed by Leech and Hanlon.

The five lines of assurance are different from the three lines of defence in the following ways:

◆ The word defence is not used – defence implies that risk is a bad thing to be defended against. Exposure to risk can bring gains as well as losses for organisations and effective risk management governance is as much about how risk is taken as it is assessed and controlled.

◆ The five lines make more explicit the role of the board and an organisation's executive directors in relation to risk management governance.

Three of the lines within the five lines approach are very similar to the three lines approach. These are:

1. Work units, meaning business unit/function/department managers.
2. Specialist units, such as the risk function, compliance function and company secretary or governance professional.
3. Internal audit.

The remaining two lines are:

1. the CEO, managing director and other senior directors and managers; and
2. the board of directors or trustees.

Within the five lines approach, the CEO or equivalent is responsible for building and maintaining a robust risk management framework. They ensure that the most significant value creating and value destroying risks to the organisation's (strategic) objectives are managed. Responsibility for the management of these risks is assigned to senior directors and managers who act as the 'risk owners', ensuring that their teams identify, assess, monitor and control these risks in an effective way.

The board has ultimate responsibility for ensuring that an organisation has an effective risk management framework and that the other four lines are performing their roles in an appropriate way. The board also has responsibility for identifying, assessing, monitoring and controlling the residual risk associated with an organisation's objectives, as well as other organisation-wide issues such as succession planning and the performance of the CEO or equivalent.

The roles for the other three lines are similar to the three lines of defence approach, except that the focus is on risks that offer value creating opportunities as well as the potential for value destroying losses.

Test yourself 8.4

Compare and contrast the three lines of defence approach with the five lines of assurance.

4.3 The role of the board

Governance codes often discuss the role of the board in terms of risk governance. The five lines of assurance approach mirrors the common themes in these codes. The UK Corporate Governance Code emphasises the following:

◆ Boards are responsible for determining the nature and extent of the principal risks an organisation is willing to take in pursuit of its strategic objectives.

◆ Boards should maintain sound risk management and internal control frameworks.

◆ Boards should provide entrepreneurial leadership within a framework of prudent and effective controls that enable risk to be assessed and managed.

◆ Non-executives should satisfy themselves that financial controls and an organisation's wider risk management framework are robust and defensible.

◆ Where appropriate, to set up a board delegated audit committee that reviews internal financial controls. Unless a risk committee is present the audit committee also reviews the organisation's internal controls and risk management framework.

Boards have an active and participatory role to play in the management of principal risks. They also have an oversight role in relation to ensuring the effective management of less significant risks.

4.4 Governing risk management within a group structure

The governance of risk management activities within a group structure can be complex. Groups are organisations that have multiple business units operating under a parent organisation. These business units are often geographically dispersed on a multinational basis. Business units may operate within different industry sectors. Examples of multinational groups include Apple, Honda, IBM, Santander, Sony and Virgin.

The dispersed nature of many groups can make effective risk management governance difficult. Business units far from the attention of head office may find it relatively easy to ignore group level policies, processes and procedures for risk management, or to implement them ineffectively. Business units from different industry sectors may have different risk management priorities and objectives, making it hard to implement a one-size-fits-all risk management framework for the whole group.

To help govern risk management activity within a group structure, it is common to have a group risk management function supported by a series of divisional, country-level or business unit risk functions. These satellite risk functions may report fully or partially, known as dotted-line reporting, to the group risk function to ensure that they follow the group risk management framework. The satellite risk functions may be granted a degree of discretion to modify the group risk management framework to meet the needs of different industry sectors. This is common where one of the sectors is financial services, given the high levels of risk management regulation in this sector.

Group structures may have a hierarchy of risk management policies and procedures to ensure consistent, but locally relevant, risk management activity across the group. This may consist of a 'group risk management policy', divisional risk management policies and business unit specific policies.

5. ISO 19600:2014 – compliance management systems

ISO 19600:2014 is the international standard for compliance management systems. The standard provides guidance for establishing, developing, implementing, evaluating, maintaining, and improving an effective and responsive compliance management system within an organisation.

The ISO takes the view that effective compliance is an essential part of maintaining the long-term sustainability of an organisation. It should create a culture of integrity and compliance where non-compliant behaviours are not tolerated.

Effective compliance management is linked to the values, ethics, and corporate governance activities of an organisation. The role of leadership from the board and senior management is emphasised. On leadership, the standard says that leaders must demonstrate a clear commitment in terms of the language they use and the actions they take to ensure effective compliance management.

The standard offers a continuous improvement framework for compliance management that is based on the management improvement philosophy of 'plan-do-check-act'.

The framework is divided into establishment and implementation phases, where compliance management processes and controls are first established, then implemented and improved.

Plan	Establish the decision objectives and plan the processes necessary to deliver the results required. For example, compliance with a law or regulation.
Do	Implement the planned processes and check the outcome – collecting data to support this. For example, compliance monitoring data.
Check	Study the results of the 'do' phase and compare against what was expected from the 'plan' phase.
Act	Where the actual outcomes are better than planned, or at least better than previous outcomes, then establish a new baseline on which the organisation should act. If outcomes are not as good as expected or as before then determine ways to improve these.

Table 8.1 Improvement framework for compliance management

In terms of the establishment phase, five tasks are highlighted:

1. Identification of internal and external compliance issues, for example, regulatory change.
2. Identification of interested parties requirements, notably stakeholders.
3. Determining the scope of the compliance management system and establishing the system, for example determining the relevant laws and regulations that must be complied with.
4. Establishing the compliance policy.
5. Adopting good governance principles.

This implementation phase moves onto:

6. Identification of compliance obligations and evaluation of the compliance risks.
7. Leadership commitment to compliance and the establishment of other roles and responsibilities.
8. Planning to address compliance risks and achieve compliance objectives.
9. Operational planning and control of compliance risks.
10. Performance evaluation and compliance reporting.
11. Managing non-compliance and continual improvement of the compliance management framework.

The compliance management standard was designed to be compatible with other ISO management standards, including ISO 31000, the standard for risk management.

6. Combining governance, risk, and compliance

Larger organisations, especially those in highly regulated sectors like financial services, may implement management frameworks that combine governance, risk management and compliance management activities. These are known as GRC frameworks. The concept of GRC is attributed to Michael Rasmussen of GRC2020. For more information, please see the directory at the back of this text.

6.1   The rationale for GRC

Governance, risk management and compliance management are inter-related sub-elements of an organisation's wider management framework. Where these elements are not co-ordinated or integrated in an effective manner, the problem of silo-based management may occur. With a silo approach, tasks may be repeated reducing efficiency. For example, an organisation might have separate arrangements for compliance risk assessments than for other types of risk assessment. Another problem is that reporting may not be integrated, meaning that separate but very similar reports are produced for governance, risk and compliance related issues. In some cases, the number of GRC relevant reports can be substantial, for example:

◆   project risk reports

◆   health and safety reports

◆   strategic risk (board level) reports

◆   operational risk reports

◆   compliance risk reports

◆   governance effectiveness reviews

◆   COBIT reports

◆   financial misstatement risk report

◆   internal audit reports

◆   financial crime reports

◆   business continuity management reports

◆   incident reports

◆   data protection reports

◆   financial reports.

By not integrating reporting, management may fail to see the linkages between governance, risk and compliance, leaving important risk exposures or control weaknesses undetected. In extreme cases of silo management, an organisation may have separate governance, risk and compliance functions as well as multiple functions within these three areas, for example health and safety, IT security and financial crime, that do not co-ordinate their activities, resulting in significant duplication of effort and a failure to communicate potential concerns that cross multiple functions.

A GRC framework that is implemented effectively should help to prevent a silo management approach. One way to achieve this might be to create a single function for governance, risk and compliance. However, that can lead to segregation of duties problems where roles such as internal audit and risk or compliance management are combined. A common solution is to maintain separate functions but make use of a GRC computer system to help co-ordinate activities and to produce common reports.

Test yourself 8.5

Explain the benefits of implementing a GRC management framework

6.2 The scope of GRC

In some cases, an organisation will implement a GRC management system that covers every single aspect of its operations. In others, the scope of GRC integration may be more limited. Three areas are especially common:

◆ financial GRC

◆ information technology GRC

◆ legal GRC.

Financial GRC
Financial GRC usually relates to financial reporting. Many organisations produce financial reports. The production and distribution of these reports can be subject to a range of governance requirements and other laws and regulations. Various risks are associated with the production of financial reports, such as financial misstatement risks. Large, 'material' inaccuracies may occur within the accounts that may over or underestimate an organisation's financial performance.

Most countries have rules about how financial reports should be produced, often known as accounting standards, such as the International Financial Reporting Standards (IFRS). In addition, there are rules about what information must be provided, how frequently this information must be provided (usually annually), the activities that must be taken to ensure that accounts are accurate, such as requirements for external auditing, and board sign-off.

Information technology GRC
Information technology GRC is focused on the governance, risk and compliance management of an organisation's IT systems, processes, policies and procedures. IT-related activities may be regulated: for example, data protection requirements. In addition, an organisation may have internal IT governance and compliance processes to ensure that employees follow internal policies and procedures about concerns such as the acceptable use of the internet, data security and password protection. In addition, there are a wide range of IT risks to consider such as hacking attacks, systems failures or data corruption. New HR-related IT risks are also growing in importance,

such as cyber bullying and the acceptable use of social media when discussing work-related activities.

Legal GRC

Legal GRC focuses on combining the work of an organisation's legal department or legal specialist with other compliance management work. Legal issues, whether criminal or civil, have a compliance related element. This might include a breach of company law, environmental law or health and safety law.

6.3 GRC information systems

GRC information management systems are used to help co-ordinate and integrate an organisation's governance, risk and compliance management activities.

GRC systems often consist of the following elements:

- a repository of all relevant policies and procedures, such as risk management policies, compliance management policies, risk appetite and internal audit procedures;
- a library of the governance, risk and compliance controls used across the organisation (this may also include information on the effectiveness of these controls);
- governance, risk and compliance metrics, such as information on reported loss events or compliance breaches;
- the results of risk assessments;
- incident management, to record any loss events that may have occurred;
- financial performance data;
- internal audit modules to track identified audit issues; and
- action planning to address control weaknesses or audit issues.

Governance, risk management and compliance systems are typically cloud-based to allow employees from across an organisation to access them quickly and easily. This also ensures that all data is held in one location. Cloud-based systems are usually hosted by the system vendor, who maintains very high levels of security and data backup protocols.

Many different GRC systems are available from software vendors. The nature and design of these systems changes frequently. An organisation looking to purchase a GRC system should weigh up the costs and benefits of several different systems before making a purchase. Systems can cost very large amounts of money to implement and maintain. Certain systems may be incompatible with an organisation's internal structure and processes.

Stop and think 8.3

Search the internet for examples of GRC information management system providers. How many can you find? What are their advantages and disadvantages?

Chapter summary

◆ Risk management, governance and compliance arrangements protect an organisation and its stakeholders from a range of adverse events including fraud, legal liability claims, regulatory sanction and reputation damage.

◆ Effective policies and procedures are an important part of risk management governance and compliance. These policies and procedures should make clear how risk is to be managed within an organisation.

◆ Policies and procedures may be complemented by a risk appetite framework which highlights what risks may be taken within agreed limits, and those that must be avoided.

◆ An organisation should establish and implement risk management compliance frameworks to ensure that all laws and regulations are complied with and that any other compliance risks are managed effectively. This includes drafting a compliance management policy, as well as allocating roles and responsibilities for compliance management.

◆ Organisations may, as part of their risk management compliance framework, ensure that internal company policies and procedures, as well as external standards guidance and codes of conduct, are complied with.

◆ An organisation should implement procedures and controls for its compliance risks. This includes compliance reporting, compliance reviews, internal audits and control monitoring.

◆ ISO 19600 provides guidance on the establishment and implementation of effective compliance management systems. This guidance can be used to help benchmark existing organisational practices.

◆ To complement compliance management activities, an organisation requires risk management governance arrangements. These arrangements should ensure that risks are managed in accordance with an organisation's objectives and the expectations of its stakeholders.

◆ Various approaches to governance exist depending on the nature, scale and complexity of an organisation's activities. One common approach for larger organisations, especially within financial services is the 'three lines of defence' approach. An alternative is the 'five lines of assurance' approach.

◆ Some organisations use GRC systems to co-ordinate their governance, risk and compliance activities. GRC systems provide a mechanism for storing common resources and data (such as policies or risk metrics). GRC systems may be used to facilitate integrated reporting of governance, risk and compliance issues.

Part two

Managing risk and compliance

Overview

Part two outlines the tools and techniques that can be used as part of a risk management and compliance framework. There are many different tools and techniques. Some are technical and very visible, while others are focused on changing behaviours and may be intangible. An organisation must select the best possible combination of tools, yielding the maximum level of benefit for the least cost.

Chapter nine outlines some of the common tools and techniques that an organisation can use to identify, assess and report on risk. Risk reporting is an important output of risk management activity. Risk reports help managers, senior managers, directors and boards to make effective decisions about which risks to control, as well as the level of control needed.

Chapter ten investigates the concepts of risk appetite and risk culture. These concepts are relatively new in risk management and help an organisation to enhance its risk control and risk reporting activities.

Chapter eleven considers the tools and techniques that are used to support compliance management in an organisation. Risk management and compliance management are closely related. Compliance management tools and techniques help to support the management of risk in an organisation, ensuring that its risk management activities are compliant with internal and external policies, rules and guidelines.

Learning outcomes

At the end of this part, you will be able to:

◆ Explain the techniques that may be used to identify risk.

◆ Appreciate the range of techniques that can be used to assess risk.

◆ Consider the role of risk reporting and the characteristics of different approaches to reporting.

◆ Understand the concept of risk appetite and how it can help to support risk management activities.

◆ Consider the factors that may influence the risk appetite of an organisation.

◆ Appreciate the role of the board in setting risk appetite and in monitoring whether an organisation is within its appetite for risk.

◆ Identify definitions of culture and risk culture.

◆ Demonstrate the importance of managing culture and risk culture.

◆ Explain how risk culture can be assessed and controls and the problems associated with assessing and controlling risk culture.

◆ Appreciate how compliance management supports risk management in an organisation and the various roles and responsibilities for compliance management.

◆ Understand the concept of risk-based compliance.

◆ Consider some common tools and techniques for managing compliance risk.

Chapter nine
Evaluating and reporting risk

Contents

1. Introduction
2. Techniques for identifying risk events
3. Identifying emerging risk
4. Risk assessment techniques
5. Risk registers and risk and control self-assessments
6. Risk reporting

1. Introduction

This chapter outlines the tools and techniques that an organisation can use to identify, assess and report on risk. It only explores common tools and techniques: you may come across other tools and techniques in some organisations.

The focus is non-technical, with an emphasis on how tools are used, as well as their potential strengths and weaknesses. No detailed statistical or technical knowledge is required.

2. Techniques for identifying risk events

An organisation is exposed to a wide range of risks. The purpose of risk identification is to determine the nature of these risks and the specific types of risk event that may occur. Potential risk events might include:

- a fire
- workplace accident
- fraud
- a creditor defaulting on a loan or credit agreement
- economic recession
- cyber attack
- a sudden reduction in consumer demand.

Positive risk events may also occur – such as a sudden increase in consumer demand – but upside opportunities are rarely the focus of formal risk event identification activities, outside of narrow applications to risks like energy price fluctuations. This focus on the identification of downside risk is not necessarily desirable. Organisations should be identifying positive and negative risk events to support strategic decision making (see Chapter 1). The risk identification techniques discussed here may be used to identify positive as well as negative risk events if desired.

A variety of different techniques can be employed to help identify risk events. These techniques vary in their sophistication. More sophisticated techniques are not necessarily better and can be costly to implement. An organisation's choice of techniques will depend on the nature, scale and complexity of its activities, as well as regulatory requirements.

2.1 Expert judgement

Expert judgement relies on the skills and experiences of relevant specialists, either in isolation or working as a group. For example, an IT specialist should have a good understanding of the types of IT-related risk events to which an organisation may be exposed. Equally, finance specialists should have a good understanding of any financial risks, such as the risk of making a financial misstatement.

Most organisations will use their own internal specialists to provide expert judgement but in some circumstances external experts, such as risk management consultants, may be used.

It is helpful to have a facilitator to work with experts to help them identify all relevant risks. The facilitator may be an internal risk specialist or an external consultant.

2.2 Focus groups and surveys

Focus groups may comprise a mix of specialists, such as IT, finance and HR specialists. They may also include functional and departmental managers, such as operations managers or marketing managers.

The idea behind a focus group is to share a range of different perspectives and experiences to achieve a consensus view. This should ensure that a greater number of relevant risk events are identified. The cost is that focus groups take up more specialist or management time due to the greater number of people involved.

An alternative way to collect a range of views is via a risk survey. Here, relevant specialists and managers are asked a series of questions and their responses are consolidated and analysed to identify relevant risk events.

A simple risk identification survey may ask respondents to list the risk events that they believe could occur or may provide a checklist of potential risk events. More sophisticated surveys may ask about how organisational processes and procedures are designed and controlled to identify the potential sources of risk events. Risk events are often linked to weaknesses in process design or control failures. Surveys may be created by internal or external risk management specialists.

Test yourself 9.1

Compare the costs and benefits of using the judgement of one expert versus a focus group.

2.3 Checklists

Checklists provide a prepared list of potential risk events. Checklists are used to support other risk identification approaches such as expert judgement, focus groups and surveys.

A checklist ensures that particular types of risk event are not forgotten. Experts, focus groups or survey respondents may accidentally overlook certain types of risk event. A checklist ensures that all relevant sources of risk are given consideration.

An organisation may draw up its own checklists based on their past experience of risk events or use checklists provided by an external agency, such as risk management association, consultant, or regulator. The advantage of external agencies is that they are able to learn from the experiences of multiple organisations.

One example of an external checklist is the Basel loss event types (Basel Committee, 2009: Annex 7) that are used by most banks, other financial and non-financial institutions to help them identify operational risks.

One feature of the Basel event types is that they are presented in different levels. Level 1 and Level 2 are shown in Table 9.1. An even more granular Level 3 list is available.

This approach allows an organisation to choose a more or less detailed checklist, assisting with the categorisation of identified risks. It is clear from the table how a specific Level 2 risk event relates to the Level 1 risk events.

More detailed checklists facilitate more targeted risk assessment monitoring and control activities. They also reduce the chance that important risk events may be overlooked but they increase the amount of time that must be devoted to risk identification. An organisation must balance the costs and benefits of more or less detailed checklists and choose the approach that works best for its circumstances.

Level 1	Level 2
Internal fraud	Unauthorised activity (such as breach of policies and procedures)
	Theft and fraud
External fraud	Theft and fraud
	Systems security (cyber-attacks)
Employment practices and workplace safety	Employee relations (strikes and so on)
	Safe environment (health and safety)
	Diversity and discrimination
Clients, products and business practices	Suitability, disclosure and fiduciary (breach of privacy, aggressive selling and so on)
	Improper business or market practices (insider trading or money laundering)
	Product flaws (faulty products)
	Selection, sponsorship and exposure (exceeding client risk limits)
	Advisory activities (providing poor advice)
Damage to physical assets	Disasters and other events (natural disasters, terrorism and so on)
Business disruption and systems failure	Systems (hardware, software, telecoms, internet failure)
Execution delivery and process management	Transaction capture, execution or maintenance (data entry error, accounting error and so on)
	Monitoring and reporting (financial reporting misstatement or reporting error to regulator)
	Customer intake and documentation (errors in product documentation or marketing campaign and so on)
	Customer/client account management (negligent loss of client funds or some other management error)
	Trade counterparties (poor performance or dispute)
	Vendors or suppliers (poor performance or disputes)

Table 9.1 Basel operational loss event types

Table 9.2 summarises the benefits and costs of using checklists.

Benefits of checklists	Costs of checklists
A cheap and efficient way of collating large amounts of information.	Can be used by someone who may not be skilled in the subject of the checklist.
Simple and easy to use. Ensures that relevant sources of risk are not missed	Can be completed by someone who may not understand precisely the objectives and ultimate use of their answers.
A useful way of updating information for current use and for monitoring trends against previous surveys.	Can focus the user's attention simply on completing the checklist, without keeping the overall reason for the checklist in mind, causing the task to be seen as just a 'form filling' exercise.
Can be adapted to individual areas of risk focus (such as health and safety, environment and so on).	May be ambiguous to the reader, however careful the design.
Useful for putting diverse sources of information into a common format.	May be completed too quickly, and thus without much thought, by someone who considers that their own time is better spent elsewhere.
Can be used to provide evidence of compliance with relevant risk management regulations.	May be completed by someone who has their own reasons for suppressing risk information.

Table 9.2 Benefits and costs of checklists

2.4 Physical inspections

Physical inspections of workplaces are a common way to assess health and safety-related risks or risks relating to fire and other physical hazards.

Physical inspections are usually completed by qualified risk identification specialists such as a building surveyor, fire safety professional or health and safety expert. Inspections are often supported by the use of questionnaires or checklists to ensure that nothing important is missed.

There is a clear advantage when a workplace and its employees are visited, particularly by someone who has the specialised knowledge to take a professional view of what is there. A formal inspection report will normally conclude with recommendations to improve the control environment and reduce the probability and impact of loss.

The disadvantages of inspections are:

◆ An inspector can only see risk exposures that are visible on the day of the visit. A visit is a snapshot in time and can capture only the activity of the day.

◆ An inspection programme can be expensive, especially when visits are needed across many different workplaces.

◆ Some of an organisation's greatest types or sources of risk may be those where third party suppliers provide goods and services. The organisation may have difficulty obtaining authority to conduct detailed inspections in third party premises unless this permission is negotiated within the original contract.

◆ Risk management is and should remain the responsibility of every manager and employee throughout an organisation. Regular visits by an inspector, if not carefully managed, could encourage managers and employees to believe that they can abdicate responsibility for risk management to the inspector.

2.5 Analytical approaches

Analytical approaches use a range of research and logic structuring methods to make risk identification more scientific and less prone to human error. Techniques include:

◆ the structured what-if technique;
◆ the Delphi technique;
◆ root cause analysis; and
◆ system and process mapping.

Structured what-if technique

The structured what-if technique (SWIFT) is a systematic, team-oriented technique commonly used for the identification of health and safety and environmental-related risks in areas like chemical processing and manufacturing. The technique uses a series of structured 'what-if' and 'how-could' type questions to consider deviations from the normal operation of systems and processes.

The activity is supported by checklists to help identify potential risk events. SWIFT relies on expert input from the team to identify risk events. The SWIFT leader's function is to structure the discussion. The SWIFT recorder keeps an on-line record of the discussion on a standard log sheet.

There is no standard approach to SWIFT. One of its strengths is that it is flexible and can be modified to suit each individual application.

A common protocol for the SWIFT analysis of a risk event is as follows:

1. Define the operational systems/processes being analysed.
2. Consider each in turn.
3. Brainstorm possible risk events. List but do not discuss (yet).

4. Structure the risk events into a logical sequence for discussion. Start with the major ones and prioritise selection of others.

5. Consider each risk event in turn.

6. Consider possible causes of each risk event.

7. Consider the possible consequences should an event occur.

8. Consider safeguards that are planned to be in place to prevent the event occurring.

9. Consider frequency and consequence.

10. Record discussion on SWIFT log sheets

11. Reconsider whether any risk events have been omitted.

12. Use checklists and, where available, previous risk event experience to check for completeness.

SWIFT is an expensive technique to use because of the time and people involved, but it is more likely to identify all relevant risk events. This is why it is used in hazardous sectors like chemical processing or nuclear power generation to ensure that all risks are identified.

Delphi technique

The Delphi technique is an information-gathering tool that is used to reach a consensus of experts on a subject, in this case the identification of risk events. Each expert participates anonymously and a facilitator uses a questionnaire to solicit ideas about the important points related to the subject. The responses are summarised and re-circulated to the experts for further comment. Consensus may be reached in a few – or many – rounds of this process.

In relation to risk identification, the Delphi technique helps reduce bias and keeps any one person from having undue influence on the risks that are identified. A range of experts can be used including risk management specialists, other functional specialists (IT, HR, governance and so on) and department and functional management (operations managers, accountants and so on).

A Delphi approach to risk identification could proceed as follows:

1. Agree the function, department, project or process to be analysed.

2. Select a panel of experts and keep the membership anonymous.

3. Send out background information and a questionnaire that asks them to identify the relevant risks.

4. Facilitator compiles responses.

5. Facilitator sends out compiled information to experts for comment. Experts invited to revise their views based on responses.

6. Repeat until a consensus is reached.

Anonymity is essential to encourage each expert to be as honest and open as possible. Studies have shown that the technique can be effective at predicting risk events but it is time consuming, especially if a consensus is hard to reach.

Root cause analysis

Root cause analysis focuses on investigating the root causes of risk events. It may be applied to hypothetical risk event scenarios or actual risk events that have occurred, either within the organisation or in similar organisations.

Root cause analysis is based on the assumption that many risk events have multiple causes. For example, a fire risk event needs material to burn, a spark and oxygen before it can cause damage. Root cause analysis adds depth to the identification of risk events by exploring how and why the event may occur. If organisations can find ways to prevent these causes, such as by keeping an area clean of combustible materials or smoking bans in the case of fire risks, the event may be stopped from occurring.

Root cause analysis approaches vary but are based on four principles:

1. Identify the causes of the event.
2. Establish the timeline from normal operations to a risk event.
3. Distinguish between root causes and more immediate causes.
4. Use the results to improve controls and to help manage future risk events.

Often, the causes of an event, as well as the order in which the causes arise, are identified using the 'five whys' technique. This asks questions such as:

1. Why did a fire occur? Because combustible material started to burn.
2. Why did the material burn? Because a spark caught the material alight.
3. Why did the spark occur? Because an electrical fault occurred in the building's wiring.
4. Why did the electrical fault occur? Because the wiring was old.
5. Why was the wiring old? Because the wiring had not been safety inspected.

More or less why questions than five may be used to get to the root cause but usually it is possible to get to the root cause in five questions. Further questions could be used in the above example to identify why a safety inspection was not carried out, for example.

Root cause analysis is time consuming. It is rarely practical or cost effective to use it to identify all risks but it is a good technique to use when investigating the causes of large and negative risk events that have occurred. This allows an organisation to learn from these events and hopefully prevent a similar chain of causes from occurring in the future.

System and process mapping

All organisations have systems and processes. In some organisations, considerable time is spent on mapping these systems and processes into flow charts. An example is provided in Figure 9.1, which provides a flow chart for supply of a manufactured product to a distributor.

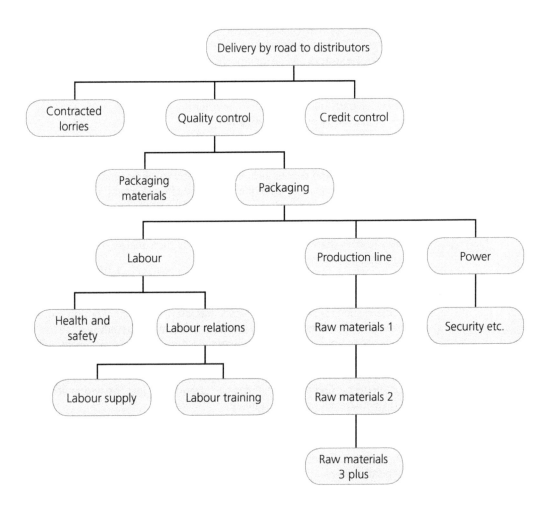

Figure 9.1 Example process flow

Systems and process mapping involves putting all of an organisation's systems and processes into flow charts. These charts are then investigated to identify potential sources of risk to the various systems, processes, activities or objectives.

A common investigation technique is fault tree analysis, which looks at what might cause a systems or process flow to fail. The fault tree does not look at the system or process leading to the end result. Instead, it tries to identify potential system or process failures (risk events) and then looks backwards to search out the possible causes of that failure.

Fault tree analysis begins with each element in a system or process flow and then considers what might happen if this element fails. The aim is to identify key points of failure and whether these can be overcome by adapting other parts of the system of process flow.

The fault tree approach can be used in different ways by mathematicians, engineers and scientists through to health and safety and business continuity managers. Fault trees can be long or short, simplistic or highly technical, and analogue or computerised as required. Fault trees have been adapted into more advanced tools such as hazard and operability studies (HAZOP) that can be used to focus on particular elements within systems and processes, such as a vital piece of machinery or a key IT system.

An advantage of the fault tree approach is that it can highlight connected risk events that could combine to cause much larger risk events. Diverse connections between system and process failures are unlikely to be recognised by individuals working on one aspect of an organisational system or process, unless they use a fault tree or similar approach.

A disadvantage of the fault tree approach is that it can take a lot of time and money to flow-chart systems and processes and then analyse them for points of failure that may cause risk events.

2.6 Loss event and near miss investigations

All organisations experience risk events that result in monetary or non-monetary losses. These could include faulty machinery, liability claims, adverse media attention or employee injury. Organisations also experience near misses, which are risk events that occur but which do not result in a loss. A small fire that is extinguished before damage can be done is an example of a near miss, as might be recovering money that has been transferred into the wrong account or averting an accident at the last minute.

Loss events and near misses are learning opportunities. Whenever they occur, an organisation may decide to identify the causes of these events using techniques such as root cause analysis. These investigations may help an organisation to identify new risks; they may also signify an increase in exposure to a previously identified risk or a control weakness. It is imperative that organisations learn quickly from losses and near misses to help prevent more serious risk events in the future.

Test yourself 9.2

What is a near miss and why should they be investigated?

3. Identifying emerging risk

Emerging risks are either significant new risks, or risks that were known about previously, but which were not considered to be significant (see Chapter 13).

Emerging risks are characterised by high levels of uncertainty, as there is not yet much experience gained, and may therefore be ignored or under/over-estimated. Techniques for identifying emerging risks can help to prevent them from being ignored or underestimated (see Chapter 13).

3.1 PEST analysis

A common technique for assessing emerging risks is PEST analysis, which analyses changes in the following key areas:

◆ political
◆ economic
◆ social
◆ technological.

Political change can be a key source of emerging risk (in terms of both opportunities and threats), whether this is changes in legislation and regulations or major changes in political philosophies and regimes. The UK Brexit referendum and subsequent political decision to leave the European Union is a good example of the latter.

Economic change can create new opportunities and downside risks. The financial crisis of 2007–08 is an example of this, as might be periods of high or low inflation, high or low interest rates or high unemployment.

Social and technological risks such as the rise of the Internet, smart phones and social media can be sources of emerging risks. The rise in hacking attacks and reputation risks linked to social media discussion trends are examples of emerging risks linked to social and technological change.

PEST analysis is usually completed by a group of participants. This might be a focus group of managers or senior managers from relevant functions supported by an expert facilitator. It is common to involve an organisation's board of directors or trustees in the case of large-scale emerging risks that can have a far-reaching strategic impact.

Analytic tools like the Delphi technique may be used to support PEST analysis.

3.2 SWOT analysis

SWOT stands for:

◆ Strengths
◆ Weaknesses
◆ Opportunities
◆ Threats

SWOT analysis is a strategic tool used to identify business objectives. It can also be used to identify emerging risks.

SWOT analysis begins by identifying an organisation's strengths and weaknesses. This may include things like its finances, the abilities of key personnel, market power, reputation and customer goodwill or the efficiency or inefficiency of its operations.

The focus then shifts to identifying potential opportunities and threats which may be on the horizon. This might be opportunities and threats relating to consumer demand, distribution channels, system and process innovations or anything else deemed relevant.

An organisation's strengths and weaknesses are compared to identify opportunities that may be exploited and threats to existing objectives. The technique helps an organisation to identify emerging risks that could be exploited using its strengths and those that are most likely to cause losses, because the organisation's weaknesses may intensify their adverse effects.

3.3 World Economic Forum Global Risk Report

The annual World Economic Forum Global Risk Report is a useful source of current and emerging risks. Issued each year, this report provides a strategic view of risk supplemented by in-depth analyses of specific 'hot topics'.

The top five risks from recent years are provided in Table 9.3.

2015	2016	2017	2018
Inter-country conflict with regional consequences	Large scale involuntary migration	Weapons of mass destruction	Weapons of mass destruction
Extreme weather events	Extreme weather events	Extreme weather events	Extreme weather events
Failure of national governance	Failure of climate change mitigation and adaptation	Water crises	Natural disasters
Country level collapse or crisis	Inter-country conflict with regional consequences	Major natural disasters	Failure of climate change mitigation and adaptation
Unemployment and underem- ployment	Major natural catastrophe	Failure of climate change mitigation and adaptation	Water crises

Table 9.3 WEF top five risks 2015–18

Stop and think 9.1

Which of the risks in Table 9.3 do you consider to be emerging risks? What are the reasons for your decisions?

Test yourself 9.3

Provide a definition for emerging risk and two current examples of potential emerging risks.

4. Risk assessment techniques

Risk assessment techniques assess the probability and impact of a risk event to help determine the level of exposure. A range of risk assessment techniques are available. Most are statistical and beyond the scope of this study text. You only need to understand the main categories of risk assessment techniques.

ISO 31010:2009 'Risk Management – Risk Assessment' provides guidance on the use of these and other techniques.

4.1 Qualitative risk assessment

Qualitative risk assessment involves a significant degree of judgement. Similar techniques to those used for risk identification are often used, including expert judgement, focus groups and surveys. Occasionally, more analytical techniques such as the Delphi technique or fault trees may be used to facilitate qualitative risk assessment.

The dominant qualitative technique is to estimate probability and impact using an ordinal scale, as per Table 9.4.

Probability		Impact	
1	Low	1	Low
2	Medium	2	Medium
3	High	3	High

Table 9.4 An ordinal scale for probability and impact

Ordinal scales may be of any length but the most common are scales of three and five. Scales of four and six are used in some organisations but rarely do these scales exceed six levels.

Data is shown in order of magnitude only, meaning that two is larger than one. It is not possible to determine how much bigger two is than one, because there is no standard of measurement for the differences between these two values. Sporting leagues are another example of ordinal scales. It is possible to say that the team at the top is the best team but not how much better this team is relative to the others in the league.

Some organisations may dispense with numbers altogether and just use words to describe the level of probability and impact. Different terms may be used in organisations such as 'almost certain', 'severe' or 'extreme' for higher values or 'minor', 'insignificant' and 'negligible' for lower ones. The exact terms used are not important, as long as their order of magnitude is clear. It is common to provide definitions for these terms to help improve the accuracy and consistency of risk assessment activities across an organisation. Table 9.5 provides an example.

Probability		Impact	
Low	Chance of occurrence not expected to exceed once per year	Low	Financial loss not expected to exceed 1% of cash flows and can be easily absorbed into day-to-day running costs.
Medium	Chance of occurrence not expected to exceed five times per year	Medium	Financial loss between 1% to 5% of cash flows and may require moderate cost cutting.
High	Chance of occurrence expected to exceed six times per year	High	Financial loss exceeds 5% of cash flows and may require major cost cutting or the cancellation of strategic projects.

Table 9.5 Defining probability and impact in an ordinal scale

Organisations may separate financial and non-financial impacts, such as reputation or customer satisfaction.

For further detail two levels of assessment may be performed, one for inherent risk and another for residual risk. This is to show the potential exposure to the risk should controls not be in place and the current effectiveness, in terms of reduced probability and impact, of the controls that have been applied to the risk.

A final extension combines probability and impact to arrive at an exposure score. Usually the ordinal values are multiplied together to arrive at an order of magnitude for exposure, for example:

		Negative Impact		
		1	2	3
Probability	1	1	2	3
	2	2	4	6
	3	3	6	9

Table 9.6 Ordinal values for exposure

It is important to stress that these are ordinal values. An exposure value of nine is larger than six, which is larger than four and so on. A value of nine does not mean that the level of exposure is 33.3% larger than a value of six.

4.2   Quantitative risk assessment

Quantitative assessment applies a standard of measurement to probability and impact to allow a more precise and objective analysis of risk. With qualitative methods, it is possible to determine how much bigger a given probability or impact value is than another. It is also possible to model an infinite number of probability and impact combinations rather than be limited to three, four, five or six values for probability and impact.

Quantitative risk assessment uses the principles of statistical analysis. It is concerned with building and analysing complex distributions for probability and impact, combining these distributions to arrive at an objective assessment of risk exposure.

In theory, quantitative risk assessment is superior to qualitative approaches. It is precise in mathematical terms and does not rely on subjective judgement. Instead, quantitative risk assessment uses historical data. For example, data regarding past stock price movements are used to assess market risks and insurance companies use claims data to assess things like the risk of property fires or vehicle collisions.

In practice, quantitative risk assessment is problematic. Data is not always available, especially for very low probability risk events. In addition, there is no guarantee that what has happened in the past will happen in the same way in the future, especially in complex and changing risk environments. The effect of global warming is a good example of this – extreme weather events appear to be on the increase, meaning that historical weather data is much less effective at predicting the future than it should be.

Quantitative risk assessment is used most in the financial services sector for assessing financial risks such as market and credit risk where data is plentiful, or for the risks insured by insurance companies (again because of their access to data). Even here, data can be hard to come by or is a poor predictor of the future. The global financial crisis was not predicted by the supposedly sophisticated risk models that were used by banks in 2007.

Test yourself 9.4

Compare and contrast the strengths and weaknesses of qualitative and quantitative risk assessment approaches.

4.3   Hybrid approaches – stress testing and scenario analysis

Hybrid approaches combine elements of quantitative and qualitative risk assessment. The aim is to provide a relatively consistent and objective method for assessing risk, which does not rely on large amounts of data.

Hybrid approaches are used for extreme risk events, meaning those with a low probability, but a high impact (whether positive or negative). Two approaches are used:

◆ stress testing
◆ scenario analysis.

Stress testing

Stress testing involves assessing the impact that extreme movements in key financial variables may have on an organisation, either in isolation or together. Common variables include:

◆ a fall in income
◆ rising inflation
◆ rising or falling interest rates
◆ fluctuations in cash flows
◆ a sudden increase in costs.

Stress tests are often performed by the finance function to assess the affect that extreme movements in financial and economic variables may have on an organisation's income statement or balance sheet.

An extension of standard stress testing is the reverse stress test, which establishes the point at which an organisation's objectives are no longer achievable. Reverse stress testing is a useful tool for corporate financial resiliency planning. There are two approaches to reverse stress testing.

1. Define a series of events, which may happen independently or as a sequence, which will cause the business plan to fail, then measure the implications on the business plan for each of the identified events.

2. Start with the income statement and balance sheet of an organisation and investigate each line item. Identify the factors that would affect that line item to such a degree that the business plan fails or the organisation becomes insolvent.

Stress testing is a good way to assess the financial strength of an organisation, especially when faced with extreme events. It can help an organisation to prepare for extreme events should they occur, helping to reduce the chance of significant financial distress or bankruptcy.

Scenario analysis

Scenario analysis was first used as a strategic planning tool to help organisations identify potential futures and to prepare for them. Organisations such as Royal Dutch Shell make extensive use of scenario analysis to help predict future energy demand and the technology used for energy production in the future. The military in many countries use scenario analysis to play out and prepare for different wartime, disaster support, and peacekeeping scenarios.

In a risk management context, a scenario is essentially a story, an outline, description or model of a possible sequence of risk events. Relevant experts and managers determine plausible but extreme future scenarios and then assess the impact on an organisation should the scenario manifest itself.

There are two principal types of scenarios: single variable scenarios and multi-variable or multi-variant scenarios. Single variable scenarios focus on a specific event or occurrence. The assessment looks at both the possible frequency of occurrence and impact from that single event. An example would be an internal fraud that loses an organisation a substantial amount or the breach of some specific regulation in a given location.

Multi-variable scenarios are more complex and examine the occurrence of multiple inter-related events which may occur at the same time or as a chain of linked events. An example of this would be a serious system failure at a critical point in time, coupled to the urgent need to process a strategically important transaction, while key senior managers are engaged in an off-site meeting.

Scenario analysis is time consuming to do properly and may involve a number of functional specialists and managers but the benefits are considerable. Scenario analysis can help organisations to anticipate and prepare for extreme scenarios. It is especially well suited to testing business continuity plans and for estimating the maximum level of loss, which can help to determine the level of insurance cover. More accurate probability and impact values for extreme events may also be determined, allowing an organisation to rank scenarios in order of significance. This allows scarce management and control resources to be targeted at the scenarios that an organisation has a higher exposure to.

Stop and think 9.2

For an organisation that you know well investigate whether it uses stress testing and scenario analysis. What stress tests and scenarios does it use?

---

5. Risk registers and risk and control self-assessments

Risk registers and risk and control self-assessments are tools that are used by organisations to store and monitor the results of their risk assessment activities.

5.1 The risk register

Most organisations have one or more risk registers. These registers may be spreadsheets or database applications and are used to store information on the risk events that have been identified and assessed. Where more than one register exists, it is important to ensure that data is collected and organised in a way that allows data to be aggregated across different registers. Risk registers are updated on a regular basis. The frequency varies depending on how often risk exposures change. Typical frequencies are monthly or quarterly.

A simple risk register may include:

◆ a description of the risk event that has been identified;

◆ the risk category that the risk event is linked to;

◆ the person responsible for managing the risk event on a day-to-day basis, often known as the risk owner;

◆ a qualitative probability and impact assessment of the risk event; and

◆ any actions currently under way to control the probability or impact of the risk event.

More comprehensive risk registers many include:

◆ a qualitative probability and impact assessment of inherent risk;

◆ a qualitative probability and impact assessment of the residual risk;

◆ any maximum exposure limit that has been assigned for residual risk exposure;

◆ information on the potential causes of the risk event;

◆ information on the potential financial and non-financial impacts of the risk event;

◆ any risk metrics that are used to monitor the organisation's exposure to the risk event; and

◆ recent trends in terms of any movements in residual risk exposure up or down.

Risk registers may be extended further into risk and control self-assessments.

5.2 Risk and control self-assessments

Risk and control self-assessment (RCSA) is a process that combines risk identification, qualitative risk assessment and an assessment of control effectiveness.

Risk and control self-assessment provides a systematic means for identifying control weaknesses and gaps that may threaten the achievement of an organisation's objectives or the operational efficiency of its systems and processes. A key output is the production of action plans that help to allocate scarce resources to address control gaps or weaknesses where the benefits of doing so (in terms of reduced residual risk exposure) exceed the associated costs of increased control.

Risk and control self-assessment can be used to support internal audit and governance activities. By identifying control gaps and weaknesses in a proactive way (such as before an internal auditor picks up the issue) and by prioritising these on cost-benefit grounds an organisation can demonstrate that it is using its resources effectively.

Risk and control self-assessment documentation will include the typical components of a risk register, plus an assessment of the effectiveness of the controls that are in place. This assessment is used to estimate the residual risk exposure.

It is common to link risk events to organisational objectives in a RCSA document. This ensures that the effect that a risk may have on an organisation's objectives is understood and supports the board in its governance responsibilities. This includes ensuring that the board are managing any risks that may threaten the achievement of an organisation's objectives.

Stop and think 9.3

Find an example of a risk register and an example of an RCSA document online. Identify the fields of information recorded on these documents.

6. Risk reporting

Risk reporting is an important element of risk management. However, it is not an end in itself nor is it an activity that should be done in isolation. Effective risk reporting exists to support decision making in an organisation. All decisions involve an element of risk. Decision makers need information on the nature and extent of these risks to make the best possible choices, whether this is in relation to the achievement of strategic goals like business expansion or operational considerations such as delivering a service or manufacturing a product.

It should be stressed that there is no single best approach to the design or presentation of risk reports, nor is there an optimum number of risks to report. The best approach is context-specific and will depend on the nature, scale and complexity of an organisation's activities and risks.

A wide range of risk reporting tools are available. An organisation will select these tools based on regulatory requirements and the needs of their decision makers.

6.1   RAG Reporting

RAG stands for Red, Amber and Green, the colours of a traffic light. The concept may be used to help prioritise risk exposures, control weaknesses, internal audit issues or any other aspect of an organisation's risk management activities. RAG ratings are used extensively in a variety of risk reporting tools.

A common interpretation of RAG is outlined in Table 9.7.

Red (R)	The level of risk exposure is very high (or low) and could threaten the achievement of an organisation's strategic objectives. Immediate action is required on the part of management to manage the risk in question.
Amber (A)	The level of risk exposure is higher/lower than normal. Management attention is required to determine whether action needs to be taken in the near future.
Green (G)	The level of risk exposure is within normal parameters. No action is required – the risk is under adequate control.

Table 9.7 RAG ratings

6.2 Risk reporting tools

Examples of risk reporting tools include:

◆ heat maps;
◆ loss and near miss databases;
◆ risk, control and performance indicators;
◆ risk dashboards and balanced scorecards; and
◆ narrative reporting.

Heat maps

Heat maps use the concept of RAG reporting. Occasionally heat maps add additional colours, such as black to denote extreme risks and blue to show insignificant risks.

Many types of heat map are used in organisations. Some heat maps show the status of risk, control or performance indicators. Others are used to show trends in risk exposure, as in Table 9.8.

Risk	Month 1	Month 2	Month 3	Month 4
Employee injury	G	G	A	R
Non-compliance	A	A	G	G
Competition	A	R	R	G

Table 9.8 Example heat map

It is common to include the relevant RAG initial to help people who are colour blind. Large heat maps can be difficult to interpret, but smaller ones can help management to focus on the most significant 'red' or 'amber' risk exposures or control weaknesses.

It is also possible to produce objective heat maps which illustrate the level of risk that is currently associated with not meeting each objective. Table 9.9 provides an example of this.

Objective	Month 1	Month 2	Month 3	Month 4
Profit	G	G	A	R
Customer Service	A	A	G	G
Compliance	A	R	R	G

Table 9.9 Objective heat map

Risk event and near miss databases

Statistics collected from risk event and near miss databases may be reported on. Usually the focus is on negative risk events and near misses: in other words, risk events or near misses that have or could have resulted in a financial or non-financial loss.

Organisations may report the number of risk events or near misses, as well as the value of any financial or non-financial loss. Non-financial losses may be estimated using ordinal impact scales or in terms of the number of complaints or negative media stories.

If there is sufficient data, it may be possible to provide reports by risk category or business unit and function. This can help to focus management attention on key categories of risk or high-risk business units and functions.

Risk, control and performance indicators

Many organisations monitor and report performance indicators to different levels of management. For example, the board and senior management may receive a range of financial performance indicators such as revenues, profit or surplus, return on equity, debt to equity and so on. Functional and department managers may receive HR information on staff absences or operational information relating to the efficiency of the systems and processes that they manage (customer waiting times, production rates and employee absence levels, for example).

Organisations may also monitor and report a range of risk and control indicators:

◆ risk indicators provide information on an organisation's inherent risk exposure to one or more risks; and

◆ control indicators provide information on the effectiveness of one or more controls.

Common risk indicators include staff turnover (because new staff are more likely to make mistakes), the number of attempted IT firewall breaches or the credit scores of any suppliers or customers that owe money to an organisation. Common control indicators include the frequency of electrical testing, unresolved internal audit issues and number of breaches of policies or procedures. As with performance indicators, different reports may be produced for different departments and functions, as well as different levels of management.

Stop and think 9.4

Find examples of performance, risk or control indicator reports for the organisation that you work for or another that you are familiar with. Be sure to ask the permission of your line manager or another manager with the appropriate level of authority.

Test yourself 9.5

What are the differences between risk, control and performance indicators?

Risk dashboards and balanced scorecards

Risk dashboards are risk reports that combine various risk and control indicators, as well as heat maps, risk event and near miss data.

Risk dashboards may be presented thematically. For example, the board may receive a strategic risk dashboard. Senior managers may receive dashboards on topics like health and safety and departments, and function managers may receive dashboards relating to their area of responsibility.

Effective dashboards are not long. People can find it very hard to process dashboards that run over more than two or three pages. Care is needed to provide the most relevant sources of information in the clearest way.

Balanced scorecards are used for strategic planning. As part of this, they provide a means of structuring a risk dashboard around an organisation's objectives so that the risks to these objectives can be monitored and reported. Balanced scorecards typically use four focus elements, although some use more than four. For example, an organisation may distil the achievement of its objectives into the following balanced scorecard factors and then structure its risk monitoring and reporting around these elements:

◆ financial performance
◆ operational efficiency
◆ human resources
◆ compliance.

Balanced scorecards may be linked to employee development and performance reviews. This ensures that an organisation's employees make risk taking and control decisions that are consistent with its objectives.

Narrative reporting

Narrative reporting involves using words to explain how a risk exposure is changing.

Narrative reporting is common where there is no numerical data that can be reported. It may also be combined with numerical data to help provide context. Table 9.10 provides a simple example in the context of a risk indicator report.

Indicator	Trend	Value last month	Previous value	Commentary
Staff Turnover (% of Total)	⬆	10%	8%	Staff turnover has increased significantly, HR are investigating the reasons for this and will report soon. A system of exit interviews has already been implemented.
Number of New Customer Complaints	⬇	100	104	Customer complaints remain relatively high. Some recent glitches with our telephone management system were the reason for this. These glitches have not delayed any customer transactions, but they have affected the quality of our service, and complaints were still being received on this last month. Now this problem has been rectified we expect complaint levels to fall in the next few months.
Value of Reported Operational Loss Events	⬌	£45,460	£50,950	Despite our recent telephone system problems the value of reported losses remains low. A recent audit report confirmed that our reporting procedures were appropriate and are being complied with. This provides assurance that these figures are accurate.

Table 9.10 Example narrative report

The trend arrows show whether the risk is increasing or reducing. They are RAG rated to provide further context.

6.3   Designing and implementing risk reports

Key factors to consider when designing risk reports are:

◆   the audience and its requirements;
◆   the size of the report and level of detail;
◆   the degree of statistical complexity; and
◆   reporting frequency.

Audience

Different audiences will require different types of report depending on the decisions they have to make and their competencies. Figure 9.2 illustrates the main audiences for risk reports.

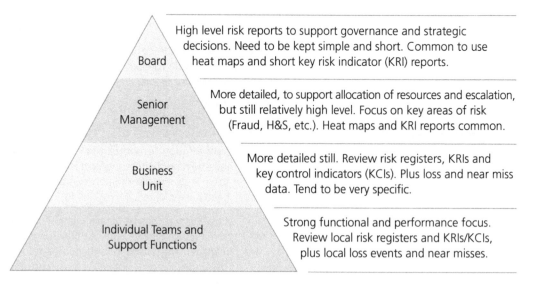

Board
High level risk reports to support governance and strategic decisions. Need to be kept simple and short. Common to use heat maps and short key risk indicator (KRI) reports.

Senior Management
More detailed, to support allocation of resources and escalation, but still relatively high level. Focus on key areas of risk (Fraud, H&S, etc.). Heat maps and KRI reports common.

Business Unit
More detailed still. Review risk registers, KRIs and key control indicators (KCIs). Plus loss and near miss data. Tend to be very specific.

Individual Teams and Support Functions
Strong functional and performance focus. Review local risk registers and KRIs/KCIs, plus local loss events and near misses.

Figure 9.2 Risk reporting audiences

Size and level of detail

More data is not necessarily better in a risk report. Include too much data and the report's audience will not be able to make sense of it. They will also have to spend more time reviewing the report and less on other matters. The key is to determine the essential pieces of data, including any narrative reporting, that is needed by the report's audience. This should involve consultation with the intended audience to ensure that they have the length of report and level of detail that they need.

Level of statistical complexity

Risk reports can get very complex, especially when quantitative risk assessment approaches are used.

Not every audience for a risk report will understand statistics or need a statistically complex report, even where data is available that can be analysed and reported using statistical methods. Again, consultation with the report's audience should help to determine their requirements.

Frequency

The frequency of a risk report depends on the frequency with which risk exposures change. In volatile areas like financial markets, reporting may be daily or on a real-time basis. For areas like cash flow/treasury management or credit risk, weekly or monthly is common. Monthly or quarterly is normal for other risks like health and safety.

Chapter summary

◆ Organisations face a wide range of risks. The purpose of risk identification is to determine the nature of these risks, in particular the specific types of risk event that may occur.

◆ Various risk identification approaches exist, including expert judgement, focus groups, surveys and more analytical tools like the Delphi technique.

◆ Emerging risks are significant new risks or risks that were known about previously, but which were not considered to be significant. An organisation can identify emerging risks using tools like PEST and SWOT analysis.

◆ Qualitative risk assessment involves a significant degree of judgement. The dominant qualitative technique is to estimate the probability and impact of a risk using an ordinal scale.

◆ Quantitative assessment is concerned with applying a standard of measurement to probability and impact. This enables a more precise and objective analysis of risk. Quantitative assessment requires large amounts of historical data to work effectively and may not be effective when historical data is an unreliable predictor of the future.

◆ Most organisations have risk registers. These registers may be spreadsheets or database applications and are used to store information on the risks that have been identified and assessed. Organisations may use risk and control self-assessments to collect information on the effectiveness of their controls.

◆ Risk reporting is an important element of risk management. Effective risk reporting exists to support decision-making in an organisation.

◆ A wide range of risk reporting tools are available including RAG reports, heat maps, risk and control indicator reports and risk event and near miss reports.

◆ Report design is important. Reports must meet regulatory requirements and the needs of their intended audience. Reports must be produced with an appropriate level of frequency (daily, weekly, monthly and so on).

Chapter ten
Risk culture, appetite and tolerance

Contents

1. Introduction

This chapter outlines the concepts of risk appetite, risk tolerance and risk culture and how they can be used to support the management of risk in an organisation. Many organisations have risk appetite frameworks and statements; the idea is to help them to keep their risk profile within acceptable parameters, while at the same time exploiting upside opportunities that help them to achieve their objectives.

Culture is an important intangible asset of all organisations. Organisations that have addressed their cultures have reported benefits beyond improved financial performance, including improved employee performance, a reduction in incidents and near misses and reduced regulatory issues. (Governing Culture, EY, 2016)

The Financial Stability Board identifies effective risk governance and risk appetite frameworks as essential to promoting culture. Risk appetite and culture must align. Both may vary at a business and functional level: for example, a business development team may have a risk-taking appetite, whereas a support team may be more conservative.

The 2018 UK Corporate Governance Code puts the relationships between companies, shareholders and stakeholders at the heart of long-term sustainable growth in the UK economy. One of the main changes in the new Code is that boards are asked to create a culture which aligns company values with strategy and to assess how they preserve value over the long term.

2. Risk appetite as a mechanism for balancing risk and return

Exposure to risk can create the potential for positive as well as negative outcomes. Strategic level risks such as developing a new product or service, increasing output, implementing a new IT system or merging with another organisation come with the potential for profit and loss. Financial risks like market and credit risk also have the potential for upsides and downsides.

Even where risks only have a downside, as in the case of health and safety, compliance or environmental risks, it is rarely possible to eliminate these risks completely. This may be because the cost would be too high or because whatever the expenditure on control a degree of residual risk will remain as long as a particular activity or process remains in operation.

Because exposure to risk may have positive and negative outcomes and because it is rarely practical to eliminate risk, an organisation should decide what risks to take and the level of risk exposure that is optimal. By determining and communicating its appetite for risk, an organisation can ensure that risk and return is balanced in a logical and consistent way and ensure that downside risks are controlled in a cost-effective way.

2.1 Defining risk appetite

There are many definitions of risk appetite within standards, regulations, documents from professional associations and academic research. Most fall into two perspectives:

◆ definitions that define risk appetite in terms of the level of risk exposure that an organisation is prepared to *accept*; and
◆ definitions that define risk appetite in terms of an organisation's *willingness* to take a defined level of risk in the pursuit of its strategic objectives.

Definitions that focus on the acceptability of risk tend to focus on downside risks that may only result in losses. As it is impossible to eliminate most risks completely, a degree of risk exposure must be accepted and an organisation's appetite for risk denotes the level of risk exposure that it is prepared to accept.

Definitions that talk about a willingness to take risk recognise that exposure to risk can be good, as it can lead to positive outcomes. In this context, an organisation must determine the risks that yield the highest possible outcomes but remember that with the potential for large positive outcomes comes the potential for large negative ones.

An organisation must decide the level of risk exposure that provides an optimal balance between the upsides and downsides of risk taking. Most organisations can only achieve their objectives if they take risk. Without risk there would be no opportunities to exploit, no products and services and no returns to earn. The trick is to take the right risks and the right level of exposure to these risks. The concept of risk appetite is about helping organisations to articulate and control this. Without risk there would be no opportunities to exploit, no products and services and no returns to earn. The trick is to take the right risks and the right level of exposure to these risks. The concept of risk appetite is about helping organisations to articulate and control this.

2.2 The role of risk appetite

Figure 10.1 illustrates three roles that risk appetite plays.

Figure 10.1 The role of risk appetite

Risk management decisions

A common role for risk appetite is to act as a benchmark for risk management decisions. This helps to determine whether a given level of risk is 'within appetite'.

Risk appetite can be used to identify:

◆ the risk events that an organisation should reduce its exposure to, because the exposure to downside losses is too high;

◆ the risk events that need relatively little attention because exposure is 'on appetite'; and

◆ the risk events that an organisation should increase its exposure to, because opportunities may otherwise be missed.

By determining its appetite, an organisation can allocate its limited risk management resources more efficiently – targeting resources where they are needed the most – to reduce the exposure to risks that are above appetite or to increase exposure where the level of risk is too low. In addition, determining risk appetite should help to improve buy-in for risk management activities by highlighting the negative consequences of not maintaining appropriate levels of risk exposure.

Managers and employees can perceive risk management as a tool that leads to excessive control and conservatism. The concept of risk appetite provides a clear benchmark for risk-reducing and risk-increasing activities, preventing over-control and excessive risk taking.

Risk governance and internal control

The concept of risk appetite has an important role to play in maintaining appropriate corporate governance. By expressing, setting and monitoring its appetite for risk an organisation can constrain management decision making, ensuring that they do not expose it to an excessive amount of risk or make overly conservative decisions that generate an insufficient return. This should help an organisation to achieve its objectives and satisfy the needs of stakeholders.

Within a governance and internal control context, it is common to use risk appetite as a mechanism for limit setting, where limits are set for an organisation's total exposure to risk or for specific categories and types of risk event.

Care should be taken when using the concept of risk appetite to set absolute limits for risk exposure. Logically it does not make sense to set absolute limits for risk exposure, since increased levels of risk may be associated with higher levels of return. It is more logical to set relative limits in terms of the rate of return that may be required for a specific level of risk. This is sometimes known as the risk premium. This risk premium helps to further clarify the balance that an organisation needs to maintain between risk taking and generating a return or delivering a service.

In finance and accounting terms, the concept of risk-adjusted return is one way in which a risk premium can be expressed. A return that is risk adjusted is discounted to reflect the potential for downside losses. The greater the exposure to downside loss, the greater the discount rate. The returns on risky financial market investments are often risk adjusted to reflect the level of risk exposure.

Strategic decision making

Determining an organisation's appetite for risk supports strategic decision making and the achievement of its objectives.

An organisation without a clear appetite for risk might pass up value-adding opportunities because they do not have a clear understanding of how to balance risk and return. In contrast, another organisation might make strategic decisions that exposes it to high levels of risk in order to generate positive returns, but the level of return that is generated may be relatively low.

An organisation cannot make effective strategic decisions if it does not have a consistent benchmark to help it weigh up the positive and negative outcomes that might occur as a result of these decisions. It is not sufficient to assess returns and risk exposure: an organisation must decide whether the level of return is sufficient for the risk taken. Without an understanding of its appetite for risk, an organisation may make inconsistent decisions that expose it to too much or too little risk.

By helping to articulate the degree of risk that it is willing to take for the returns that may be generated, risk appetite can be used to ensure that an organisation:

◆   does not enter into investments or activities that expose it to an excessive amount of risk, where the potential for return is too low to compensate for the potential for downside losses; and

◆   is not overly conservative: stifling innovation, promoting excessive bureaucracy and passing up investments or activities that should add value.

Stop and think 10.1

Search the internet for examples of organisations that have failed because they did not take enough risk or because they took too much risk.

Examples of organisations that took too much risk include Northern Rock or Lehman Brothers prior to the 2007–08 financial crisis. Examples of organisations that took too little risk include Kodak, which failed to develop the digital camera, and IBM, who were slow to develop the personal computer.

Test yourself 10.1

How can using the concept of risk appetite add value to an organisation?

3. Risk tolerance and capacity

An organisation may use the concepts of risk tolerance and risk capacity instead of, or to provide extra dimensions to, its risk appetite framework.

3.1   Risk tolerance

The term risk tolerance may be used instead of risk appetite, especially where the focus is on downside risk. More accurately, the concept complements risk appetite and can be used to set tolerance limits for specific categories of risk, or for metrics such as risk, control or performance indicators.

Tolerance limits are best understood in the context of downside risks. An organisation may set tolerance limits for health and safety incidents. Minor incidents may be tolerated but major incidents such as a death or serious injury may not be tolerated.

In terms of metrics, tolerance limits may be set for a range of risk, control or performance indicators including staff turnover rates, staff absence rates, customer complaints, system availability, late audit items or cash flow volatility.

Tolerance limits can be linked to the concept of RAG reporting (see Chapter 9, page 184). Any risk or metric that is in the red zone will generally be considered intolerable, with the boundary between amber and red denoting the limit of tolerance. The boundary between green and amber may be used to show the preferred limit of tolerance.

Case study 10.1

An organisation does not normally experience work-related health and safety incidents that result in employee absence of more than three days. It decides that it would prefer not to tolerate absences that exceed four days.

Where an absence may exceed four days this is reported as an amber health and safety risk. An absence of six days or more is considered to be the absolute limit of tolerance. Where there is concern that an absence of six days or more could occur, this is reported as a red risk.

3.2 Risk capacity

Risk capacity denotes the maximum enterprise-wide level of risk to which an organisation may be exposed.

Decisions that increase an organisation's exposure to risk can add up. An organisation may get into trouble if several of these result in unfavourable outcomes at the same time. An organisation may need to take risk to achieve its objectives but if it takes too much risk in aggregate it will risk serious financial distress and ultimately bankruptcy.

Risk capacity is usually a function of an organisation's financial strength. Organisations that have significant financial reserves or low levels of debt can normally take more risk. Risk capacity may also be determined by governments, regulators or other stakeholders (such as shareholders and consumers). For example, public concern about the risks associated with activities such as fracking or genetically modified foodstuffs may mean that organisations decide against investing in them despite the potential financial returns. Equally, banks may wish to lend more money to generate greater profits, but regulators may prevent them from doing so because of concerns about the risk to the financial system.

Test yourself 10.2

Compare and contrast risk appetite, risk tolerance and risk capacity

4. Expressing risk appetite

Organisations articulate their appetite for risk in different ways. There is no one agreed approach. Different risks may require different means of expression. How an organisation assesses its exposure to risk will affect the approach that is chosen.

4.1 Metric-based expressions of risk appetite

An organisation can use metrics to express its appetite for risk. Two approaches are common:

◆ probability and impact boundaries; and

◆ targets, limits and thresholds.

Probability and impact boundaries
Where probability and impact are assessed quantitatively or qualitatively, it is possible to establish risk appetite limits for probability or impact.

Table 10.1 illustrates this in the context of a qualitative ordinal scale approach to assessing probability and negative loss impacts. This is common for operational risks, including health and safety and pollution risks:

Negative Impact				
		1	2	3
Probability	1	1	2	3
	2	2	4	6
	3	3	6	9

Table 10.1 Example probability and impact boundary

The boundary between 'in' and 'out' of appetite is set at a combined probability and impact (exposure) score of six or more. Risks with an exposure value that is six or more are out of appetite. This may be combined with a RAG rating as illustrated. Risks scoring six or more are coloured red, highlighting that they are outside an organisation's appetite for risk. Risks scoring three or four are coloured amber to reflect the concern that the level of exposure may increase into the red range. Ideally, risks should be controlled when in the amber range to prevent the level of exposure moving to red.

Targets, limits and thresholds
The targets, limits and thresholds set by an organisation are a reflection of its appetite for risk.

A target is a value or range of values that an organisation is aiming for. Targets are most often set for strategic risks that may have a positive or negative outcome. For example, an organisation may set a profit, surplus, growth or market share target. Targets may be for a single objective – for example, to grow market share by 5% – or expressed in ranges and linked to the concept of RAG reporting.

Case study 10.2

An organisation has a target for growing its asset base by £10 million per year. It decides that it would prefer for the rate of growth to vary by no more than 10% (£1 million). In years where asset growth may be less than £9 million or greater than £11 million this is reported as 'amber'. Low asset growth may generate a low level of return and very rapid growth can lead to increased operational risk exposures if systems, processes and productivity levels cannot keep up.

An increase or reduction in asset growth of 50% (£5 million) is considered to be the absolute limit of appetite. Years that may lead to growth of £5 million or less, or £15 million or more, are reported as a red risk.

A limit denotes the maximum or minimum value that an organisation is prepared to accept. Limits are most commonly applied to downside risks and there is a strong link here with the concept of risk tolerance. Limits may be applied to customer complaints: for example, unexpected losses or the frequency and severity of health and safety incidents.

Thresholds are often linked to the concept of RAG reporting. For a given risk or risk, control and performance indicator an organisation may set a green-amber threshold and an amber-red threshold that denotes when the risk or indicator is moving from green to amber and then red. Thresholds may be used in conjunction with targets and limits. The above example of how targets can be used incorporates a red and amber threshold.

Stop and think 10.2

For the organisation that you work for or another that you are familiar with, identify examples of the targets, limits and thresholds that it uses. If the organisation is not one that you work for look in its annual accounts, if these are made public. Many organisations will talk about key targets, limits and thresholds in their annual accounts.

Government organisations may publish performance and risk metrics online, along with any associated targets, limits and thresholds.

4.2   Non-metric expressions of risk appetite

The risk appetite of an organisation is reflected in the words that it says externally and to its employees. An organisation may express its risk appetite in one or more of the following:

◆   statement of values;

◆   risk management policy, which will often contain principles for the management of risk; and

◆   a formal risk appetite statement.

Values

Many organisations have statements which explain their values. Values explain what an organisation stands for and believes in. Values are at the core of an organisation's being and underpin its policies and procedures, as well as its culture. Examples of values include:

◆   to behave honestly, ethically or sustainably;

◆   to treat people with fairness, integrity and respect;

◆   to put safety first;

◆   to put the customer first; or

◆   to continuously look for ways to improve.

Many of an organisation's values will relate to how risks are taken and managed across the organisation. For example, values like honesty are relevant in terms of compliance and internal control. Sustainability is concerned with taking a long-term view of the organisation's performance, as well as its impact on its local community and the environment. Risk management is often also about taking a long-term, forward-looking view of potential risks.

Risk management principles

An organisation may include risk management principles in its risk management policy (see Chapter 4). These principles are an important expression of risk appetite. For example, risk appetite-related principles might include:

◆   only taking risks where the benefits from doing so outweigh the costs;

◆   not taking risks that might result in criminal prosecution;

◆   maintaining a specific credit rating; or

◆   ensuring that risk management activities maximise stakeholder value.

The risk appetite statement

An organisation may draft a formal risk appetite statement. This statement will usually explain:

◆   the organisation's values and risk management principles that relate to its risk appetite;

◆   any risks that the organisation has zero appetite for (such as risk of regulatory non-compliance or insolvency);

◆ the stakeholders that the organisation has considered in determining its appetite for risk (shareholders, customers or employees);

◆ how the organisation monitors its risk profile relative to its risk appetite; and

◆ the measures that the organisation will take where risks exceed appetite.

Stop and think 10.3

Search the internet for examples of risk appetite statements that have been published by organisations. You may find them on their own or as part of a risk management policy or annual report and accounts.

Test yourself 10.3

Why should risk appetite be expressed quantitatively as well as qualitatively?

5. Determining risk appetite

Care is needed when determining an organisation's appetite for risk. If risk appetite is set too low then valuable opportunities may be missed. If risk appetite is set too high, then an organisation may become financially distressed and have to cease operating.

5.1 Factors to consider when determining appetite

Various factors may influence the level of risk appetite chosen by an organisation. Common factors include:

◆ legal and regulatory requirements;

◆ the risk preferences of key stakeholder groups such as shareholders, customers and employees;

◆ the specialist knowledge, skills and experience of the organisation's risk, compliance and governance specialists (highly skilled specialists may be able to help an organisation take risks that have a greater upside potential);

◆ the strength of an organisation's balance sheet, which will influence its ability to withstand unexpected losses, high levels of capital resources are especially significant, as is the ratio of debt to equity; and

◆ external factors such as technological change or economic growth.

Technological change, such as the internet and social media, can present significant upside opportunities and downside losses – examples of high risk appetite companies looking to exploit technological change include Tesla and Uber.

Organisations may decide to increase their appetite for risk in the face of technological change, risking large losses in the hope of exploiting opportunities that may generate big financial gains. Periods of high economic growth may also promote risk taking because of the increased opportunity for profit. Investment risk appetite levels tend to increase during periods of economic growth. Should this growth stop, then an organisation may experience larger than expected losses. Great care is needed when deciding whether to exploit a period of economic growth, as illustrated by the losses some banks suffered during the 2007–08 financial crisis.

5.2 The role of the board

An organisation's risk appetite should usually be set by the board or trustees. This expectation is reflected in many governance codes, including the UK Governance Code.

In some organisations risk appetite is decided below board level and sent to them for approval. This is not good practice. The board should play an active role in determining an organisation's appetite for risk. When setting an organisation's appetite for risk, the board should consider the factors highlighted in the previous section.

The board is best placed to determine risk appetite because it has a broad organisation-wide view and exists to represent the interests of stakeholders. The board is also often responsible for determining strategy and an organisation's objectives. These are factors that influence and are influenced by risk appetite.

5.3 The role of the chief risk officer and risk function

Where an organisation has a CRO or risk function, they should help to facilitate the board's role in setting risk appetite. This might include organising a workshop or providing information to help the board make a decision.

The CRO or risk function plays a key role in helping an organisation to monitor its risk profile relative to its risk appetite. This can be achieved through the production of risk reports. The CRO or risk function can provide expert risk control advice where an organisation is taking too much or too little risk relative to its risk appetite.

6. Good practice guidance on implementing risk appetite

A wide range of good practice resources focus on risk appetite. Three helpful resources are published by:

◆   the Chief Risk Officers Forum
◆   the Institute of Risk Management
◆   the COSO thought leadership series.

6.1   Chief Risk Officers Forum

The CRO Forum is a group of insurance company CROs from across Europe. The Forum produces a range of high-quality papers on important risk management topics such as risk appetite and risk culture.

Although the members of the Forum come from the European insurance industry, the work that they produce is relevant for other sectors. The members are experienced risk management professionals and the guides are practical in focus.

The CRO Forum paper on risk appetite is written in conjunction with the North American CRO Council (CRO Forum and CRO Council, 2013). The paper offers definitions for key terms such as risk appetite, risk tolerance and risk capacity. It also provides guidance on how to determine and express risk appetite in an effective way. Some of the key messages in the paper are:

◆   There is no single best approach for risk appetite. An organisation needs to implement what is right for it, depending on the needs of its stakeholders and the nature, scale and complexity of its activities.

◆   The diverse interests and risk preferences of all stakeholders should be considered.

◆   Risk appetite levels should be realistic, meaning not too high or too low relative to the current risk profile. Large changes in risk appetite levels are hard to implement and can be risky if the organisation does not have appropriate controls in place to manage the change in risk exposure.

◆   The level of risk appetite should be reviewed at least annually by the board.

◆   An organisation's risk appetite should be communicated to all of its decision makers to ensure that they make appropriate and consistent decisions.

◆   Quantitative risk limits should be set where possible.

◆   Qualitative boundaries should be used where risks cannot be quantified.

6.2   Institute of Risk Management

The Institute of Risk Management (IRM) provides an online resource and white paper on risk appetite (IRM, 2011).

The IRM's work builds on the risk management guidance within the UK Corporate Governance Code and argues that all organisations should determine their appetite for risk and monitor this against their risk profile. The IRM's paper suggests that:

◆   Risk appetite should be expressed quantitatively.

◆   Risk appetite is not a single fixed concept. Different appetites will be required for different types of risk (such as strategic, operational and financial).

◆   Risk appetite is a function of an organisation's financial strength and risk management maturity, meaning the effectiveness of its risk management framework.

◆   When setting risk appetite, an organisation must consider its strategic and operational objectives.

◆   Risk appetite should be integrated into an organisation's governance and internal control arrangements.

The paper provides some helpful self-assessment questions that organisations can use to check the effectiveness of their risk appetite framework.

6.3   COSO risk appetite thought leadership paper

The COSO paper discusses the use of risk appetite within an ERM framework. The paper argues that:

◆   Risk appetite is an essential part of an effective ERM framework.

◆   Risk appetite and strategy setting decisions should be integrated. Organisations must consider their appetite for risk when deciding on their objectives.

◆   Decision makers across the organisation need to understand its appetite for risk so they are clear on the risks that are acceptable and those that are not.

◆   The board should set an organisation's appetite for risk and monitor the risk profile to ensure that it remains within appetite.

◆   Organisations should review their appetite for risk on a regular basis.

7. Culture and risk culture

Effective risk taking and risk management is about more than policies, procedures or processes. It is an organisation's employees – its people – that have to implement and comply with these policies, procedures and processes. If they do not do this effectively, significant adverse risk events can occur. An organisation's employees are also the ones who make risk taking and risk reduction decisions: poor quality decisions may lead to an organisation taking too much or too little risk.

People's behaviour and the decisions that they make are influenced by a range of factors – such as their education, work and life experiences, or family background – but most of these can be boiled down into one key influence: culture, meaning how they have learned to relate to other people when in a social setting. In an organisational context this frequently means an organisation's culture.

Figure 10.2 illustrates the various cultural layers that can influence individuals and the decisions that they make.

Macro-cultures relate to things like:

◆   the country or region where a person grew up;

◆   religious or family influences;

◆   where they were educated and the level of that education; and

◆   their professional training and experiences, for example, company secretary, lawyer or accountant.

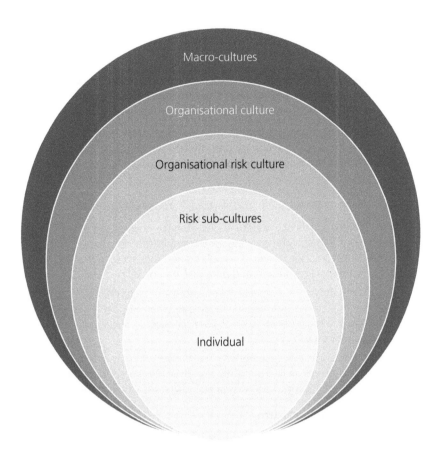

Figure 10.2 Culture onion

7.1 Defining organisational culture

An organisation's culture relates to how its employees collectively think, feel, perceive, act and behave. Humans are social animals and most exhibit a strong desire to fit in. An organisation's culture provides an implicit but powerful co-ordination mechanism for how its employees live and work together. People that resist the cultural norms of an organisation will typically be brought into line very quickly through their interactions with other employees, including line managers and their peers.

An organisation's culture is a shared phenomenon but it is also a process that is open to influence. All of the people that make up an organisation can influence its culture, especially those in positions of power and influence. In addition, an organisation's past experiences, including the decisions made and the outcomes of these decisions can have a major influence. Organisations that have been successful on their decision making may be bold, confident and entrepreneurial. Organisations that have experienced some very unsuccessful decisions may be much more reflective and cautious.

Stop and think 10.4

For an organisation that you have worked for, reflect on the culture that was in place there – what words would you use to describe it? Collegiate, hierarchical, aggressive, reflective, and so on.

If you worked for this organisation for a number of years, reflect on how this culture may have changed and what caused this change, for example a major business success or failure.

Organisational cultures are often multi-layered. Three key layers exist:

1. The visible products of the culture – for example how people dress, the design and layout of the organisation's premises (offices or open plan), the jargon in use and the design of its policies and procedures (detailed and prescriptive, or more flexible and principles-based).

2. The beliefs and values that are spoken about – a major influence here is the tone that comes from top management, what they say is important to them and the organisation (such as financial success, social values, taking a short or a long-term view and so on).

3. The deeper underlying assumptions – behaviours that are so ingrained that people do not realise that they are exhibiting them. Examples might include competitiveness, aggressiveness, politeness or friendliness.

7.2 Defining risk culture

The risk culture of an organisation is a subset of its wider organisational culture. Risk culture can relate to many different types of behaviour and attitude in relation to risk taking and risk management, including:

◆   the level of risk taking that is considered to be desirable (high or low);

◆   how different types of risk are perceived and whether they are considered to be high or low, or good or bad;

◆   the level of risk control that is considered to be desirable (high or low);

◆   why risk management is perceived to be necessary, such as whether it is seen as value enhancing or simply a box-ticking compliance exercise;

◆   whether or not risk compliance and risk governance are viewed as important activities;

◆   the general importance attached to risk management and risk management goals;

◆   the level of awareness that an organisation's employees have about the risks to which it is exposed;

◆   how employees respond to policies and procedures (whether they are seen as helpful or unnecessary red-tape);

◆   whether risk events are perceived as learning opportunities or an opportunity to blame others; and

◆   whether employees are prepared to report risk events and control
     weaknesses.

Risk culture and appetite are related concepts. The risk culture of an
organisation can have a significant influence on its appetite for risk, and the
risk appetite is often a reflection of the organisation's risk culture. Risk cultures
characterised by high levels of risk aversion will tend to set low levels of risk
appetite and vice versa.

Test yourself 10.4

What is the difference between culture and risk culture?

7.3   Risk sub-cultures

Most organisations have risk sub-cultures that fit under the overall
organisational risk culture. These sub-cultures may emerge in different countries
of operation, business lines, functions, departments, teams or workplaces.

Risk sub-cultures are influenced by the broader organisational risk culture but
significant deviations can occur. These deviations are not necessarily a problem
and may facilitate the smooth functioning of risk taking and risk management in
different parts of the organisation. However, issues can occur from time to time.
The Barclays LIBOR scandal illustrates the problem of a deviant risk sub-culture.

7.4   The consequences of risk culture 'failures'

There is no such thing as an ideal or optimal risk culture. However, the
consequences of having an inappropriate risk culture can be disastrous.
Significant problems can arise when a risk culture works against an
organisation's risk management framework, associated governance and
compliance arrangements. The Barclays LIBOR scandal (see Case study 5.6 on
page 101) is an example of the consequences of risk culture failure.

The LIBOR scandal cost Barclays a lot of money in fines. It also damaged the
reputation of the banking group and led to major structural and management
changes. Scandals in other sectors, such as the VW emissions scandal, have
also been caused by failures in the risk cultures and risk sub-cultures of these
organisations. Many major health and safety incidents have also been linked to
failures in risk culture, such as the BP Deepwater Horizon case.

8. Assessing, monitoring and controlling risk culture

The assessment, monitoring and control of risk culture is difficult because of
its subjective nature. As you get deeper into the beliefs, values and underlying
assumptions that people have about risk taking and risk management, it can be

hard to evaluate these with any degree of accuracy. It is difficult to ask the right questions – or even a sufficient number of questions – to arrive at an accurate assessment.

Even though the accuracy of assessment is a problem, organisations do try to assess, monitor and control risk culture. Common tools include:

◆ employee surveys (such as employee satisfaction questionnaires)
◆ employee focus groups
◆ interviewing staff
◆ analysis of HR information (staff turnover, exit interviews, grievances and so on
◆ internal audits.

Specialist risk culture surveys and metrics may be used in some cases. These are often developed by risk culture specialists and psychologists working for external consultants.

8.1   Risk culture surveys and metrics

Risk culture surveys and metrics provide mechanisms that help an organisation assess its risk culture and monitor how risk culture changes over time. An organisation's risk culture is rarely static; it is important to monitor how it is changing to ensure that inappropriate behaviours, values or underlying assumptions do not emerge.

Risk culture surveys
Risk culture surveys are specialist staff surveys designed to assess an organisation's risk culture. Surveys may be built in-house by the HR and risk specialists of an organisation or they may be facilitated by an external consultant. Many consulting organisations offer risk culture assessment tools to their clients.

Risk culture surveys can help to make more visible the beliefs, values and underlying assumptions that characterise an organisation's risk culture. Organisations can then highlight the positive elements that they may want to strengthen, such as risk awareness or a concern for compliance, along with the elements that may be deemed inappropriate, such as unsafe working practices.

In terms of disadvantages, risk culture surveys are time consuming to design and to administer, taking up valuable employee time. There is no guarantee that a survey will provide an accurate picture of an organisation's risk culture. If incorrect or insufficient questions are asked, or if respondents do not understand the questions, then a false picture of the risk culture may be created.

Metrics
Risk culture metrics might include data on policy breaches, the number of overdue internal audit actions, or losses and near misses caused by inappropriate employee behaviour.

There is no formal list of risk culture metrics. Organisations that make use of risk culture metrics should decide for themselves the metrics that are appropriate.

The monitoring of risk culture metrics is common in the financial services sector, but less common in other sectors.

8.2   Controlling risk culture

The constantly changing nature of an organisation's risk culture requires regular control interventions to ensure that it remains appropriate. Risk culture is not something that can be controlled via a large change project and then left for months or years. A variety of tools can be used to control risk culture. One way to structure these tools is via Simons' levers of control (Simons, 1995).

Simons' levers and some example risk culture controls are presented in Table 10.2.

Lever	Description	Example controls
Belief systems	Used to inspire employees and direct the search for new opportunities (risk taking)	Tone and action from the top (how the leaders of the organisation talk and act about risk and the importance of risk management) The organisation's values Codes of conduct
Boundary systems	Used to set limits on risk taking behaviours	Risk appetite Policies and procedures Mandates and limits of authority
Diagnostic systems	Used to motivate, monitor and reward behaviours and the achievement of organisational outcomes	Employee performance evaluations Remuneration arrangements Disciplinary and grievance processes
Interactive systems	Used to stimulate organisational learning and the emergence of new ideas and strategies	Training and development Risk communication and escalation processes Lessons learned – evaluations of successes and failures

Table 10.2 Simons' levers of control

The key point about Simon's levers is that the effective control of risk culture is about controlling intangible beliefs and values, as well as creating tangible incentives for the right behaviours or barriers for the wrong ones. There is a strong psychological element to controlling risk culture. Some organisations bring in experts in occupational psychology to facilitate the control of their risk culture.

Test yourself 10.5

How often should organisations attempt to assess, monitor and control their risk culture?

8.3 Practical guidance on assessing, monitoring and controlling risk culture

Practical guidance on the assessment, monitoring and control of risk culture is provided by a variety of organisations. Some resources are outlined in Table 10.3.

Organisation	Description	Web link
Association of Certified Chartered Accountants (ACCA)	Guidance from ACCA on how to improve risk governance and oversight through the creation of a risk challenge culture. A risk challenge culture is one where inappropriate behaviours, beliefs and values are challenged and where risk management processes and procedures are improved on a continuous basis.	www.accaglobal.com
CRO Forum	The CRO Forum consists of senior risk specialists working in the insurance industry, but its guidance on the assessment, monitoring and control of risk culture is relevant to other sectors. The document provides definitions for culture and risk culture and best practice on how to talk about and manage risk culture within an organisation.	www.thecroforum.org
Financial Stability Board	The FSB provides guidance on how to assess risk culture. The document is especially useful for organisations looking to develop metrics on risk culture. The FSB structures its guidance around four topics: tone from the top, accountability for risk taking and control decisions; effective challenge in relation to risk taking and control; and incentives for appropriate risk management behaviours.	www.fsb.org

Health and Safety Executive	The UK HSE provides resources on the management of risk culture in relation to health and safety within organisations, which is also known as 'safety climate'. The HSE provides good practice guidance on controlling safety climate and a survey tool to help assess safety climate.	www.hse.gov.uk
Institute of Risk Management	The IRM has provided a white paper on the management of risk culture. The IRM suggests that there are 10 elements of success to managing risk culture which includes factors like: tone from the top, willingness to learn from mistakes, risk awareness and aligning risk culture management with HR strategy.	www.theirm.org

Table 10.3 Guidance on assessing, monitoring and controlling risk culture

Stop and think 10.5

Consider the organisation that you work for or another that you are familiar with. Reflect on the work that it is doing to assess, monitor and control its risk culture – what are the tools and techniques that it uses?

Consider an organisation that you do not work for. Take a look at its annual accounts to see what is said about its culture and risk culture. Some organisations include a section on culture. This may include information in its risk culture.

Chapter summary

◆ Exposure to risk can create the potential for positive as well as negative outcomes. It is important that an organisation understands the level of risk taking that is appropriate, along with the risks and outcomes that it wishes to take and those it should limit.

◆ Risk appetite can be defined in terms of a willingness to take risk or the acceptability of risk. Organisations in areas where there are significant safety or environmental hazards will often definite risk appetite in terms of the acceptability of risk. Most other organisations will find it more appropriate to talk about a willingness to take risk, since risk taking is needed to achieve most business objectives.

◆ Determining an organisation's risk appetite should help it make better strategic, governance and risk management decisions. This is because an organisation will have a clearer understanding of the risks that need to be taken and those that need to be reduced.

◆ Organisations may set risk tolerance and risk capacity levels. Risk tolerances are usually set for specific types of risk or risk indicator and denote the levels of risk that are tolerable and intolerable. Risk capacity denotes the total amount of risk that an organisation can be exposed to without risking its long-term future as a going concern.

◆ Risk appetite can be expressed in a variety of quantitative and qualitative ways including risk matrices, RAG ratings, organisational values and codes of conduct.

◆ An organisation should determine its appetite for risk, considering factors such as financial strength and the risk preferences of its stakeholders. The board of directors or trustees should normally be in charge of this process.

◆ Culture and risk culture are as important as risk management frameworks and processes in influencing how risks are taken and managed within an organisation.

◆ Inappropriate risk cultures can lead to excessive risk taking or insufficient risk taking, it may also lead to compliance breaches. It is very important that an organisation takes steps to prevent inappropriate risk cultures from forming.

◆ Risk cultures can be assessed, monitored and controlled using a variety of tools and techniques. These tools and techniques are not perfect. Care must be taken when interpreting the results of risk culture assessments and metrics or attempting to manipulate a risk culture. Mistakes can be made very easily and this may have an adverse effect on a risk culture.

◆ Practical guidance on the assessment, monitoring and control of risk culture is available via a range of good practice sources, including the IRM and UK HSE.

Chapter eleven
Compliance management

Contents

1. Introduction

This chapter outlines how an organisation can manage its compliance-related activities. All organisations have to comply with a range of laws and regulations. Non-compliance can have serious consequences, including fines, the imprisonment of key staff, and the closure of the organisation. Non-compliance can lead to lengthy legal disputes, liability claims, negative media coverage, loss of reputation and can affect the share price of quoted companies.

Complying with all applicable laws and regulations is time consuming and costly, especially as laws and regulations change. Over-compliance is a possibility and can affect the efficiency of an organisation and its processes. Compliance management helps an organisation to balance the costs and benefits of compliance to ensure that its compliance activities are cost effective and support the achievement of all its other objectives.

Compliance management does not have the same focus or objectives as risk management. Not all compliance activities may be connected with risk management. Nevertheless, there are many circumstances where the boundaries of compliance and risk management cross. Risk managers often get involved in relevant compliance activities and compliance managers may find themselves involved in risk management. Company secretaries and other governance professionals will often get involved in both risk management and compliance management as part of their role.

2. Linking compliance and risk management

Compliance management and risk management are linked in two ways:

1.　In many countries and organisational sectors there are laws and regulations that are related to the practice of risk management in organisations (which need to be complied with).

2.　Whenever there are laws and regulations, there is a risk that an organisation will face sanctions where it is found to be non-compliant, This is often termed compliance risk. It can be managed using risk management tools and techniques.

2.1　Risk management rules and regulations

Organisations are subject to a variety of laws and regulations that relate to the practice of risk management and the risks that their stakeholders are exposed to (see Chapters 2 and 3). Examples include:

◆　company law and governance regulations;

◆　health and safety laws and associated regulations;

◆　environmental laws and associated regulations; and

◆　prudential regulation and conduct of business regulation within the financial services sector.

Compliance management ensures that:

◆　all applicable laws and regulations are identified; and

◆　that the implications of these laws and regulations for an organisation's decisions and processes are assessed and understood.

Compliance management includes:

◆　putting mechanisms in place to assess whether the risk management policies, procedures and practices within an organisation are compliant with applicable laws and regulations; and

◆　designing and implementing controls which monitor and maintain compliance.

Where risk management policies, procedures and practices are found to be non-compliant, compliance management can help ensure that actions are taken to make these policies, procedures and practices compliant and to manage any related dialogue with the relevant supervisory or regulatory agencies.

2.2　Managing compliance risk

Where there are laws and regulations there is compliance risk. Potential compliance risk events include:

◆ An organisation does not realise that a law or regulation exists or applies to it. This may be because the law or regulation is new or changed, or the organisation is operating in an unfamiliar legal jurisdiction. In countries where laws may be modified by judicial rulings (so-called case law), it may be that the compliance implications of a particular law change as a result of a ruling.

◆ An organisation is aware of the existence of a law or regulation, but there is a lack of certainty concerning how to comply with the law or regulation. This is quite common in relation to principles and outcomes-based regulation, where there is no single way to comply. Laws and regulations in new areas, such as data protection, can also create uncertainty because there may not yet be an established process for ensuring full compliance.

◆ Uncertainties may exist over when or how a law or regulation may apply to different contexts. This is especially common when dealing with new regulations in new areas, such as data protection or the Modern Slavery Act in the UK.

◆ An organisation's management makes a conscious decision not to comply with a law or regulation. This may be because compliance with the law or regulation is deemed to be overly costly or inefficient, or conflicting with other rules and regulations, for example.

◆ Staff members within the organisation take decisions or actions that cause the organisation to breach a law or regulation. This behaviour may be accidental or deliberate. For example, a staff member may accidentally lose sensitive personal information or they might decide to sell it, illegally, to a third party.

◆ Complexities and conflicting priorities within processes and procedures may make it hard to design them to ensure full compliance while at the same time achieve organisational objectives. For example, financial crime rules have made it harder for people to open bank accounts. The account opening process is now much longer and greater amounts of documentation are required. This can cause frustration for new customers and may prevent legitimate and law-abiding customers from opening an account where they lack the required documentation.

For one or more of the reasons above, even the best managed, most ethical and law abiding organisation may find itself at risk of sanction because they have breached laws and regulations. Equally, concerns about compliance risks may lead to over-compliance. Over-compliance increases the costs of compliance and may also lead to inefficient and ineffective processes. Compliance management exists to help prevent non-compliance (or partial compliance) and over-compliance.

Case study 11.1

The following are examples of data protection breaches that have led to sanctions by regulators:

- an organisation was named and shamed when an employee lost a digital camera that contained the pictures of six job applicants;

- a financial services firm was fined when it lost unencrypted IT backup tapes that contained account information on 500,000 customers;

- an organisation was fined when a malicious hacker breached their IT security and stole sensitive personal information;

- a bank was fined when a branch repeatedly sent customer information to the wrong recipients; and

- a council employee posted information relating to the care of vulnerable children on his/her personal social media account.

These examples highlight how, as technology changes, organisations can find it hard to keep up with the compliance risks associated with data protection laws and regulations. All of these breaches were accidental, and in some cases the organisation may not have considered them to be potential breaches before the imposition of sanctions (such as the loss of a camera or how a staff member uses social media) but these events still highlighted significant compliance risk exposures.

Recent developments in data protection rules across Europe, including Ireland and the UK, are creating new uncertainties and compliance risks for organisations. Current issues include:

- The management of automated decision making (such as automated lending decisions). Currently it is unclear how organisations can demonstrate that these decisions are made in a fair and consistent manner without providing commercially sensitive information about their decision processes.

- A person's right to be forgotten. An organisation may find it very difficult to find and delete every single reference to an individual. Challenges include back-up tapes taken prior to the erasure of a person's records (to erase the data the whole tape must be destroyed), as well as the increased use of personal devices for things like work emails.

- Uncertainties over what information may be retained on people and for how long. Here conflicts may arise between data protection regulations (the right to have personal information deleted) and conduct of business regulations (the need to prove that an appropriate service was provided).

Data protection laws are important from a human rights perspective but it is hard for law makers to keep up with developments. Equally, it is hard for organisations to futureproof their systems and processes to maintain compliance as technologies and social attitudes change.

3. Roles and responsibilities for compliance management

The structure of compliance management roles and responsibilities within organisations varies according to their nature, scale and complexity. In some organisations, individuals and functions may have multiple roles and will combine compliance management with a range of other responsibilities. In others, especially larger organisations, compliance management may exist as a separate function – although other parts of the organisation will continue to have compliance management related responsibilities.

Common individuals, groups and functions that have roles and responsibilities in relation to compliance management include:

- the board of directors;
- the audit committee;
- the company secretary and other governance professionals;
- the compliance function;
- the risk management function;
- the internal audit function;
- other specialist functions, for example health and safety or IT security;
- line managers across the organisation; and
- staff members.

3.1 Board of directors

The company laws, governance regulations and codes of many countries make it clear that the board of directors has ultimate responsibility for ensuring that an organisation is compliant with all relevant laws and regulations. In some countries, board members may have legal duties to ensure that an organisation is compliant with relevant laws and regulations. Failure to fulfil these duties may lead to fines and the dismissal or imprisonment of directors.

Boards rely on a variety of assurance mechanisms to oversee the compliance management activities of an organisation. This may include receiving compliance-focused internal audit reports and reviews for specific business areas, processes or areas of regulation, such as health and safety and environmental protection. Boards may receive compliance monitoring reports outlining the range of laws and regulations that the organisation is expected to comply with and the effectiveness of the controls that have been put in place to ensure compliance. Where new laws or regulations are created, or weaknesses found in compliance management controls, a board may receive reports on these and regular progress updates on the actions taken to address them.

3.2 Audit committee

Where appropriate, an organisation may have an audit committee. An audit committee is typically delegated by the board and is made up of board directors, often exclusively non-executive directors (NEDs).

Audit committees have a specific compliance management role to ensure that an organisation complies with the laws and regulations that relate to financial reporting. The audit committee, supported by the internal and external auditors, provides assurance to the board that the annual accounts are accurate and contain all the information necessary to comply with financial reporting rules.

Many audit committees have additional compliance responsibilities delegated to them by the board. This may include receiving internal audit reports and compliance reviews. The audit committee will often have more time to focus on these reports than the main board and may be involved in deciding where to target the time of internal auditors and compliance managers, such as focusing their attention on specific laws or regulations, or processes and functions, that are deemed to have high levels of compliance risk.

Audit committees that are responsible for overseeing risk management activities may have responsibility for overseeing the management of compliance risk via the compliance management function or another function responsible for compliance management.

3.3 Company secretary and other governance professionals

In a smaller organisation, the company secretary or equivalent governance professional may take on the role of the compliance function or a compliance manager may report to them.

In an organisation that has a separate compliance function, the company secretary or governance professional may retain certain compliance management responsibilities. These responsibilities may include ensuring that the organisation is compliant with company law and other governance-related laws and regulations, and reporting on this to the board. In many countries, a company secretary is required under company law and is held responsible for ensuring that an organisation's directors operate within the law. It is usually the company secretary that is the named representative on any legal documents.

3.4 Compliance function

Where present, the compliance function should have primary responsibility for the day-to-day compliance management activities of an organisation. This may include:

◆ keeping up to date with new laws and regulations or changes to existing laws and regulations;

◆ supporting the work of the internal audit function in relation to the compliance elements of internal audit reports;

◆ performing compliance reviews to assess whether the organisation and specific processes, procedures, activities and functions are compliant with key laws and regulations;

◆ the identification, assessment and monitoring of compliance risks;

◆ designing and implementing controls to mitigate the probability and impact of compliance risk events;

◆ working with police, lawyers, regulators and other relevant authorities to help resolve any compliance breaches;

◆ relationship management with regulatory and supervisory agencies: this may include providing information to them about the organisation as required;

◆ supporting the work of the company secretary and other governance professionals: this may include producing compliance monitoring reports for the board and senior management; and

◆ providing advice, guidance and training to other functions in the organisation in relation to compliance issues and the management of compliance risks.

Stop and think 11.1

Consider an organisation that you are familiar with. Investigate whether it has a compliance function. If the function is present, identify the roles and responsibilities of this function. If the function does not exist, identify where responsibility lies for compliance management. Is it the company secretary or governance professional?

If you work for the organisation, look on the intranet or ask your line manager. For other organisations, look on their website and, if available, the annual report. Look for a webpage or report section on governance. The presence of a compliance function and its roles and responsibilities should be discussed there.

3.5   Risk management function

An organisation's risk management function may have responsibility for overseeing the management of any compliance risks that relate to laws and regulations on risk management.

The risk management function may support the compliance function and other specialist functions by providing advice on how to manage compliance risks. The risk management function may help the compliance function to design tools and techniques for the identification, assessment, monitoring and control of compliance risks, and to design relevant risk reports. In some cases the compliance function may be part of the risk management function.

3.6   Internal audit function

Many internal audits will include assessments of compliance management related controls and monitoring tools. For example, IT-related audits might include an assessment of the controls used to ensure compliance with data protection laws. In addition, the internal audit function may complete thematic audits that look at specific aspects of an organisation's compliance management arrangements, such as arrangements for regulatory reporting or for assessing compliance risks.

Internal audit may work with the compliance function to complete compliance reviews, which look in detail at the controls used to ensure compliance with laws and regulations. Internal audit will be expected to escalate any concerns that they may have in relation to compliance management across the organisation, or the organisation's exposure to specific compliance risks.

3.7   Other specialist functions

An organisation may have specialist functions in areas of high risk and regulation like health and safety, financial reporting or information security.

Where specialist functions are present, they have a central role to play in the control of relevant compliance risks. This will include supporting the design and implementation of controls that ensure compliance with relevant laws and regulations.

Specialist functions may provide technical advice to the compliance function, company secretary and other governance professionals in relation to specific laws and regulations and on how to manage the associated compliance risks. Given the range of laws and regulations that exist, it is not possible for the compliance function to have expertise in every area. For example, an information security function may have staff members who are experts in data protection regulations and on how to comply with these regulations in an appropriate and cost-effective way.

3.8   Line managers across the organisation

All line managers have the responsibility to ensure that their direct reports comply with applicable laws and regulations, and that compliance-related controls are used in an effective manner. This will include ensuring that compliance-related policies are complied with, and that processes and procedures are performed in a compliant manner. This will also include ensuring that their employees have the skills and training they need to conduct their duties in a compliant manner.

Line managers are responsible for ensuring that the decisions they make do not expose the organisation to compliance risks. For example, a line manager that implements unsafe manual handling practices may be responsible for exposing the organisation to the risk of accidents and subsequent legal sanctions in the event of any injuries.

3.9   Staff members

All employees within an organisation are responsible for conducting their duties in a way that is compliant, or at least not knowingly non-compliant, with applicable laws and regulations. This will include complying with compliance-related organisation policies and procedures, as well as ensuring that they exercise due care, skill and diligence while at work.

An employee cannot be expected to know every law and regulation that applies to their organisation. That is why organisations have compliance functions and other compliance-related specialists to support their work. However, employees should, at all times, follow the instructions of the compliance function and other compliance-related specialists to ensure that their actions or inaction does not expose the organisation to unnecessary or excessive compliance risks. Compliance education and training may be provided to help employees understand their responsibilities and to conduct their role in a compliant manner.

Stop and think 11.2

Have you been made aware of your compliance management responsibilities in the organisations where you have worked? How was this done: at induction, via policies, procedures and training or through your line manager?

Test yourself 11.2

Are all employees within an organisation equally responsible for compliance management, irrespective of their role and responsibilities?

4. Risk-based compliance monitoring

Organisations must do all they can to comply with applicable laws and regulations. That does not mean that the distinction between compliance and non-compliance is clear cut. In practice, it may not be possible to guarantee that an organisation is fully in compliance with every law and regulation. Such guarantees are not always necessary or beneficial when compared to the costs involved. This is especially the case where there is no clear distinction between compliance and non-compliance, such as in the case of regulatory guidance, principles, and codes.

This does not mean that an organisation should be making a conscious decision to not be compliant. This refers to the level of assurance that the organisation looks to maintain over the monitoring and control of its compliance activities. For some laws and regulations, considerable compliance management resources may be needed to provide the necessary assurance, for others significantly less resources may be devoted.

Compliance management is costly. Organisations may have to invest in compliance management experts, design and implement compliance management policies, procedures and tools, and ensure that these policies, processes, and tools are working as intended.

A large part of this compliance management cost relates to the monitoring of an organisation's compliance activities. Organisations need to know that staff and management at all levels understand their compliance-related responsibilities and that they are taking all necessary measures to ensure that compliance with applicable laws and regulations is maintained. This will include conducting compliance reviews, where the day-to-day operation of compliance-related controls is investigated. It may include detailed internal audits and the monitoring of compliance indicators, such as measuring the number of unauthorised policy or procedure breaches.

Organisations do not have limitless resources to monitor compliance. In addition, the act of monitoring compliance can be disruptive to the operations of an organisation. Compliance reviews and audits take up valuable staff and management time. Senior managers and directors also have limited amounts of time to devote to reviewing the output of an organisation's compliance monitoring activities and to initiate subsequent corrective actions.

The concept of risk-based compliance monitoring helps an organisation to allocate its compliance monitoring resources in a cost-effective way. The idea is that the greatest amount of resource is devoted to the largest compliance risks, such as the risk of criminal sanctions. Smaller amounts of monitoring resource are then devoted to smaller compliance risks. In this regard risk-based compliance is a mechanism for assessing the costs and benefits of compliance monitoring. Where the benefits outweigh the costs, monitoring resource is increased. Where costs exceed the benefits, resource is decreased.

As with any other type of risk, an organisation's exposure to compliance risk will depend on the probability of non-compliance and the resultant impact of non-compliance in terms of fines, liability claims or other sanctions. High levels of exposure may be the result of a high probability of non-compliance, a high impact of non-compliance or a combination of the two.

Where risk-based compliance is used, it is common for compliance risks to be assessed using a risk matrix, as illustrated in Table 11.1.

	Impact of compliance sanction		
		1	2	3
Probability of compliance sanction	1	3	6	9
	2	2	4	6
	3	1	2	3

Table 11.1 An example compliance risk matrix

In the above example, compliance risks in the 'red' zone will have the greatest level of monitoring resources devoted to them. This means that monitoring will be more frequent and may be more in-depth. This may mean that an extensive range of indicators are used to monitor compliance. Individual decisions may also be reviewed to determine whether they are fully compliant or not.

Compliance risks assessed to be in the 'amber' and 'green' zones will have proportionately less monitoring resources devoted to them. In the case of green compliance risks, monitoring may be light touch (a high level review of policies and procedures to ensure they are kept up to date) and may only occur every few years.

Each organisation that decides to use risk-based compliance will need to assess the probability and impact of all its compliance risks. In general, the compliance risks that are associated with a failure to prevent a criminal act are much higher than those associated with civil misconduct. There are exceptions to this. Breaches of civil law can have consequences as serious as criminal law in some cases. Breaches of employment law, such as a case of unfair dismissal, can have significant financial implications, especially when linked to employee discrimination.

Case study 11.2

Many countries have laws and regulations that are designed to prevent criminals from using the proceeds of their illegal activities. This can include regulations around the purchase and sale of high value assets (cars and houses), and the opening and operation of bank accounts and bank loans (see Chapter 14).

Organisations that are found to be in breach of these regulations can face significant fines and other criminal sanctions. As a result, the associated exposure to compliance risk can be very high.

Compliance monitoring can be frequent and in-depth in relation to proceeds of crime regulations. Every single transaction (such as bank account transactions) may need to be monitored on a real-time basis to check for suspicious activity. Any such activities are then escalated to the compliance function or the Money Laundering Reporting Officer (MLRO) where required. The decisions made by staff members may also be assessed in detail. For example, regular checks may be made to ensure that a customer's identify is confirmed using multiple sources of verification. This can include recording and analysing phone conversations to provide additional assurance that staff members are using the necessary controls in a consistent and effective manner.

Test yourself 11.3

Does the concept of risk-based compliance monitoring mean that organisations do not need to comply in full with laws and regulations where the level of compliance risk is low?

5. Compliance management tools

A range of tools may be used to support the compliance management activities of an organisation. These include:

◆   compliance policies and procedures

◆   compliance codes of conduct

◆   compliance reviews and audits

◆   compliance impact analysis

◆   gap analysis and action planning

◆   compliance reporting

◆   HR related controls

◆   whistleblowing procedures

◆   establishing an appropriate compliance culture.

5.1   Compliance policies and procedures

An organisation may have policies and procedures that are focused on compliance management, or it may have policies and procedures focused on other activities that have a compliance element. For example, risk management policies and procedures may include elements that relate to compliance with relevant risk management laws and regulations (health and safety laws or prudential regulation).

Policies that are focused on compliance management will specify how compliance risks are to be identified, assessed, monitored and controlled. They will also explain the various roles and responsibilities that exist for compliance management.

Compliance management procedures will specify how particular compliance risks are to be monitored and controlled. For example, there may be 'know-your-customer' procedures which relate to the verification of a customer's identity, or complaints handling procedures which specify how complaints should be managed in a fashion that complies with relevant conduct of business regulation. Procedures for monitoring and reporting on suspicious transactions (suspected money laundering activities) are a further common example of compliance management procedures.

5.2   Compliance codes of conduct

An organisation may have one or more codes of conduct in place. These are often compliance related. In addition, professional associations may have codes of conduct that they expect their members to adhere to. These codes cover professions such as medicine, law, accountancy, finance and governance. Regulators may implement codes of conduct for specific roles, such as board directors and the functions that provide assurance to them, notably the risk function, compliance function and internal audit function. This is common in financial services.

Codes of conduct specify the type of conduct that is expected of relevant staff members, managers and directors within an organisation. Codes may include rules which must be followed at all times, as well as guidance on the standards of behaviour that are expected. Codes may cover:

◆ general principles such as behaving lawfully, ethically, honestly, without bias or discrimination;

◆ the use of organisational assets and information;

◆ declaring and managing conflicts of interests;

◆ receiving corporate hospitality;

◆ dealing with customers and service users, including the handling of complaints;

◆ behaviour when using the internet and social media; and

◆ reporting concerns about the conduct of staff members and other stakeholders.

Staff members found to be in breach of a code of conduct may be subject to disciplinary action including an official warning letter, loss of a bonus or pay rise, or dismissal in more extreme cases.

Test yourself 11.4

Why does an organisation need compliance policies, procedures and codes of conduct?

5.3 Compliance reviews and audits

Compliance reviews are a form of internal audit that review and report on the effectiveness of compliance-related controls. Reviews may look at specific laws and regulations or specific operational areas, such as payments, payroll, health, and safety or IT security.

Compliance reviews will investigate whether compliance controls are used in an appropriate manner and whether additional controls are required. Where weaknesses are identified, these may be ranked in order of priority from low to medium and high. Actions will be agreed with the relevant managers to ensure that any weaknesses are addressed in a timely manner.

Other internal audits of key organisational processes and functions may identify compliance-related issues linked to weaknesses in these processes or associated controls. For example, an audit of an organisation's treasury function or data integrity processes may identify compliance issues relating to financial crime regulations or data protection laws.

5.4 Compliance impact analysis

A compliance impact analysis is a form of risk assessment that investigates the impact of a compliance breach.

Compliance impact analyses will assess the direct and indirect financial costs of a breach. They may also assess non-financial impacts such as reputation effects.

The direct financial costs relate to any fines or direct financial costs that are incurred in the event of a breach. This includes legal and court costs.

The indirect financial costs include the costs associated with managing the effects of a breach. One key indirect cost is the cost of staff time that may be devoted to managing the aftermath of a breach, such as dealing with regulators, lawyers, and the media.

In terms of non-financial impacts, organisations found to be in breach of a law or regulation may suffer adverse media and social media coverage. This may affect how they are perceived by stakeholders and consequently damage their reputation.

Compliance impact analyses may attempt to quantify in broad monetary terms the direct and indirect financial costs of a breach. Alternatively, an ordinal scale (one to three or one to five) may be used to provide a rough estimate of the financial impacts. Non-financial impacts are usually calculated using an ordinal scale because of the difficulties associated with adding numerical values to intangible factors like reputation loss.

The completion of an effective compliance impact analysis requires:

◆ input from a cross-functional range of experts, such as compliance managers, risk managers, finance specialists and public relations experts;

◆ the analysis of any existing information within the organisation, such as pre-existing risk assessments, information on historical breaches (internal and external – where reported in the public domain) and compliance reviews; and

◆ regular updates as new information is obtained, for example information about compliance breaches perpetrated by similar organisations.

5.5 Gap analysis and action planning

A compliance gap analysis helps an organisation to assess whether its existing policies, processes, procedures and compliance controls are sufficient to comply with relevant laws and regulations.

Gap analyses may be performed on specific laws or sets of regulations. In each case, the law or regulation is broken down by article, subsection or paragraph and an assessment is made as to whether existing policies, processes, procedures and compliance controls are sufficient to ensure compliance with each article, subsection or paragraph. Where gaps are identified these may be prioritised in terms of 'low', 'medium' or 'high' gaps.

Action plans may be included within a compliance gap analysis where gaps are identified. Table 11.2 provides an example compliance gap analysis template.

Requirement	Currently in place	Gap Y/N?	Priority	Evidence	Action	Action owner	Due Date
The various legal articles or regulatory requirements that need to be assessed	The policies, procedures, etc. that are currently in place to ensure compliance	Whether a gap exists	The level of priority associated with a gap	Evidence to support the gap assessment. This might be a recent review of a policy or an audit report	Actions required to close a gap	An owner ensures an action is completed	Date action is due

Table 11.2 Example compliance gap analysis template

A gap analysis works best when completed by a small team of relevant experts. This will include a compliance manager and the relevant business managers that are responsible for the processes, procedures and activities subject to the relevant legal requirements or regulations.

Compliance gap analyses are common for new laws and regulations, or where there are major changes to existing laws and regulations.

5.6 Compliance reporting

Compliance reports may include the output from a range of other compliance activities, including risk-based compliance assessments, compliance impact analyses, compliance reviews and compliance gap analyses.

Compliance reports include a summary of any new laws and regulations, or changes to existing laws and regulations. In addition, a range of metrics may be monitored to assess the effectiveness of existing compliance controls. Metrics might include the number of reported compliance breaches or near miss breaches, delays in identified internal audit actions or metrics related to specific topics such as data protection or customer complaints.

Compliance reports will be produced by the compliance function (where this function exists). Alternatively, the company secretary or other governance professional may oversee the production of reports. Reports should be provided to the board and audit committee where relevant to help provide assurance that the organisation is compliant with relevant laws and regulations. Reports may also be provided to senior management and department or functional management to help them monitor the effectiveness of their compliance management activities and take action to address any weaknesses.

5.7 HR related controls

Many HR related controls are relevant from a compliance management perspective. Example controls include:

◆   recruitment controls to ensure that fit and proper employees are recruited;

◆   performance management and personal development planning processes
to help ensure that employees have the incentives, skills and training that
they need to support an organisation's compliance management activities;
and

◆   disciplinary procedures to take action where a member of staff is not
fulfilling their compliance management responsibilities – such as where
a staff member is found to be in breach of a policy, procedure or code of
conduct or where they are found to have engaged in criminal activities.

HR related controls in relation to promoting diversity, preventing discrimination
or workplace bullying and other employee relations and conduct issues are
important because they can help to prevent breaches of employment laws and
diversity and discrimination laws.

5.8   Whistleblowing policies and procedures

Whistleblowing policies and procedures outline how staff members should
report any concerns that they may have about the conduct of a colleague,
manager, director, other employee or third party contractor working with an
organisation. This might include reporting criminal activities, observed breaches
of policies and procedures and poor behaviour such as workplace bullying or
discrimination.

Whistleblowing policies and procedures should explain where and how
a member of staff is expected to report any concerns. This might include
providing a whistleblowing phone hotline or email box that provides access to a
senior manager, such as the Head of Compliance. Whistleblowing policies and
procedures should explain how a whistle-blower will be protected when they
report a concern.

Stop and think 11.3

**Investigate whether an organisation that you are familiar with has a
whistleblowing policy or procedure. If you work for this organisation,
you should find a policy or procedure on the staff intranet or ask your
line manager.**

The BSI provides a publically available specification (PAS) on the
establishment and implementation of whistleblowing policies and procedures
(PAS 1998:2008). PAS publications are free to access.

Test yourself 11.5

**What role do HR controls, and whistleblowing policies and procedures,
play in controlling compliance?**

5.9 Establishing an appropriate culture

A compliance culture is an element of an organisation's wider organisational culture and related risk culture (see Chapter 10).

A compliance culture relates to the general attitudes and behaviours that staff members have in relation to compliance and compliance management. An organisation's compliance culture will affect the conduct of staff members and their willingness to support the effective implementation of compliance related policies, procedures and controls.

There are various ways to ensure an appropriate compliance culture. Mechanisms include:

- having a clear set of organisation values and related codes of conduct that reinforce the importance of behaving with honesty and integrity and the need for effective compliance management;

- performance management and bonus arrangements that reinforce an organisation's values and codes of conduct;

- a commitment from directors and senior managers to maintaining a compliant organisation, this includes a consistent 'tone from the top' in relation to the importance of compliance management and directors and senior managers demonstrating through their own actions the tone that they set;

- providing staff training to ensure that all staff are aware of the importance of compliance management and their roles and responsibilities in relation to compliance management;

- explaining to employees the benefits of effective compliance management and how it contributes to organisational success; and

- reinforcing openness and honesty via a no-blame ethos where employees are encouraged to report potential or actual compliance breaches without fear of reprisal.

Chapter summary

- All organisations have to comply with a range of laws and regulations. Non-compliance can have serious consequences including fines, legal liability suits and a loss of reputation.

- Compliance management and risk management are linked because:
  - there are many laws and regulations that relate to the practice of risk management in organisations; and
  - whenever there are laws and regulations there are compliance risks that need to be managed.

- Compliance management exists to help prevent non-compliance, under-compliance and over-compliance. Over-compliance is a problem because it is unnecessarily costly and may reduce the efficiency and effectiveness of an organisation's processes and procedures.

◆ An organisation may have a specialist compliance function. The structure of compliance management roles and responsibilities within an organisation varies according to its nature, scale and complexity.

◆ The board of an organisation has a key role in overseeing its compliance management activities. The board should seek assurance that compliance management arrangements are effective and appropriate.

◆ All employees, especially managers, have roles and responsibilities in relation to compliance management. The specific nature of these roles and responsibilities depends on the business unit or function that they work within and their job description.

◆ The concept of risk-based compliance monitoring helps an organisation to allocate its compliance monitoring resources in a cost-effective way. The idea is that the greatest amount of resource is devoted to the largest compliance risks, such as the risk of criminal sanction. Lesser amounts of monitoring resource are devoted to smaller compliance risks.

◆ A range of tools may be used to support the compliance management activities of an organisation, including compliance management policies and procedures, compliance impact assessments, compliance gap analyses and action plans, compliance reports and establishing an appropriate compliance culture.

Part three

Risk and the business environment

Overview

The third and final part of this study text focuses on the application of risk management in real-world organisations. It considers how risk exposures can be controlled, as well as a number of specific applications of risk management that you may encounter.

Chapter twelve explores the risk control strategies used by organisations to influence their exposure to risk. Control strategies may be used to influence probability or impact and to mitigate the secondary effects of risk events, such as business disruption and reputation losses.

Chapter thirteen looks at practical applications of risk management in an organisation, including project risk management, supply chain risk management and cyber risk management.

Chapters fourteen and fifteen provide an overview of current trends and future developments in risk management. This includes an investigation into how contemporary trends are sources of emerging risks for organisations, along with developments in risk management technology such as the use of 'big data'.

Learning outcomes

At the end of this part, you will be able to:

◆ Understand how risk control can influence an organisation's exposure to risk.

◆ Explain the four Ts approach to risk control and a range of risk treatment strategies.

◆ Identify a variety of common risk controls.

◆ Understand the role of risk financing and common risk financing strategies.

◆ Appreciate how risk management can be used to support a range of common activities in organisations including internal control, project management, and supply chain risk management.

◆ Demonstrate the links between risk management, corporate social responsibility, and sustainability.

◆ Consider the implications of risk reporting for risk and compliance management.

◆ Understand the relationship between risk and opportunity management.

◆ Explain the role of risk management in supporting the prevention of financial crime.

◆ Identify the sources of emerging risks and a range of current emerging risks.

◆ Appreciate the role of behavioural risk management.

◆ Explain how developments in information technology may support risk management and be a source of risk.

Chapter twelve
Risk control strategies

Contents

1. Introduction

This chapter considers how risk can be controlled in an organisation. Risk control involves the application of tools to influence the probability and/or impact of a risk event. The mitigation of follow-on effects that risk events may have on the continuity of an organisation's operations or its reputation is also a key part of risk control.

A wide range of tools can be used to control risk – more than can be covered in this chapter. Even so, it is possible to categorise these tools into a manageable set of control strategies.

2. Reasons for risk control

All organisations make use of risk control strategies and their associated control tools. These strategies and tools are used to reduce the probability and impact of loss events, such as fires, fraud or IT system failures.

Risk control strategies may also be used to increase the upside of risk events. From a risk management perspective, risk control in organisations is focused on the prevention and reduction of loss event probabilities and impacts. Section 2.2 provides a brief discussion of how risk controls may be used to seize upside opportunities.

2.1 Managing probability and impact

An organisation may reduce its exposure to loss events by lowering the probability that a given event will occur or by mitigating the impact of any event that does occur.

Risk control tools that reduce the probability of a loss event occurring are known as loss prevention tools. Tools that reduce the impact of loss events are known as loss reduction tools. Table 12.1 provides examples of these tools.

Loss prevention tools	Loss reduction tools
IT system firewall	Data backup arrangements
No smoking policy	Fire extinguishers
Segregation of duties	Whistleblowing arrangements
Door locks	Burglar alarm
Driver safety training	Motor insurance

Table 12.1 Examples of loss prevention and reduction tools

To distinguish between loss prevention and loss reduction tools, consider the life cycle of a loss event.

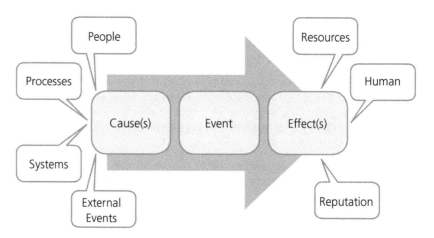

Figure 12.1 Life cycle of a loss event

Loss prevention tools reduce the probability of a loss event by targeting its causes. The causes of a loss event are usually linked to the actions or inactions of people, failures in processes and systems or external events (weather, politics and so on). Loss events often require more than one cause to occur. For example, a fire may require faulty electrical wiring to cause a spark, plus combustible materials to burn.

Loss reduction tools target the effects of loss events. Loss events may have financial and non-financial effects. In financial terms, they can affect the resources (physical assets and cash assets) of an organisation. Physical assets may be damaged or destroyed, requiring repair or replacement. Cash assets may be lost via fines or liability claims.

Loss reduction tools reduce the financial effects of loss events by limiting the physical damage that is caused (such as by having a sprinkler system to put out a fire as quickly as possible) or by helping to fund the repair or replacement of loss assets, compensation payments or legal liability claims as cost effectively as possible. Insurance is one way in which the repair or replacement of lost assets and compensation and liability claims can be funded.

In non-financial terms, loss events may cause death and injury. Loss events may also affect the reputation of an organisation via lost customer goodwill or adverse media coverage, for example. These can have an indirect financial value (such as loss of sales). The non-financial effects of loss events may be mitigated by shortening the duration of a loss event or by helping an organisation to recover quickly from events. Loss reduction tools may also help to prevent death or injury, such as the use of evacuation arrangements in the event of a fire.

An organisation will employ a range of loss prevention and loss reduction tools to control particular loss events. In part, this is due to the fact that events are the result of multiple causes and have multiple effects. It is rare for any one risk control tool to combine probability and impact reduction.

Stop and think 12.1

Can you identify any risk control tools that help to reduce the probability and impact of loss events?

Think carefully about where a control is employed in the cause-event-effect chain. Tools will typically influence the causes or the effects of a loss event, not both. This includes risk detection tools like fire alarms. An alarm does not prevent fire; it signals that a fire has occurred.

Test yourself 12.1

What are the common causes and effects of loss events?

2.2   Using controls for loss events to help seize opportunities

From a risk management perspective, risk control is focused on preventing the causes and reducing the effects of loss events. From a wider strategic management perspective, risk control may help an organisation to seize opportunities for higher levels of financial and non-financial performance, allowing it to achieve and sometimes exceed its objectives.

Traditional loss prevention and loss reduction tools can help an organisation to seize opportunities by protecting its cash flows. An organisation needs cash to help it to exploit opportunities, such as exploiting new technologies, markets or opportunities to develop new products.

Mechanisms such as market research, and strategic investments like flexible manufacturing systems or IT systems, can help organisations to seize new opportunities. As a risk control tool, market research can be used to highlight and take advantage of potential opportunities for new product ideas and markets. Flexible manufacturing and IT systems allow organisations to adapt their production processes, modifying their products and services to exploit changes in customer needs and wants. For example, technological innovations that allow an organisation to supply products and services over the internet is a form of risk control, as it helps to protect an organisation's market share from competitors developing similar delivery mechanisms.

3. The four Ts of risk control

Controlling risk to manipulate the probability or impact of loss events, or to exploit opportunities, is not a given. The ISO's international standard on risk management (ISO 31000:2018) provides the description of a mechanism for categorising the options that are available. This mechanism is known as the 'four Ts':

◆   tolerate
◆   treat
◆   transfer
◆   terminate

3.1   Tolerate

To tolerate a risk exposure means to take no formal action to control it.

Risks may be tolerated where they are known and accepted by an organisation. This may be where a risk exposure is considered to be within an organisation's appetite for risk.

In addition, an organisation may tolerate a risk where active controls are considered uneconomic or impractical, or where the risk is necessary to support the achievement of organisational objectives. Objectives like the development of new products, process change or the implementation of new technology systems will always require a degree of risk. The issue is that risk should be accepted on an informed basis.

Where risk exposures are tolerated, it is good practice for senior management to approve and periodically review the decision. It is rare for a risk exposure to be tolerated indefinitely.

3.2 Treat

Risk treatments are actions taken to manipulate an organisation's exposure to one or more risks. Risk treatments include many of the loss prevention and loss reduction tools that can be used by an organisation. It can also mean the increase of risk by increasing exposure or lowering controls.

3.3 Transfer

Risk transfer passes the impact of loss events to a third party. This may involve passing on:

◆ the financial impacts of a loss event; or

◆ the financial and non-financial impacts of a loss event.

Passing on only the financial impacts of a loss event is achieved via insurance or equivalent risk financing contracts. Insurance contracts provide either full or partial **indemnity** against certain pre-specified loss events in return for the payment of a consideration or premium. The purchaser of an insurance contract, called the policyholder, is able to pass on the financial liability of one or more loss events to the insurance company, swapping volatility in their cash flows for a known cost in the form of an insurance premium. Other forms of risk financing work in a similar way (see section 6).

Passing on the financial and non-financial impacts of a loss event involves a contract with a different type of third party, usually a supplier or outsourced service provider. Whenever an organisation uses an external supplier to provide goods and services, it is effectively transferring the risks associated with the production and supply of these goods and services to the third party. For example, by purchasing electricity from an electricity supplier rather than generating power for itself, an organisation is effectively transferring all of the risks associated with electricity generation to the supplier. Similarly, an organisation might decide to outsource certain hazardous activities to third parties, such as asbestos removal.

indemnity
Financial security or protection from the financial effects of a loss event. Full indemnity ensures that a person or organisation is put back in the same financial position that they were in pre-loss. Partial indemnity means that they will receive only a fraction of the money they have lost.

3.4 Terminate

Termination includes any action taken to stop an activity or leave a location that is creating a particular risk exposure or combination of exposures. For example, an organisation might decide to vacate premises with a high risk of flooding or it might decide to stop using an operational process that creates a risk of environmental pollution or new technology that has a high risk of failure.

The decision to terminate a risk exposure is a very serious one. The only way to terminate an exposure is to terminate the activity or location that is creating the exposure. This could mean that an organisation passes up valuable opportunities and it may fail to achieve its objectives. The achievement of organisational objectives will always require activities that involve exposure to risk.

The decision to terminate a risk exposure should only occur where no level of risk exposure is considered to be tolerable, or where the risk exposure is considered to be untreatable or non-transferrable.

Test yourself 12.2

Under what circumstances may risk be tolerated? Contrast this with termination.

4. Risk treatment techniques

Risk treatment (the second of the four Ts) is a common choice for organisations looking to control their exposure to risk. This choice includes loss prevention and loss reduction tools. To get the most from risk treatment it is helpful to categorise the prevention and reduction tools that are available. This can help an organisation to develop optimal risk control strategies that address the range of causes and effects associated with different loss events.

4.1   PCDD hazard risk typology

PCDD stands for:

◆   Preventive
◆   Corrective
◆   Directive
◆   Detective

The PCDD hazard risk typology is used to help classify the range of controls that can be used to control health and safety or environmental hazards.

A similar approach is used to classify the internal controls that an organisation will use to control its employees, processes and activities to comply with laws, regulations and internal policies and to achieve organisational objectives.

Preventive controls focus on addressing the causes of loss events and are a type of loss prevention tool. Preventive controls are designed to prevent things like accidents, human error, misconduct, or other sources of hazard or internal control failure. Preventive controls include:

◆   staff training (such as manual handling training);
◆   personal protective equipment;
◆   asset maintenance (such as servicing);
◆   shredding confidential documents; and
◆   security arrangements (locks, passwords and so on).

Corrective controls help to correct the adverse consequences of a hazard or similar loss event that has occurred (such as a fire, pollution event or a compliance breach). Corrective controls are a type of loss reduction tool.

Corrective controls include mechanisms to learn from loss events that have occurred, such as post-event investigations into what went wrong and why.

The investigation of near-misses and the actions taken to address the causes of these misses are corrective controls. Near-misses provide valuable learning opportunities.

Examples of corrective controls include:

◆ fire extinguishers;

◆ disciplinary procedures;

◆ business continuity and recovery plans;

◆ data recovery procedures; and

◆ occupational health arrangements.

Directive controls are controls that are used to enforce desirable outcomes. From a hazard perspective, this might include the design and implementation of health and safety policies and procedures. More broadly, they might include all of an organisation's policies and procedures that are related to risk management, governance or compliance. Other directive controls might include codes of conduct, instructions from line managers, or the roles and responsibilities assigned to employees within their job description. Directive controls address the causes of loss events and are a type of loss prevention tool.

Detective controls help to indicate the onset of a hazard or subsequent loss event such as a fire or pollution. Detective controls may be used to highlight deficiencies in preventive or directive controls that may influence their effectiveness. A detective control is a form of loss prevention tool where it helps to detect the causes of potential loss events, and a loss reduction tool where it helps to detect the occurrence of an actual loss event.

Detective controls provide an indication that something is wrong. They function best when combined with corrective, preventive or directive controls. By taking prompt action, an organisation may either help to correct the adverse effects of a loss event or help to prevent future events by addressing weaknesses in preventive or directive controls. Detective controls include:

◆ fire and burglar alarms;

◆ internal audits and compliance reviews;

◆ tests of business continuity and disaster recovery plans;

◆ health and safety inspections;

◆ inventory checks, to confirm that all equipment is in place and is in good condition; and

◆ bank reconciliations to detect loss events such as fraud.

Test yourself 12.3

Categorise the following controls using the PCDD approach:

◆ **Smoke alarm**

◆ **Financial reconciliation**

◆   **Internal audit action plans**

◆   **Insurance**

◆   **Building security**

◆   **IT acceptable use policy.**

4.2   Other categories of risk treatment techniques

Another way to categorise risk treatment techniques is in terms of their formality or informality. This can help an organisation ensure a good balance between the formal and informal aspects of its approach to treating risk exposures.

Formal controls
Formal controls have one or more of the following characteristics:

◆   they have a physical presence, for example door locks or a sprinkler system;

◆   they are documented within a policy or procedure; or

◆   they involve tangible sanctions, such as disciplinary arrangements.

Formal controls provide a clear and tangible mechanism for risk control. They include a wide range of preventive, corrective, directive and detective controls.

Informal controls
Informal controls are social mechanisms of control. These controls are almost never documented and they do not have a physical presence. The sanctions for informal control violations are intangible, meaning that they are hard to define or quantify.

Informal controls include the culture and risk culture of an organisation. They relate to the social norms, beliefs, values and perceptions that staff members and other stakeholders have concerning the control of risk. For example, safety violations may be tolerated and justified in some organisations to avoid 'unnecessary' red tape. In other organisations, safety violations of any kind may not be tolerated because safety is seen as an essential part of a smooth, efficient and ethical operation.

Informal controls tend to be human-oriented and social in nature. They relate to how people communicate, exert power and influence over each other, and work together. Sanctions tend to be intangible. Individuals who do not comply with informal controls may find that their peers are unfriendly, non-communicative or unhelpful rather than imposing tangible sanctions like disciplinary arrangements, although repeat violations of informal controls may lead to formal sanctions.

Informal controls are an important complement to formal controls. Informal controls help to ensure compliance and correct implementation of formal controls. In addition, informal controls can act as a substitute for formal controls where there are weaknesses in the formal control environment– such as where formal controls are absent or they are not working effectively.

Stop and think 12.2

Write down a list of as many formal controls that you can think of, then do the same for informal controls. It is likely that you will come up with a much longer list of formal controls. Is this because formal controls are more visible and easier to identify?

There is no easy answer here. Informal controls can be hard to identify because they are less tangible. Alternatively, it may be that there are fewer informal controls. Either way, informal controls are a very important part of any control environment, especially when formal controls are absent or are at risk of being ineffective.

5. Common risk treatment controls

Table 12.2 provides a list of some common risk treatment controls. A brief explanation is provided for each control, as well as whether it is a formal or informal control. Formal controls are further classified as preventive, corrective, directive or detective.

Control	Description	Formal or informal	PCDD
Action plans	Plans that are put in place to address identified weaknesses in the identification, assessment, monitoring or control of risk. Action plans often follow the completion of an audit, test or review.	Formal	Directive
Alarms	Includes smoke and heat alarms, burglar alarms and IT-related alarms (such as virus infection).	Formal	Detective
Automation	The automation of systems and processes to remove the potential for human error.	Formal	Preventive
Audits and reviews	Internal audits and reviews designed to assess the effectiveness of an organisation's internal controls and its exposure to compliance risk.	Formal	Detective
Business recovery plans	Plans that specify how an organisation should manage its recovery from a major loss event such as a fire or IT systems failure.	Formal	Directive
Communica-tion	Mechanisms that help and encourage people to communicate with each other. These mechanisms may be formal (meetings and committees) and informal (a chat over lunch or coffee). Communication helps people work together to identify and find ways to address the causes of loss events and their effects.	Formal and informal	All

Computer firewall	Software-based protection for an IT network or system against unauthorised access and virus attacks.	Formal	Preventive
Data backup	The electronic back up of data. This may be via the use of real time backups (mirrored servers) or periodic (daily or weekly) backups using external storage devices (tapes, external hard drives and so on).	Formal	Corrective
Due diligence	A comprehensive appraisal of a business or third party prior to signing a contract. This almost always includes appraisal of financial performance and strength. It may also include reviewing business strategies and management capabilities.	Formal	Detective
Emergency shut down	Mechanisms that ensure the rapid shutdown of systems that are failing or which are unsafe. This includes 'red button' emergency shutdown switches on machinery.	Formal	Corrective
Financial provisions	Money that is set aside to cover expected future losses from a loss event. Provisions are often set aside to cover costs such as liability claims or compensation payments. These costs can take some time to crystallise after an event has occurred. For example, it may take time for the full costs of a pollution event to emerge.	Formal	Corrective
Inspections	This may include site inspections or inspections of specific pieces of machinery. The aim of an inspection is to look for any faults in working practices, buildings or machine operations that may cause future loss events.	Formal	Detective
Insurance contract	In exchange for a known premium, full or partial financial protection is provided against an agreed set of loss events. Common insurance contracts include motor (third party, fire, theft and damage), buildings and contents (theft or damage to property) and employer's liability (compensation claims made by injured workers).	Formal	Corrective
Maintenance	Maintenance of physical assets to ensure that they perform efficiently and effectively. This includes maintaining buildings and machinery.	Formal	Preventive
Policies and procedures	Policies explain high level principles and responsibilities in relation to a specific area of focus (such as a health and safety or IT security policy). Procedures provide more specific direction on how to conduct a specific task or operation (such as manual handling procedures or procedures for reporting an IT security breach).	Formal	Directive
Property protection devices	Physical devices that help to protect property. This includes flood and fire protection (such as a wind break).	Formal	Preventive

Redundancy	Building spare capacity into a system or process. This includes maintaining stocks of spare equipment, using two or more live computer servers and internet connections or having multiple sources of power generation (such as backup generators).	Formal	Corrective
Segregation of duties	Separation of key duties, such as the authorisation and processing of financial transactions. This helps to prevent fraud and compliance-related breaches.	Formal	Preventive
Safety equipment	Physical equipment such as safety clothing and mechanical guards that protect people from injury.	Formal	Preventive
Safety training	Training on how to work in a safe way – this includes training on fire safety, manual handling and IT security.	Formal	Directive
Skills and professional training	Training that provides people with the practical and professional skills and knowledge that they need to perform their job. This might include training on operating machinery, IT systems and financial reporting or tax changes for accountants.	Formal	Preventive
Soft skills training	Training related to areas such as communication, ethical behaviours, inter-personal relationships, social graces or cross-cultural awareness.	Informal	All
System-based validation	Validation checks that are built into a system. This includes checks to ensure that all fields are completed and checks for accuracy such as check digits or the multiple entry of key information to ensure consistency.	Formal	Detective
Team building	Team building exercises and training that is designed to build trust and co-operation between the members of a team.	Informal	All
Testing	The testing of processes, procedures and physical devices. This includes testing fire alarms and business continuity plans, as well as the testing of electrical equipment and wiring or gas appliances.	Formal	Detective
Tone and action from the top	The words and expressions that are used by senior management and directors in relation to areas such as openness, honesty, integrity, tolerance, compliance and ethical conduct. The tone set, and actual behaviour displayed, by senior management and directors can have a significant impact on employee attitudes and behaviours in these areas.	Informal	Preventive, Directive.

Table 12.2 Common risk treatment controls

6. Risk financing

Organisations use risk financing mechanisms to help fund the financial consequences of loss events. Loss events can be very expensive to recover from: assets may need to be repaired or replaced, including buildings and machinery. There may be clean-up costs, compensation payments, liability claims and fines.

Table 12.3 uses the four Ts framework to explain how risk financing fits into an organisation's risk control strategies.

It is common to further break down the risk financing options into specific strategies. These strategies are illustrated in Figure 12.2.

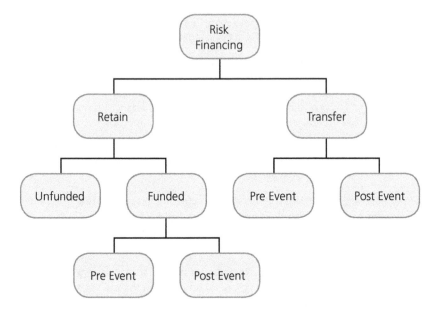

Figure 12.2 Risk financing strategies

6.1   Retained risk financing

Treating, tolerating or terminating the effects of loss events with the aid of risk financing tools is called retained risk financing.

Retained risk financing involves retaining rather than transferring the financial effects of a loss event. Organisations that use retained risk financing make the decision to keep the financial impacts of one or more types of loss event within the legal and financial boundaries of the organisation. This means that these financial effects will affect one or more of the following:

◆   organisational cash flows;

◆   profit or surplus; and

◆   the balance sheet, reducing assets or increasing liabilities.

Strategy	Role of risk financing
Treat	Risk financing may be employed to protect an organisation's cash flows from the financial impacts of a loss event. An organisation can ensure that loss events do not affect its ability to meet its liabilities as they fall due by maintaining sufficient cash surpluses in the current year or capital on the balance sheet. Equally, cash funds can be used to replace lost assets quickly, minimising any business disruption effects.
Tolerate	An organisation may be able to tolerate loss events more easily where finance is available pre-loss – or can be obtained post-loss – to help restore lost assets. Where the decision is made to not replace assets, risk financing can be used to help clean up the loss – such as funding the costs of clearing a site where a fire has occurred.
Transfer	Many forms of risk transfer involve a financial element. This is most obvious in the form of insurance-related risk transfer mechanisms – where the insurer agrees to provide funds to the insured in the event of certain pre-specified risk triggers. In the case of risk transfer via some other third party supplier or outsourced service provider, responsibility for financing risk events is transferred to this supplier/provider. An organisation that has transferred risks to third parties/ service providers, including insurers, may decide to put financing mechanisms in place to help mitigate the risks associated with the failure of or disruptions to the continuity of a supplier/provider, or in the case of an insurer, their refusal to pay a claim.
Terminate	Even where a decision is made to terminate an activity that is considered to be high risk, risk financing may be needed. For example, there may be redundancy and asset disposal costs and it may be that the full extent of these costs is unknown at the time that the decision is taken to terminate. The decision to terminate may carry with it associated risks that need to be financed. For example, the decision to not update a computer system on the grounds that transferring the data to a new system is too risky might mean that the organisation has to finance the consequences of an increased risk of systems failure from the aging system. Equally, the decision to stop producing a high risk product may expose an organisation to business risk, including the risk of losing market share to rivals.

Table 12.3 Risk financing options linked to the four Ts

Retained risk financing is funded or unfunded. Funded means allocating a pot of funds before a loss has to be financed. Unfunded means not putting funding in place and relying on current cash flows or unallocated capital.

Funded retained risk financing may be chosen because risk transfer (in the form of insurance or similar) is not needed, not available or too expensive. Unfunded risk financing may occur because:

◆ the potential for a given loss event has not been identified (a failure in risk identification);

◆ the full effects of a loss event are not understood (a failure in risk assessment);

◆ there is a failure in risk transfer, such as where an insurer disputes a claim or refuses to pay out in full; or

◆ an organisation decides that the financial effects of a loss event are small enough to not require funding.

Funded retained risk financing can be implemented before (pre-event) or after (post-event) the occurrence of a loss event. Funding may be implemented post-event where a loss event has occurred but the full effects of the loss event are not yet known or have not been fully realised. The time period between the loss event and the realisation of all the losses that are associated with the event can give an organisation time to put in place plans to fund these losses when they are incurred.

A variety of retained risk financing mechanisms are available. Table 12.4 provides a summary of common retained risk financing tools. It also indicates whether they may be applied pre or post-event, and whether they can be used on a funded or unfunded basis.

Funded risk financing tools may be combined to form layers of finance for losses of varying sizes. Unfunded risk financing and risk transfer provide further layers of finance. For example, an organisation may decide to use unfunded risk finance for smaller losses, including any within an agreed insurance deductible, then insurance up to a given loss size, known as the 'limit of indemnity'. A contingency loan might be used for losses that exceed this loss size.

The potential combinations are many and there are no strict rules as to which tool should be layered on top of which. It is up to an organisation to decide how best to layer different financing tools in relation to specific risks.

Stop and think 12.3

For one or more specific types of loss event, such as pollution or motor vehicle accidents, examine the different retained risk financing tools that are used by the organisation that you work for or another that you are familiar with. How are these different tools layered to achieve an optimum risk financing strategy? If possible, speak to the organisation's insurance manager for help.

Tool	Summary	Funded or infunded?	Pre or post-loss?
Allocated reserves	Profit or surplus that is allocated to help fund a specific project or loss event. Financial provisions are a form of allocated reserve.	Funded	Both
Captive insurance	A virtual insurance company that is created by an organisation to help fund and manage its loss events. Some types of captive insurance arrangement offer limited degrees of risk transfer but in their purest form, known as a single parent captive, there is no risk transfer outside of the organisation.	Funded	Both
Capital	Capital may be generated from retained profits or surpluses. Capital may also be generated from shareholders and creditors in the form of loans. Surplus capital that is not used to operate or grow an organisation may be allocated to fund specific types of loss event or it may be retained on an unallocated basis to help deal with any type of loss event that occurs. It is common for financial institutions to hold a significant amount of surplus capital to help fund loss events. This is often a requirement under the prudential regulations applied to these institutions.	Funded	Both
Cash flows	The cash that flows into an organisation may be used to finance loss events. Cash may be generated by sales, donations, grants and loans or similar. Where cash flows are used to pay for loss events this may mean that planned projects have to be cancelled, savings must be made and, in extreme cases, an organisation may have to cease operating temporarily or permanently.	Unfunded	Both
Contingency loans	The purpose of a contingency loan is to provide credit if certain events occur, such as a large fire or a major lawsuit. Contingency loans provide an organisation with a line of credit but only in relation to certain pre-specified risk events. Usually a retainer fee is payable to ensure that a line of credit is available but only when credit is provided is interest payable. The retainer fee is usually much less than the fees associated with more general lines of credit.	Funded	Both

Contingent capital	Contingent capital is a form of debt that is converted into equity when certain triggers are met, such as at the onset of a loss event that may bankrupt an organisation if left unfunded.	Funded	Usually pre-loss
	The recent growth of contingent convertible (coco) bonds in the banking sector is a good example of the use of contingent capital. Coco bonds are a form of debt; in this case, a commercial bond that can be converted to equity if a bank's capital ratio falls too low. The threshold for conversion is specified in the contract. Coco bonds are accounted for as a form of debt and are thus tax deductible. They can be relied upon in a similar way to equity in that the funds cannot be withdrawn by the counterparty providing the loan facility.		
Deductibles	An organisation may choose or be required to hold a deductible as part of an insurance agreement. Where a deductible is in place an organisation must pay for the initial amount of any insurance claim. Deductibles are common in areas such as motor insurance and claims for property damage and theft. Deductible amounts for organisation range from £0 to £millions for larger organisations. Where deductible amounts are small it may be possible to pay for them on an unfunded basis. Larger deductibles may require funding.	Both	Usually pre-loss
Mutual funds	Mutual funds are hard to categorise because they combine retained risk finance and risk transfer. Mutual funds are set up by similar organisations to help pool their limited risk financing resources. Mutual funds are used by professions (such as lawyers and medical doctors) to help provide professional indemnity funds. Mutual funds are used by financial institutions to facilitate the **securitisation** of financial risks.	Funded	Usually pre-loss
Self-insurance	The term self-insurance is a misnomer. as it does not mean that the financial effects of a risk are transferred. Self-insurance is a term often used to refer to funded risk financing arrangements such as capital insurance companies.	Funded	Both
Unallocated reserves	Profit or surplus that is generated and which is not allocated to a specific project or fund.	Unfunded	Both

Table 12.4 Retained risk financing tools

Test yourself 12.4

Distinguish funded from unfunded risk finance.

6.2 Insurance risk transfer

Insurance risk transfer means purchasing insurance from an insurance company. Insurance companies provide insurance against a range of potential loss events, including:

◆ motor accidents, fire and theft;

◆ property damage and theft;

◆ building defects, like subsidence;

◆ employer's liability – legal liability payments to staff suffering health and safety problems;

◆ professional indemnity covering legal liability claims and compensation payments due as a result of malpractice or professional negligence;

◆ fraud; and

◆ business interruption, which covers lost sales and other costs when a business' activities are disrupted as a result of fire or flood.

An organisation will normally use an insurance intermediary, known as an insurance broker, to help them to design an insurance program, purchase insurance and to process claims. Organisational insurance purchases are complicated and a broker can help the organisation to achieve the best possible combination of cover and premium cost.

Large organisations may have an insurance professional to help support the purchase of insurance contracts and to process claims. Alternatively, the risk function or company secretary or governance professional may be involved in purchasing insurance.

It is rare for an organisation to purchase full indemnity insurance cover. To help reduce premium costs and to ensure that insurance is available, cover is limited to a maximum loss amount, known as the limit of indemnity or indemnity limit. Deductibles are common, requiring the organisation to pay the initial amount for a loss that is incurred, such as the first £10,000 of a claim. Insurance premiums should be cheaper if the deductible is larger and the maximum level of cover is lower, as the level of risk transfer is lower. An organisation will need to layer insurance with other forms of risk finance where high deductibles are in place or the maximum loss amount is lower than the level of loss that may be incurred,

There will be a limit at which taking a deductible is not cost effective in terms of premium discount. Deductibles and premium savings require careful cost benefit consideration.

The circumstances under which an insurance company will pay a claim are specified in the insurance contract. These circumstances may be ambiguous and

securitisation
The practice of grouping risky assets into an investment vehicle (known as a financial instrument) for sale to one or more third parties. When an asset is securitised, the third party obtains the rights to any cash that flows from these assets (such as investment returns) but they are also liable for any losses that arise. Debt is a common securitised asset. An organisation sells debts that are outstanding to a third party who gains from all future interest payments but will also lose out if the relevant creditors default.

disputes can arise, especially when the claim amount is high. Brokers can help an organisation to understand the complexities of insurance contracts, as can specialists in insurance law.

6.3   Non-conventional risk transfer for the financial effects of risk

Insurance is a common risk transfer tool but it is not the only mechanism that organisations can use to transfer the financial effects of loss events. Insurance is not available for every type of risk. It may be expensive where it is available. The alternatives that exist to insurance are termed non-conventional risk transfer tools.

Non-conventional risk transfer tools for the financial effects of risk include:

◆   financial markets, particularly in relation to derivatives and their use for **hedging** financial risks such as exchange rate fluctuations or fluctuations in the price of commodities such as electricity and oil;

◆   finite risk insurance, which provides a multi-year mechanism for sharing the financial effects of loss events with an external counterparty;

◆   protected cell captive insurance companies, which operate like finite risk insurance;

◆   catastrophe bonds, which are risk-linked securities that are used to transfer risks to financial counterparties who make a profit if the pre-specified catastrophic event fails to occur; and

◆   credit default swaps, which provide a form of insurance against creditors defaulting on their obligations, for example trade creditors.

Detailed knowledge of non-conventional risk transfer tools is beyond the scope of this study text. An organisation that chooses to use non-conventional risk transfer tools should ensure that it has the right expertise in place. This might be via an internal insurance manager or risk specialist, or an external risk specialist or insurance broker. Non-conventional risk transfer arrangements can be very complicated to set up and it is easy to make mistakes.

7. Controlling major loss events

The scale of a loss event can vary significantly. Most loss events will be relatively small scale in terms of their effects on an organisation but major events can occur on occasion.

Major loss events can have significant financial and non-financial implications for organisations. Initially they can lead to serious asset damage, injury or death, and often attract media attention. Post-event, the business activities of the organisation may be disrupted for some time as a result of the initial effects, and large regulatory fines and liability claims can follow. How effectively an organisation manages the aftermath of a loss event may also affect its reputation. Ultimately, an organisation that does not have effective crisis management arrangements and business continuity plans may not survive the aftermath of a major loss event.

hedging
An investment to reduce the risk of adverse price movements in an asset. Normally, a hedge consists of taking an offsetting position in a related financial derivative. Many organisations use derivatives to hedge risk. For example, farmers might use forwards and futures to help hedge the risk of commodity price fluctuations (to fix the price they will receive for crops they produce in the future), as do food processing companies to help stabilise their input costs. It is common for airlines and other transport related organisations to look to hedge oil price risks. Energy intensive manufacturing companies may seek to hedge energy price risks. Organisations which have loans may use interest rate swaps when they are concerned about the financing costs associated with increasing interest rates.

7.1   Crisis management

Crisis management is the process by which an organisation deals with a disruptive and potentially unexpected event that threatens to harm the organisation, its stakeholders or the general public.

The level of potential harm from a crisis is significant. Examples of crisis events include major fires, chemical spills, death or injury of people, terrorist attacks, prolonged technology systems failures or data breaches.

The process of crisis management is the same as for risk management. It involves the identification, assessment, monitoring and control of crisis risks. The tools used within the crisis management process are different, however, because crisis events are rare and are more complex in terms of their causes and effects than most other loss events.

The fact that crisis events are rare means that an organisation will have little data to help identify and assess them. Individual organisations may not have experienced a crisis event in their lifetime and may never experience one.

To help identify and assess crisis events, an organisation can use information on crises that have been experienced by other organisations. It is also common to use scenario analysis (section 4.3, Chapter 9) where relevant experts (operational managers, legal experts and risk or compliance specialists) meet to imagine the sequence of causes that could give rise to a crisis event and the resultant short and long-term effects of each identified crisis event. This relies on expert judgement, given the lack of data that is available.

The control of crisis events is built around the following areas, each of which represents a different stage in the development of a crisis.

1. *Signal detection*: looking for early warning signs that a crisis could occur. This includes investigating near misses, internal audit findings and risk monitoring reports. It may also include looking at operational performance reports and external events in the wider world (such as economic or regulatory change).

2. *Preparation and prevention*: where steps are taken to prepare for the occurrence of potential crisis events (often identified via scenario analysis) and to prevent these events by looking to control their causes.

3. *Containment and damage control*: where a loss event occurs that may or does evolve into a crisis, steps must be taken to limit the adverse effects of this event. This may include implementing business continuity plans, communicating with key staff and stakeholders, working with the emergency services, or implementing a public relations plan to deal with any media interest.

4. *Business recovery*: it can take a long time to recover from a crisis but this duration can be reduced with effective recovery arrangements. These arrangements include quickly replacing lost assets and ensuring that funds are available to support the recovery.

5. *Learning from the crisis*: assuming that an organisation recovers from a crisis, it is imperative that lessons are learned from the experience to

help prevent or reduce the effects of future crises. This might include implementing a post event review of how the crisis was managed or finding ways to improve the effectiveness of pre-crisis controls.

In the digital age, organisations must be constantly crisis-ready. For example, social media may be used to inform stakeholders of a crisis event even before the organisation itself is aware.

7.2　Business continuity planning

Business continuity plans help with containment, damage control and support business recovery.

Business continuity plans may be produced for a whole organisation but it is more common to develop plans for specific functions, systems or premises. It is common to have business continuity plans to support the recovery of disrupted IT systems or for essential operational processes, such as manufacturing and supply chains.

A business continuity plan outlines the actions that should be taken to minimise business disruption and to help recover from a major loss event as quickly as possible. For example, in the event that an organisation's IT systems fail, the organisation will need to determine the priority systems that require rapid recovery and agree recovery time objectives (the speed with which these systems must be recovered). The plan will show the order in which systems need to be recovered first and how quickly they must be recovered.

Business continuity plans should explain the roles and responsibilities that people have to support recovery efforts and reporting lines. This will include the work and home contact details for all those involved in the operation of a plan.

Business continuity plans should be tested, usually annually. Testing may be desk-based (a review of the documentation to ensure it is up to date) or a 'live' test may be performed. This involves creating an artificial business continuity scenario and investigating whether a plan and the staff involved in implementing the plan can respond to the scenario in an effective manner.

Stop and think 12.4

Search the internet for examples of business continuity plan templates. What do these templates include?

Test yourself 12.5

How does business continuity planning fit with crisis management?

8. Controlling third party risks

All organisations use third party service contracts. These include contracts for energy supply, cleaning and waste collection, or an organisation may contract elements of its core operations via long-term outsourcing arrangements. For example, an organisation might decide to outsource IT support or its customer call centre operations.

Where service contracts are entered into, there will be third party risk. The key risks are:

◆ Failure of the service provider to provide an acceptable quality of service.

◆ Disruptions to the continuity of service.

◆ Failure of the service provider (such as bankruptcy), meaning that the service can no longer be provided.

Each of these risks can have a significant impact on organisations, increasing costs, and disrupting operational continuity. Controlling these risks can be done using a variety of risk treatment tools. Table 12.5 provides a summary of some common tools.

Control	Description	Formal or informal	PCDD
Contract management	Legal review of contracts prior to signing. Ongoing legal review of contracts to ensure that they are up to date and reflect the latest legal advice.	Formal	Preventive
Dual supply arrangements	Contracting with two or more suppliers ensures that there is continuity of supply in the event of supply disruption or failure.	Formal	Corrective
Due diligence	A comprehensive appraisal of a business or third party prior to signing a contract. This almost always includes an appraisal of financial performance and strength. It may also include reviewing business strategies and management capabilities.	Formal	Detective
Escrow agreement	An arrangement by which a service provider deposits an asset (such as money, documents or software) with a third person (called an escrow agent), who, in turn, delivers the asset to the service receiver if specific contractual provisions are not met. Escrow agreements are common in IT service contracts. In the event that an IT service provider fails, the organisation that received the service is granted rights to update and maintain the software. They may also have rights to transfer staff from the provider and other assets (such as hardware).	Formal	Corrective

| Relationship management | Regular meetings between the organisation and its service providers. These meetings help to build a positive working relationship and avoid contractual disputes. | Formal and informal | All |
| Service level agreements | A documented commitment that exists between a service provider and a client. Particular aspects of the service (such as quality, availability and responsibilities) are agreed between the service provider and the service user. Where service levels are not maintained the service provider may be liable to provide a full or partial refund if the situation is not corrected promptly. | Formal | Detective and Directive |

Table 12.5 Controls for third party risks

Chapter summary

◆ All organisations make use of risk control tools. These tools are used to reduce the probability and impact of loss events, such as fires, fraud or IT system failures.

◆ Loss prevention tools reduce the probability of a loss event by targeting the causes of risk events. These are usually linked to the actions or inactions of people, failures in processes and systems or external events (weather, politics and so on).

◆ Loss reduction tools target the effects of loss events. Loss events may have financial and non-financial effects. In financial terms, they can affect the physical assets and cash assets of an organisation. In non-financial terms, organisations may suffer reputation damage and the loss of customer goodwill.

◆ In broad terms, there are four risk control strategies: treat, tolerate, transfer and terminate.

◆ Risk treatment can be further broken down into a variety of control options. These include formal and informal controls, and preventive, corrective, detective and directive controls.

◆ An organisation will use a wide range of risk financing mechanisms to help fund the financial consequences of loss events. Loss events can be very expensive to recover from. Assets may need to be repaired or replaced (such as buildings and machinery). There may also be clean-up costs, compensation payments, fines and liability claims.

◆ Retained risk financing involves retaining rather than transferring the financial effects of a loss event. An organisation using retained risk financing has made the decision to keep the financial impacts of one or more types of loss event within its legal and financial boundaries.

◆ Insurance risk transfer means purchasing insurance from an insurance company. Insurance companies provide insurance against a range of potential loss events including asset damage, theft and liability claims.

◆ Insurance is not available for every type of risk and where it is available it may be expensive. The alternatives that exist to insurance are termed non-conventional risk transfer tools.

◆ Crisis management is the process by which an organisation controls disruptive and unexpected events that threaten to harm the organisation, its stakeholders, or the general public. Crisis management is supported by business continuity planning.

◆ Most organisations make use of third party service contracts. This may be contracts for energy supply, cleaning and waste collection, or they may contract elements of their core operations via long-term outsourcing arrangements. Specialist controls are needed to reduce the probability and impact of service contract risks.

Chapter 13
Risk management in practice

Contents

1. Introduction
2. Common applications of risk management practice
3. Risk management, corporate social responsibility and sustainability
4. Regulatory reporting

1. Introduction

Risk management is a broad discipline that can be applied to all organisational activities. This chapter considers some common applications of risk management, including:

◆ operational risk management
◆ project risk management
◆ supply chain risk management
◆ cyber risk management.

2. Common applications of risk management practice

Risk management processes, tools, and techniques may be used by a wide variety of people within an organisation and applied to many different types of activities, including:

◆ production operations
◆ the management of technology systems and processes
◆ programme and project management
◆ supply change management
◆ corporate social responsibility (CSR) programmes
◆ regulatory reporting.

2.1   An overview of applications

The first four activities in the above list each have their own sub-discipline of risk management, respectively:

◆   operations or operational risk management

◆   cyber risk management

◆   project risk management

◆   supply chain risk management.

Larger organisations may have specialists for each of these sub-disciplines. Smaller organisations may have specialists which work across two or more of these disciplines, or they may use external consultants.

Where specialists exist for discrete sub-disciplines, care must be taken to avoid a silo-based approach to risk management. One way to achieve this is to incorporate these sub-disciplines into an enterprise risk management approach (see section 3 of Chapter 7, page 127).

2.2   Operations or operational risk management

All organisations have operations. In the case of manufacturing organisations, these operations are often tangible and easy to see. Manufacturers will have production lines that are used to produce the products that they sell, whether cars, televisions, bread and so on. Primary producers such as farms, mining companies or mineral extraction organisations such as oil and gas companies will also have well-defined operational processes. These types of organisations will also have less tangible processes in relation to their information systems, human resource management and supply chain arrangements (relationship management).

The operations of professional services, education and third sector organisations like charities may be less visible. Even so, these organisations still require operations that allow them to provide products like financial services, professional advice, consultancy, education and research.

Wherever there are operations, there is risk. Manufacturing, product or service delivery processes can break down, be damaged or destroyed, as can the premises within which these operations are delivered. Paper or computer-based operational processes may break down, suffer damage or be destroyed, especially when these processes rely on technology, data and networks.

People can be the biggest source of risk. People are often required to control operations or carry our manual tasks. They may make mistakes, act negligently, act wilfully or be absent due to illness. Culture in an organisation can play a major role in the management of people risks.

Table 13.1 summarises some types of loss events that may affect the operations of an organisation.

Loss event	Description	Type of operations affected
Absence or loss of employees	An organisation's employees will support one or more of its operations. This may include finance, manufacturing, HR or IT operations. Where particular employees are unavailable, for whatever reason, these operations may be disrupted or become inefficient.	All
Employee negligence or misconduct	Employee negligence or misconduct may interfere with operational performance or raise the cost of these operations, as a result of related compliance breaches, for example. Negligence might include not performing manual tasks with appropriate skill, care and diligence. Misconduct might include activities such as policy and procedure breaches or crimes like fraud.	All
Fire	Fire can destroy operational machinery and IT systems. Fire may also damage or destroy the buildings within which operations are performed.	All
Human error	All operations require a degree of human intervention. This might include undertaking manual tasks or programming automated systems. Human error can increase costs, reduce efficiency and result in product and service-related faults.	All
IT systems failure	Operations may be solely IT-based (most financial services operations) or physical operational processes may rely on IT systems (robotised manufacturing).	IT operations and any operation that relies on IT systems
Machine breakdown	Any physical machinery (vehicles, robots, lathes, electric tools and so on) that is required for an operational process may break down for a variety of reasons. Breakdowns can be costly to repair and disruptive, affecting productivity levels.	Primary mining and extraction operations and secondary manufacturing, operations, including construction.
Power failure	Power failures will disrupt almost all modern operational processes. Even processes that do not require electricity may not be possible where electric light is required (such as craft-related activities).	All
Weather related damage	Adverse weather can cause flooding and damage property. Employees required to support operational processes may find that they are unable to come to work due to travel disruption.	All

Table 13.1 Example operations related loss events

Where loss events affect an organisation's operations, one or more of the following adverse effects may be experienced:

◆ increased costs, such as the costs of repairing or replacing machinery;

◆ a reduction in operational efficiency, increasing the unit cost of production and reducing productivity levels;

◆ business interruption, meaning that goods and services cannot be delivered;

◆ customer complaints, which may result in compensation payments where goods and services are not provided;

◆ reputation damage, where an organisation does not recover quickly or fails to deal effectively with customer complaints and media enquiries; and

◆ a compliance breach, where an event leads to injury or death of an employee, third party or customer, for example.

Operations or operational risk management is concerned with reducing the probability and impact of operations related loss events. It can be used to mitigate the above adverse effects.

The term operational risk management entered common use in the late 1990s. It was first used in financial institutions to delineate the management of risk in financial operations and related processes from financial risks such as market, credit and liquidity risk. Since then, operational risk management has entered more widespread use. There is even an Institute of Operational Risk for risk professionals that choose to specialise in the sub-discipline.

All employees or managers have some degree of responsibility for the management of the risks associated with these operations. For example, they will be expected to carry out their responsibilities with due skill, care and diligence. They will also be expected to escalate any concerns they may have about potential loss events or control weaknesses. Organisations may also have one or more specialist operational risk manager to support the management of the risks to their operations. These specialists may put together operational risk reports for senior management, develop tools to assess the probability and impact of loss events and ensure that operational risk controls are effective. These staff specialists cannot and should not assume responsibility for operational risk themselves, however, as that lies with the functionaries responsible for producing the goods or services.

Stop and think 13.1

Identify three operational processes for the organisation that you work for or another you are familiar with. Consider the risks which may disrupt these processes or the cost of delivery, and consider how they are managed.

Test yourself 13.1

Define operational risk management and explain its benefits for an organisation.

2.3 Cyber risk management

Almost all organisations use technology, networks and the internet to process, store and communicate information. An organisation is exposed to cyber risks whenever it uses IT equipment and systems, and especially a network or the internet.

Cyber risk management is concerned with all forms of digital risk. Cyber risk management traditionally falls within the field of information assurance (IA), the practice of assuring that an organisation's information and technical resources are:

◆ secure,

◆ only accessible to authorised personnel

◆ are used only for the purposes they are intended

◆ are complete and intact.

Information assurance is a well-established discipline that marries risk management with the IT systems, practices and policies of an organisation, applying aspects of corporate governance to the technical infrastructure of an organisation. Information assurance is broken down into a number of distinct areas:

◆ Integrity: information assets are accurate and complete within an organisation.

◆ Availability: information assets are available when needed.

◆ Authenticity: information assets are genuine and their sources are valid.

◆ Non-repudiation: transactions and communications of information assets are valid and cannot be denied.

◆ Confidentiality: only those who have the right to access information assets can access them.

Information technology and information security activities are a part of IA, but IA goes beyond the traditional boundaries of these activities. Security breaches are only one cause of cyber risk events. Causal factors such as power failures, data corruption, and data entry or processing errors may affect an organisation's ability to assure the accuracy, completeness and availability of its information. In addition, the rise of social media has added to the range of causal factors and cyber risk events that can occur. For example, employees may make negative comments about their organisation, their colleagues or management on social media, damaging the reputation of the organisation. Employees may also reveal sensitive information on social media platforms.

A further example of how technological change has influenced cyber risk is in the misuse of company assets. Table 13.2 summarises a range of common cyber risk related loss events.

Case study 13.1

In 2015, three UK judges were sacked for accessing pornographic material using their official IT accounts and computers. A fourth judge resigned. There was no evidence that any of the judges had acted illegally but they were dismissed on the grounds that they had misused taxpayer assets. Their dismissal was widely reported on news media.

Risk factor	Example loss events
Recruitment	Looking at potential new recruits on social media to prejudge them regarding their suitability for new positions could lead to legal disputes and compensation claims.
Liability for acts or views of employees	One or more employees using a social media platform to be abusive about another employee could lead to grievances and discrimination or cyber-bullying compensation claims. Employees using company assets to access illegal resources, for example, pornography.
Liability for treatment of employees	Employee grievances arising from colleagues or managers using social media to bully or harass them.
Reputation	One or more employees using a social media platform in an embarrassing, socially ambiguous or litigious manner.
Breaches of confidentiality	Employees using a social media platform to talk about work practices, colleagues, clients or to share commercially sensitive information. Employees losing commercially sensitive information, including the loss of a smartphone, memory stick, tablet or laptop. Employees using personal email accounts or poorly protected personal devices for work-related activities.
IT security	Systems disruptions and the loss or corruption of data as a result of hacking or denial of service attacks. This includes phishing attacks.
Productivity of operations	Systems or network failures. Data corruption or loss. Employees spending time on social media or online games when they should be working.
Privacy issues in monitoring use	Legal disputes and employee grievances where the monitoring of internet use on corporate infrastructure is not disclosed to employees.

Table 13.2 Cyber risk factors and example loss events

Table 13.2 illustrates how cyber risk is changing. Traditionally, its focus was on protecting IT assets and the information that is held on these assets. These risks remain important in the 21st century, but equally significant is how employees communicate while at work, about their work and how customers and third parties discuss organisations online, especially via social media platforms. These activities are giving rise to a range of new cyber risk events that require new types of control activities.

As cyber technologies change, cyber risk management controls must develop to include both formal IT technical controls and less formal HR-type controls. These formal and informal controls include:

◆ *Technical controls*: system-based safeguards such as access controls, malware protection, encryption and firewalls.

◆ *Physical controls*: physical prevention of unauthorised access (such as secure server rooms and keeping data backups locked away), protection from theft and fire prevention.

◆ *Procedural controls*: acceptable use policies, effective risk assessments and auditing, business continuity planning and asset management registers.

◆ *People controls*: effective recruitment practices, proper staff training and cyber risk awareness programmes.

◆ *Legal controls*: ensuring compliance with relevant legislation, including data protection laws and controls to manage any legal issues that might result from employee misconduct, such as cyber bullying.

All employees have responsibilities for the management of cyber risk; this includes ensuring that they comply with acceptable use policies, that they report potential hacking attacks and that they do not reveal sensitive information on social media. Oversight of cyber risk management activities is often within the IT team. This team may be supported by the risk function and other specialist functions like HR and compliance, especially in relation to people and legal related controls.

Test yourself 13.2

How do people-related controls help to prevent cyber risk events?

2.4 Project risk management

Project management is concerned with planning and co-ordinating the work of a team of people to achieve specific goals, within a specified time period, often with limited financial and human resources. Projects are temporary endeavours, but the changes that they bring may be permanent. Examples of projects within organisations include:

◆ designing and implementing a new IT system;

◆ moving or refurbishing a work site (office or factory);

◆ research and development of a new product or process;

◆ launching a new product;

◆ implementing new operational processes;

◆ merging with another organisation;

◆ implementing new risk management or corporate governance arrangements; and

◆ setting up a new subsidiary in a new location or market.

Multiple related projects may be grouped into a wider programme. For example, the implementation of a new risk management framework may have one project dealing with implementing a supporting IT system; another dealing with changes to governance arrangements; and further projects implementing new risk assessment and control and reporting arrangements.

All projects are conducted within a range of constraints, including financial, time and quality constraints. Projects can be complex, requiring the co-ordination of different resources, skills, knowledge and expertise, all of which is subject to a range of risks that may result in delays, cost overruns and poor quality implementation. Poor quality implementation can be especially problematic. For example:

◆ a new IT system may be unreliable or require extensive manual workarounds that negate any efficiency gains;

◆ a new location or refurbishment may prove to be unsuitable to employee needs (too hot, too cold, damp, lacking adequate light, noisy and so on);

◆ a new product or process may come with design flaws or prove to be unreliable;

◆ a merger may lead to culture clashes between the two organisations and fail;

◆ new risk management and governance arrangements may not comply with relevant laws and regulations; and

◆ the products offered by a new subsidiary may not meet the needs of consumers.

Stop and think 13.2

Search the Internet for examples of project management failures in your sector or country of work. You will find that there are many high-profile projects that fail. Investigate the causes of these failures and examine whether they were due to cost or time overruns, or failed implementation.

Project risk management ensures that project objectives are delivered on time and on budget. Project risk managers use a range of practices to identify, assess, monitor and control project risks to ensure the smooth progress of a project or programme.

Ward provides a nine-phase process for managing risk within projects and programmes. This is summarised in Table 13.3.

Phase	Description	Objective
Define	Define the scope of the project and the project constraints to avoid the risk of any misunderstanding between participants.	Ensure that project participants have a shared understanding of the project and that all project information can be accessed quickly and easily.
Focus	Focus on the agreed risk management objectives and processes.	Ensure that all participants understand the project objectives and that risk management tools are established, within any cost and resource constraints.
Identify	Identify the risks and opportunities associated with the project.	Participants must understand the potential risks, the causes and effects to manage a project effectively.
Structure	Structure risks according to their type, severity of exposure, management expertise required and so on.	Ensure that risks are categorised by type to allow appropriate expertise to be focused on them. Structure risks by probability and impact to facilitate prioritisation.
Ownership	Assign risks to owners according to type and the severity of exposure.	Ensure that the right expertise is available to manage risks. Ensure that risks are escalated to the appropriate level of management, depending on their severity.
Estimate	Continue to estimate risk exposures to keep track of any changes.	Ensure that risks are monitored on a regular basis and that the results of this monitoring activity are reported.
Evaluate	Evaluation of project risk management activities.	Evaluate the effectiveness of project risk management activities, including assessment and control activities.
Plan	Project plan and associated risk management plans.	All projects require careful planning and plans may need to be revised in the light of risks and other unplanned factors. Risk management plans ensure that mechanisms are in place to respond to changes in risk exposure or the emergence of risks during a project.
Manage	Management and control of the project through its lifetime.	Monitor project progress and manage any loss events or crises that occur.

Table 13.3 Project risk management process

The specific risk management tools that are used within the project risk management process are very similar to those for other types of risk. Common tools include risk registers, risk reports of key risk indicators (KRIs) and key performance indicators (KPIs), project risk committees and crisis management. Organisations may have specialist project risk managers, project management specialists with a knowledge of risk management or risk management specialists that support project management teams. External project management specialists may be used for technical projects or in smaller organisations.

A formal methodology for managing projects, including the risks that are associated with projects, is known as PRINCE2 (PRojects IN Controlled Environments). PRINCE2 is built on seven principles:

1. Projects must have a business justification. The benefits of a project to an organisation must be clear and ideally quantifiable (improve efficiency, reduce costs or improve revenues).

2. Project teams should learn from their experiences at every stage, to help improve future performance.

3. Roles and responsibilities are defined clearly. Everyone on a team must know what they are responsible for and what everyone else is responsible for.

4. Work in planned stages by breaking projects up into phases. This supports principle 2 and ensures that progress can be monitored.

5. Project oversight boards of senior managers manage by exception. Project managers are left to control projects except when project objectives are under threat.

6. Team focus on quality to ensure that the project delivers what is expected and that all objectives are met, in full.

7. Project management and risk management approaches are tailored to meet the needs of specific organisations and project. Large, complex projects may require more in-depth risk assessment and control, for example.

The PRINCE2 methodology builds risk management into the management of a project from the beginning and should, if applied correctly, incorporate Ward's nine phases of project risk management. Within the PRINCE2 approach, risks are captured on risk registers; issues and quality concerns are captured on issue registers and quality registers. Issue and quality registers may contain information on actual loss events as well as potential control issues. Lessons logs ensure that valuable learning experiences are not missed, so that project risks can be addressed more effectively in the future.

The Project Management Institute (PMI) is a professional institute for project managers, including experts in project risk management. The PMI provides practice standards for project managers, including a practice standard on project risk management.

Test yourself 13.3

What are the key risks associated with projects?

2.5 Supply chain risk management

A supply chain is a network of organisations and people that work together to produce a good or service, followed by distributing the good or service to the end client or consumer.

Most organisations will have, and are part of, a supply chain of some form. An upstream supply chain ensures that the inputs required for an organisation to function are available, such as electricity, equipment, software or product components. A downstream supply chain ensures that an organisation can supply its goods and services to clients and consumers further down the chain towards the end consumer.

Without a cost-effective and reliable supply chain, an organisation cannot operate efficiently. It cannot operate at all in the case of extreme supply chain disruption. Examples of supply chain loss events include:

◆ upstream suppliers are late delivering goods and services or are unable to deliver;

◆ upstream suppliers do not deliver goods and services of sufficient quality;

◆ reputation events, where a supplier is not conforming with the moral and legal conventions of an organisation, for example by using child labour;

◆ the cost of upstream supplies increases unexpectedly, perhaps as a result of exchange rate risk;

◆ payment and other legal disputes with upstream suppliers and downstream clients and consumers; and

◆ environmental risks due to pollution caused by upstream suppliers or distributors to downstream clients and customers.

In turn, these loss events may be caused by a variety of causal factors, including:

◆ bankruptcy of an upstream supplier or a supplier experiencing a major crisis;

◆ a change in specification after an order is received but is yet to be fulfilled;

◆ cyber risks such as hacking attacks;

◆ financial risks that affect costs and prices, notably exchange rate risk and credit risks;

◆ human error;

◆ socio-political risks, which may affect upstream supplies from, or the ability to distribute to, specific countries; and

◆ weather events, such as heavy snow or flooding.

Supply chain risk management is concerned with identifying, assessing, monitoring and controlling supply chain risks. If done correctly, an organisation should maintain the continuity, quality and affordability of its upstream supplies. Downstream clients and customers should also receive the quality of goods and services they expect, on time and on budget.

Supply chain risk management uses the same basic activities and tools as traditional risk management when identifying, assessing, monitoring and controlling supply chain risks. What can differ is the way in which these activities and tools are applied. A key issue within supply chain risk management is developing a detailed understanding of the complete supply chain network and the processes that connect each of the organisations and people within the network. Problems can occur anywhere within a supply chain: unknown interdependencies can cause major problems.

Case study 13.2

A fire at component manufacturer Aisin Seicki threatened to halt the production at Toyota for weeks. Aisin Seicki produced a vital braking system component for all Toyota vehicles. Toyota and Aisin Seiki operate a just-in-time manufacturing system and only a two to three-day supply of the component remained.

Disaster was averted by working with other suppliers to produce the part. Machinery was rescued from the damaged factory and transferred to the other suppliers. Supply of the component resumed after two days.

This case shows how a very small and seemingly insignificant component in a supply chain can cause major disruption – even for a large, successful organisation.

Another issue for supply chain risk management is developing a detailed understanding of the risk management and related internal control, governance and compliance arrangements of upstream and downstream organisations that work within the chain. This is important for a number of reasons:

1. To understand the effectiveness of these arrangements and each organisation's ability to manage loss events that could disrupt the supply chain.

2. To ensure that each organisation's internal control and governance arrangements are appropriate and do not expose others in the chain to compliance risk.

3. To ensure that each organisation's environmental management and health and safety management activities are appropriate and do not expose others in the chain to reputation risk.

Due diligence arrangements are important to manage these problems, as are other third party risk controls like relationship management and contract management (see page 251).

3. Risk management, corporate social responsibility and sustainability

Where an organisation has CSR or sustainability related activities, these should be supported by its risk management practices.

Corporate social responsibility is an activity that is connected with compliance, but is concerned with exceeding the minimum requirements of laws and regulations. Corporate social responsibility is a form of self-regulatory mechanism that ensures an organisation and its employees behave in a way that is ethical and consistent with national and international norms, irrespective of how well laws and regulations are designed or enforced.

CSR is related to areas such as human rights and protecting vulnerable third parties and communities. These areas may be covered by laws and regulations, but organisations with CSR programmes recognise that they need to go beyond these laws and regulations to ensure that their employees and other stakeholders receive all the benefits that they are entitled to from the organisation. At the same time, they should be protected, as fully as possible, from any risks that may affect them, such as pollution, injury or a loss of income.

CSR activities may include:

- Philanthropy: donating money to relevant charities, such as charities that support the communities within which an organisation is located or environmental charities to help mitigate concerns over carbon emissions.
- Providing free or subsidised services for employees and their families, notably health and education.
- Providing time off for employees that volunteer their time and expertise to local charities.
- Marketing campaigns designed to change social attitudes towards human rights issues or the environment. This might include promoting gender equality or encouraging recycling of product packaging.
- Providing free or subsidised goods and services to clients and customers on low incomes.

Sustainability is a parallel management philosophy that acts as an extension to CSR. The focus of CSR is social: sustainability adds a stronger environmental dimension, as well as a financial element.

Sustainability is built around the principle of the 'triple bottom line': the idea that an organisation should balance each of the following elements equally, not just aim for short-term profit or surplus maximisation.

1. *People*: providing fair labour practices, including a living wage to prevent poverty, safety and employment rights;
2. *Planet*: ensuring that the global and local environment is not damaged by the organisation and its activities; and
3. *Profit*: delivering long-term economic value for all stakeholders.

Sustainability-related activities include:

◆ fair trade initiatives;

◆ supply chain selection processes that prioritise local suppliers and distributors wherever possible;

◆ closed loop supply chains that minimise waste, re-use waste products and include end-of-life product recycling or refurbishment;

◆ proactive reduction of the organisation's own carbon footprint via recycling schemes, electric vehicles or the use of renewable energy;

◆ moving to production processes that cause less ground, air or water pollution;

◆ long-term business plans that emphasise long-term growth over short-term performance; and

◆ initiatives to improve worker health, such as subsidised, nutritionally balanced meals.

The management of CSR and sustainability is about sharing the economic value created by organisations in a fair way, across all relevant stakeholders. At the same time, the short-term adverse consequences of an organisation's economic activities, for example pollution or health and safety hazards, are minimised, especially in relation to the effects they can have on vulnerable stakeholders such as low skilled employees and poorer communities. Larger organisations may have dedicated CSR and sustainability management functions and management specialists. Smaller organisations may combine these responsibilities with other functions such as HR, governance or compliance.

Effective CSR and sustainability management requires risk management for the following three reasons:

◆ like CSR and sustainability, risk management is a discipline for creating stakeholder value over the longer term (see Chapter 1, page 5);

◆ risk management tools and techniques are essential when addressing issues relating to environmental pollution or health and safety; and

◆ an organisation that claims to implement CSR and sustainability initiatives may suffer from reputation risk where related loss events, such as pollution or employee injuries, suggest that these initiatives are implemented poorly.

In some organisations, the discipline of sustainability risk management (SRM) is emerging. Sustainability risk management uses conventional risk management tools and techniques to assess and control risks that may affect the financial, social or environmental sustainability of an organisation. The tools and techniques used to identify, assess, monitor and control sustainability risks are the same as for other types of risk, it is just the focus that differs.

It is important that an organisation's CSR or sustainability-related activities are supported by the risk function or external risk management professional.

Stop and think 13.3

Search the internet for examples of CSR and sustainability activities in organisations. Can you find evidence of how risk management is used to support these activities?

Test yourself 13.4

How can risk management support an organisation's CSR and sustainability objectives?

4. Regulatory reporting

Many organisations are required to report information to regulators. This information may include:

- information on the organisation and its directors (company address, major shareholders if any, names and addresses of directors);
- information on staff salaries and tax paid;
- financial accounts;
- business plans;
- governance and internal control arrangements;
- major risks and how these risks are managed;
- pollution and health and safety incidents; and
- major loss events or control failures.

Where an organisation is required to provide reports to regulators, it will be exposed to the following three risk events:

- missed reporting deadlines;
- reports are provided, but incomplete; and
- reports are complete, but there are errors in the information provided.

Exposure to these risk events may be increased by unclear regulatory reporting requirements, a lack of clarity over accounting conventions, differences in information management practices within an organisation and having to cope with large volumes of data that may not be managed using an efficient data storage and reporting system.

Regulatory reporting risks are a form of compliance risk and may be managed using compliance management tools such as compliance reviews and audits, or compliance-related policies and procedures (see Chapter 11, page 222). These and other controls are incorporated into the wider regulatory reporting process that is designed to mitigate reporting risk events.

4.1 Regulatory reporting processes

The specifics of an organisation's regulatory reporting process will vary according to the nature, scale and complexity of its activities, as well as the information that must be reported. The reporting process incorporates five basic activities. Table 13.4 summarises these activities and some common regulatory reporting tasks.

	Activity	Common tasks
1	Understanding and implementing the regulatory reporting requirements	Horizon scanning to identify new or changing reporting requirements. Reviewing and interpreting reporting requirements in the context of the organisation. Translating reporting requirements into internal policies and procedures. Identifying the necessary data points and establishing consistent and replicable processes to extract the data. Where appropriate, implementing IT systems to support data extraction, validation and consolidation.
2	Fulfilling specific regulatory reporting requirements	Managing data volumes, inconsistencies and other complexities to ensure that data is available on time. Data validation and other internal control checks.to ensure accuracy. Allocating clear roles and responsibilities for producing, checking and reporting data.
3	Managing the risk of process failure	Automating data extraction and reporting where possible to minimise human input or processing errors. Ensuring that the IT systems required for reporting are reliable and do not fail when required. Data backup arrangements. Maintaining the integrity and confidentiality of regulatory reports. Controls for preventing reporting errors and omissions. Audits of reporting processes.
4	Managing the reputation and financial impacts of reporting risk events	Procedures for being proactive about reporting errors and omissions where they are identified (such as reporting any mistakes to the regulator before the regulator has detected them). Preventing or mitigating regulatory enforcement in the case of reporting delays or errors or omissions in reports. Learning from previous mistakes and near-misses to prevent future problems.
5	Managing legal and resource requirements	Ensuring that appropriate legal expertise is available to control the risks of reporting delays, errors or omissions. Ensuring that appropriate resources are available to collect and validate all of the required data and to produce the necessary reports.

Table 13.4 Regulatory reporting activities

Stop and think 13.4

For the organisation that you work for or another of your choice, identify the regulatory reporting requirements that it must comply with. What process and related activities and tasks are in place to ensure that regulatory reports are timely, accurate and complete?

4.2 Roles and responsibilities for regulatory reporting

A variety of functions may be involved in regulatory reporting. Some may have responsibility for a number of reports. Others may only be involved in specific types of regulatory report. The following functions are most often involved in regulatory reporting:

◆ company secretary and other governance professionals;

◆ compliance function;

◆ finance function;

◆ health and safety function;

◆ IT function;

◆ risk function; and

◆ functions from across the wider organisation.

The specific roles and responsibilities allocated to these functions will vary according to the nature, scale and complexity of an organisation.

Company secretary and other governance professionals
Company secretaries and other governance professionals have responsibilities for a variety of reporting requirements, such as the completion of annual company returns, changes to directors and articles of association or the filing of accounts. None of these reports are directly risk management-related, though they still have to manage any compliance risks associated with reporting delays, errors and omissions.

In some small to medium-sized organisations, the company secretary or governance professional may have additional responsibilities for regulatory reporting, including the reporting of data protection breaches, health and safety incidents or an organisation's internal control arrangements.

The company secretary or governance professional will often rely on other functions within an organisation to supply information, especially when they are responsible for reporting things like health and safety incidents. This will require them to design and implement appropriate reporting systems, processes and escalation procedures to ensure that the information they require is timely, accurate and complete.

Compliance function

Where present, a compliance function may:

1. Have responsibility for producing some or all of the reports required by regulators.

2. Oversee the regulatory reporting activities of other functions within the organisation to ensure that any compliance risks are identified, assessed, monitored and controlled in an appropriate manner.

In the case of (1), the compliance function may collect, validate and collate data from across the organisation to produce the necessary reports. The compliance function should design and implement reporting systems, processes and escalation procedures (where necessary) to ensure that they receive the information they need to produce the reports.

In the case of (2), the compliance function is not directly responsible for producing and submitting reports but will oversee these activities in other functions to ensure that reports are submitted on time without errors and omissions. The compliance function will design and implement policies to ensure that the reporting processes across the organisation are appropriate. The compliance function may be involved in training to help other functions fulfil their responsibilities, as well as conducting compliance reviews and internal audits to test the effectiveness of reporting processes across the organisation.

Finance function

The finance function has a key role to play in producing reports that contain accounting or other financial information. This may include financial and management accounts, as well as a variety of accounting ratios.

Most organisations are required to provide annual accounts to a relevant authority or to shareholders and in some cases additional financial information may be required. For example, financial institutions in many countries have to provide an assessment of the adequacy of their financial resources in relation to their risk exposures as part of their prudential regulation obligations.

Health and safety function

Where a health and safety function exists, this function may be responsible for all health and safety-related reports. This will include the reporting of more serious health and safety-related incidents, where death, serious injury or ill health has resulted, as well as any other reporting requirements. In the UK, deaths and serious injuries must be reported to the HSE as part of RIDDOR (see Chapter 3, page 52).

Information technology function

In certain sectors, the IT function may have responsibilities to report any IT security breaches to regulators as part of requirements to report material risk events that may affect the financial viability of an organisation or its ability to meet stakeholder expectations (e.g. in financial services and the charity sectors).

With the development of enhanced information security laws, such as the EU's General Data Protection Regulation (GDPR), direct communication between the IT function and regulators is reducing. It is now common to have a chief information security officer or equivalent who will talk to a local regulator (such as the UK Information Commissioners Office). This may be the company secretary or general counsel of an organisation.

Risk function
The risk function may be involved in producing some or all of the regulatory reports that have a risk element. This may include health and safety and data protection-related reporting in some organisations.

In financial services, the risk function will usually work with the finance function to ensure that any prudential regulation reporting requirements are fulfilled It will also work with the compliance department to comply with the conduct of business regulation reporting requirements, such as customer complaints data.

Other business functions
Other business functions may have responsibilities for producing and supplying information for regulatory reports. They are usually not involved in collating or delivering these reports to regulators.

The internal audit function has an additional responsibility to support the compliance function in conducting compliance reviews and internal audits of reporting processes and procedures.

Test yourself 13.5

Explain the five activities that make up an effective regulatory reporting process.

Chapter summary

◆ Risk management is a broad discipline that can be applied to a range of organisational activities. Some common applications of risk management include operational risk management, project risk management, supply chain risk management and cyber risk management.

◆ Operational risk management is concerned with identifying, assessing, monitoring and controlling the risks that arise as a result of operational activities. All organisations have operations and a wide range of risks can affect the efficiency, continuity and cost effectiveness of these operations.

◆ Cyber risk management is concerned with the management of digital risks. Cyber risk management ensures that an organisation's information and technical resources are secure, only accessible to authorised personnel, are used for their intended purpose only and are complete and intact. This includes IT security and data protection.

- As internet and social media use grows, cyber risk management has changed to incorporate human resource-related issues, such as cyber bullying and other forms of online misconduct. This change means that new people-related and legal controls are required, as well as technical IT controls.

- Project management is concerned with planning and co-ordinating the work of a team of people to achieve specific goals within a specified time period, often with limited financial and human resources. Where there are projects there are risks which may prevent the project from being achieved on time and on budget.

- A formal methodology for managing projects, including the risks that are associated with projects, is known as PRNCE2 (PRojects IN Controlled Environments). The PRINCE2 methodology includes the use of risk registers, related issues logs and quality logs. Lessons logs ensure that valuable learning experiences are recorded to help manage project risks more effectively in the future.

- Supply chain risk management is concerned with identifying, assessing, monitoring and controlling supply chain risks. Supply chain risk management applies a range of common risk management tools to maintain the continuity, quality and affordability of its upstream supplies. It also ensures that downstream clients and customers receive the quality of goods and services they expect on time and on budget.

- Corporate social responsibility is an activity that is connected with compliance but is concerned with exceeding the minimum requirements of laws and regulations. Corporate social responsibility is a form of self-regulatory mechanism to encourage behaviours that are ethical and consistent with national and international norms.

- Sustainability is a parallel management philosophy that acts as an extension to CSR. The focus of CSR is primarily social. Sustainability adds a stronger environmental dimension, as well as a financial element. Sustainability is often expressed in terms of the 'triple bottom line' of people, planet and profit.

- In some organisations, the discipline of sustainability risk management (SRM) is emerging. SRM uses conventional risk management tools and techniques to assess and control risks that may affect the financial, social or environmental sustainability of an organisation.

- Where an organisation is required to provide reports to regulators, it must manage the compliance risks associated with missing reporting deadlines or providing incomplete or inaccurate reports.

- Regulatory reporting processes ensure that reports are on time, accurate and complete. These processes are supported by a variety of functions, including the compliance function, risk function and company secretary and other governance professionals.

Chapter fourteen
Trends and future developments for risk management

Contents

1. Introduction

Risk exposures change and new risks emerge. Risk management must adapt to these changes and new risks.

This chapter outlines a number of current risk trends, including:

- ◆ Crime, financial crime and the regulations and controls that exist to combat it;
- ◆ bribery, political risks and corporate gift giving perceptions;
- ◆ managing behavioural (people) risks;
- ◆ climate change and asymmetric risks;
- ◆ reputation risk management;
- ◆ the convergence between tangible and intangible risk; and
- ◆ shareholder activism.

2. Crime

A crime is an unlawful act that merits a punishment, usually in the form of a fine or imprisonment. To be convicted of a crime, certain conditions must be met:

1. The crime should take the form of an action. A person cannot be convicted of crime just because he/she is thinking of committing a crime.

2. There is no crime without intent. The criminal act must be voluntary or purposeful.

3. For an act to be a crime, both the act and the intent must occur at the same time.

Crimes can be committed by employees and non-employees such as third-party vendors, customers and cybercriminals. In the context of business, crime can be classified into the following four categories:

◆ offence against an individual;

◆ offence against property or services;

◆ violation of laws; and

◆ other offences.

2.1 Offences against an individual

While offences against an individual such as homicide or manslaughter can unfortunately occur in the workplace, it would be very difficult to charge an organisation with either crime. In addition to proving that actions of a specific individual led to people's death, it has to be proven beyond a reasonable doubt that these actions were for the benefit of the organisation and within the scope of the employment contract of the offender.

When it comes to battery or assault, a legal action can arise against the organisation as well as the offender. Damages from these offences may not be covered by employees' compensation remedy provisions. For example, it is an assault when the terminated employee is obstructed physically from taking his or her personal belongings, or he or she is removed from the workplace using physical force. The employee has a right to file a lawsuit against the organisation.

Workplace violence against an individual can also take the form of harassment, intimidation or other threatening behaviour. Victims of such violence would generally be entitled to receive monetary compensation. In certain situations, if the organisation fails to act on an initial harassment complaint that later results in (physical) assault, the mistreated employee may seek damages against the organisation for battery.

Certain occupations come with a greater risk of such offences occurring, including roles where employees are:

◆ responsible for money;

◆ working in dangerous places;

◆ working in places where alcohol is distributed; or

◆ working during times of day when crime is more likely to occur.

As employee complaints of alleged batteries and assaults in the workplace are often communicated in an emotional manner, organisations should be mindful of the legal definitions of these terms during investigations, response actions and audit trails.

2.2 Offences against property or services

Larceny, embezzlement, robbery, fraud and false pretences are all examples of theft: crime that involves taking something that belongs to someone else and keeping it. Robbery involves an act of violence, whereas embezzlement is often related to misappropriation of funds.

Theft can be committed without the other person's knowledge, (by using deceiving or intimidating techniques). Although it is often associated with tangible assets like money, theft can also be of services, such as an employee using his or her company's computer for personal needs (also known as computer crime).

Employee theft can damage an organisation financially unless it is covered by insurance, it can also harm the organisation's reputation.

Cyber crime is a relatively new but growing threat involving third parties using a computer to commit a crime. This crime can be in the form of a disruption (a hacker uploading a computer virus to disrupt manufacturing operations) or an act of theft (a hacker stealing material non-public information for a ransom) or both.

Other offences within this category include employees using stolen property to conduct day-to-day duties (given they possess the knowledge that this property was stolen), employees forging documents to commit fraud, employees breaking and entering a workplace at night to commit burglary and employees maliciously burning the employer's property (arson).

2.3 Violation of laws

Violation of certain laws can be considered a criminal offence. Examples of such laws are anti-trust and environmental laws, the Food and Drug Act, the Terrorism Act and others.

Anti-trust law covers activities that restrain trade, such as when trade participants collude to fix the market prices. It also supervises merger and acquisition activities to prevent any one single participant dominating the market.

Many environmental laws have criminal provisions, often related to health and safety requirements. Inappropriate disposal of waste from manufacturing activities can carry criminal penalties.

Under the Food and Drug Act, organisations may face a criminal punishment for misbranding and misrepresenting the benefits of their products and services.

The Terrorism Act 2006 creates crime offences for organisations that encourage and support acts of terrorism.

2.4 Other offences

Other key criminal offences to note are extortion and bribery. Government organisations specifically face the risk of their employees committing a criminal act of extortion. For example, a government employee could collect an unlawful fee under the colour of the office by threatening to revoke a liquor licence from a restaurant that greatly relies on sale of alcohol to remain profitable. Blackmail, where a victim is forced to pay to prevent certain damaging information to be released, is a form of extortion and can take place in both governmental and non-governmental workplaces.

Bribery, on the other hand, is an act of crime that involves a wilful corrupt payment (or receipt of such payment) for official action from a public official within the government. This payment does not necessarily have to be in the form of cash: it can be in the form of goods, services or other forms that the recipient would find valuable.

2.5 Countering workplace crime

To prevent crime in the workplace, organisations increasingly employ specialist firms to run extensive background checks on new applicants, including criminal checks. Clear organisational policies, checks and procedures, as well as continuous training for employees reduce opportunities for theft. Regular audits of areas that are responsible for handling money, payroll, invoices and receipts help to identify gaps and early warning signals. With the arrival of accessible technology, organisations are now able to utilise safeguards such as security camera surveillance to prevent workplace crime, while using access control systems to effectively manage employees' access to offices and working facilities.

As technology progresses, security management software solutions that help to manage risks, anticipate potential threats and produce customised risk reports will become a more common feature of the day-to-day crime risk management.

2.6 Cyber crime prevention

At a minimum, organisations are strongly advised to install password-protected firewalls and up-to-date antivirus software.

However, hackers constantly find new ways around existing defences. Therefore, many organisations employ specialist firms to help them identify and operationally manage weak spots, such as having too many employees with privileged user access or lack of back-up processes of the key records.

Continuous employee training is another proactive way to reduce the risk of cyber crime.

3. Financial crime

Financial crime covers any type of criminal conduct that relates to money, financial services, or financial markets. Examples of financial crime include:

◆   fraud or dishonesty;

◆   misconduct relating to financial markets and financial information, such as insider trading and financial misstatement risks;

◆   handling the proceeds of crime; and

◆   the funding of terrorism.

Financial crime is nothing new for banks and other financial institutions that are exposed to significant levels of financial crime risk and accompanying conduct of business regulation.

What is relatively new is the application of financial crime regulations to non-financial services organisations. Any organisation that handles significant amounts of cash, including charities, housing developers and associations, estate or rental agencies, and those involved in the sale or purchase of high value goods, may be exposed to proceeds of crime-related risks. Any incorporated company, especially quoted companies, may be exposed to market misconduct risks and all organisations face a risk of fraud or dishonesty.

Financial crime risks have three main impacts on an organisation:

1.   direct financial loss as a result of an employee or external party committing fraud, for example;

2.   reputation and brand loss, where adverse publicity may damage the public image of the organisation; and

3.   legal and regulatory sanctions due to a breach of financial crime laws and regulations.

Financial crime laws and regulation relate to the handling of proceeds of crime, or money laundering. Money laundering is used to make illegal gains appear legitimate. Historically, financial crime and money laundering regulation only applied to financial institutions; today its scope has broadened to include any organisation.

Where organisations manage client money, provide loans, investment returns, or insurance-related payments, they may be subject to additional regulations relating to the funding of terrorist organisations. High levels of current concern regarding terrorist activities mean that the scope of this regulation has increased. For example, in the UK, new anti-money laundering (AML) and countering financing of terrorism (CFT) regulation came into force in 2017.

3.1 Anti-money laundering

Most countries have AML laws and regulations intended to prevent individuals and organised crime groups from using the monetary proceeds of their illegal activities.

Many illegal transactions are cash-based, because cash is hard to trace. This might include drugs or the sale of stolen goods. Criminals may also steal cash from banks, retail premises or similar.

Successful criminals can amass significant cash sums, far more than they need to cover their day-to-day expenses. This can lead to attempts at 'laundering' the cash to make it appear legitimate. One way to do this is to pay the cash into a bank account but there are strong controls on cash payments into banks in most countries. Alternatively, the cash may be used to purchase high value goods, such as houses, jewellery, or luxury vehicles, which may then be sold on to make the proceeds appear legitimate.

Money could be laundered through a company, whereby over-inflated cash payments are made for goods and services that may or may not exist (such as a restaurant with a small number of customers but large revenues, especially as there is a wide spread between the cost of the actual ingredients and the sales price of the product). This form of money laundering requires higher levels of organisation and often individuals with accounting and legal expertise. Even so, the 'investment' can be worthwhile for many criminal gangs if it helps their illegal gains to appear legitimate.

Anti-money laundering laws and regulations attempt to combat these tactics. They require organisations that fall within the scope of these laws and regulations to use a range of control measures to prevent money from being laundered. Regulated organisations that do not implement compliant controls, or which permit money laundering deliberately or by error or omission, can face serious sanctions, including large fines and the imprisonment of senior staff and directors.

In the UK and Ireland, new AML regulations came into force in 2017, as part of the European Union's fourth Directive on Money Laundering. In the UK this is known as the Money Laundering, Terrorist Financing and Transfer of Funds (Information on the Payer) Regulations 2017. This was superseded by the Sanctions and Anti-Money Laundering Act 2018 in the UK, to ensure that UK law mirrors EU law if it leaves the EU.

The UK regulation extends the scope of the previous 2007 regulations to include all gambling providers (rather than only casinos) and the trustees of beneficial trusts. The regulation also enhanced the rules in relation to:

◆ customer due diligence;
◆ further limitations on the ability to rely on third party anti-money laundering controls;
◆ the provision of electronic money (crypto-currencies, such as Bitcoin) and pre-payment cards (common in areas like travel money, public transport, and contactless payments);
◆ improving the financial transparency of beneficial trusts; and
◆ the enforcement of sanctions against non-compliant organisations.

The emergence of electronic money and pre-payment cards have created significant difficulties for existing regulations. Criminals are always looking for ways around existing laws and regulations and they must be updated regularly to close any loopholes created by technological innovation. This includes keeping up to date with technological developments in electronic ledgers and blockchain technology.

3.2 Countering the financing of terrorism

Growing concerns about terrorism and the funding of terrorist activities have led to enhanced laws and regulations.

Terrorist activities require funds to plan attacks, purchase equipment and train attackers. In the case of more organised groups, funds may be used to 'pay' those involved in running them. Terrorist gangs can finance their activities more easily if they have access to the wider banking and payments system to facilitate the transfer of funds. Physical cash is much more unwieldy, especially for large transactions where AML laws may prevent large cash transactions.

Detecting terrorist funding can be very difficult, especially since legitimately earned funds may be used to help support terrorist activities, such as donations from sympathisers. With money laundering, a crime has to occur before the funds enter the banking system, making it easier to link funds to specific crimes. With terrorist funding, the crime occurs after the funds have been made available via the banking or wider payment system.

Many countries combine terrorist funding laws and regulations with anti-money laundering. This is the case in the UK and Ireland.

Stop and think 14.1

Search online for examples of organisations that have been fined for failing to prevent money laundering and terrorist financing. How large were these fines?

Test yourself 14.1

What types of organisation are required to comply with AML and CFT regulations?

3.3 Common AML and CFT controls

Anti-money laundering and CFT risk management activities follow a similar process to other types of risk. The starting point is identifying and assessing potential risks, followed by monitoring and controlling them.

In terms of identifying and assessing AML and CFT risks, an organisation must determine whether and how their products and services could be used to launder money or support, inadvertently or deliberately, the funding of terrorism. This will include identifying the products, services, stakeholders (customers and third parties) and physical locations that are most at risk of money laundering and terrorist financing activities, then assessing the level of exposure in terms of probability and impact.

Once risks have been identified and assessed, appropriate controls and monitoring arrangements must be put in place. These include:

◆ developing appropriate policies and procedures to help co-ordinate control activities;

◆ establishing roles and responsibilities, which may include appointing a money laundering reporting officer (MLRO) to oversee AML and CFT activities;

◆ reporting any suspicions of money laundering or terrorist funding activity to the relevant authorities;

◆ establish due diligence arrangements to help identify potential money laundering and terrorist funding activities. This will often include 'know your customer' (KYC) arrangements to verify the legitimacy of customers and other relevant stakeholders, for example via enhanced identity checks;

◆ monitoring of transactions to search for suspicious activity: for example, accounts used for money laundering may receive occasional large cash payments followed by frequent smaller withdrawals;

◆ maintaining appropriate records of KYC checks and transaction monitoring activities;

◆ reporting suspicious activity to the MLRO and subsequently to the relevant authorities;

◆ dual control and segregation of duties controls to help prevent collusion between an employee and criminals or terrorists;

◆ training for employees to ensure that they are aware of and compliant with AML and CFT regulations, and the organisation's own policies and procedures; and

◆ AML and CFT compliance reviews and internal audits.

The sophistication of these controls can be considerable in an organisation where the risk of money laundering and terrorist funding activities is high. For example, many banks employ real-time, automated account monitoring tools and artificially intelligent IT systems to identify suspicious activities and to automatically block transactions. Know your customer checks may be something as simple as providing a valid ID (passport or driving licence) or it may include detailed background checks looking at past financial records.

3.4 Reporting a suspicious transaction or activity

Where money laundering or terrorist financing is suspected, most regulatory regimes require that these suspicions are reported to the relevant authorities. The relevant authority in the UK is the National Crime Agency (NCA) and the method of contact is through the submission of a Suspicious Activity Report (SAR).

The definition of 'suspicious activity' is very broad and includes any transaction or related activity that might be considered unusual, such as a large cash payment or withdrawal, strange behaviour on the part of a stakeholder, or requests that do not make sense from a commercial perspective.

Where an employee in an organisation has concerns about a transaction or activity, they are required to report this suspicion to the nominated officer (often the MLRO) who must then decide whether to pass this onto the NCA for investigation. At this stage, the nominated officer may decide to suspend the activity or transaction if considered safe to do so.

The nominated officer may be anyone with suitable skills, training or experience. It may be a senior manager within the compliance function or the company secretary or other governance professional.

To ensure that an organisation is protected from potential prosecutions for failing to prevent money laundering or terrorist funding, it is important that its employees know when and how to escalate their suspicions to the nominated officer. It is better to report unfounded suspicions than to fail to report actual incidences of money laundering and terrorist funding. In most cases, an innocent customer or other stakeholder will not be aware that any suspicions have been raised.

In the UK, SARs can be submitted via a secure online system with telephone support from a dedicated team of professionals. This online service means that organisation-specific information need only be submitted once. Each time a suspicious activity is identified, the nominated officer provides information on:

◆   the type and nature of the suspicion;

◆   date and location of the event;

◆   whether the individual is believed to be a suspect or victim;

◆   the personal details of the individual engaging in the activity; and

◆   the individual's account details where necessary.

Where suspicious transactions or activities are identified, UK authorities have a range of sanctions under the Sanctions and Anti-Money Laundering Act 2018. This includes imposing restrictions on where money may be transferred or how much can be transferred. It also includes freezing and seizing economic assets (money, property and so on) where necessary.

4. Bribery and corruption

The UK Bribery Act 2010 established a liability for organisations whose employees commit an act of bribery of public officials, or business-to-business bribery anywhere in the world.

Organisations are expected to implement internal control mechanisms based on six principles:

1.   Proportionality
2.   Top-level commitment
3.   Risk assessment
4.   Due diligence
5.   Communication
6.   Monitoring and review.

Internal controls should reflect the size and the risk profile of an organisation. For example, a large global mining company with significant revenue-generating operations in Africa is expected to have more vigorous anti-bribery and corruption controls than a medium-sized retail clothing company based and operating in the UK.

As responsibility for compliance with applicable laws and regulations starts with the top, senior management should actively promote a zero tolerance policy towards bribery and corruption by any individual within the organisation. Organisations should be proactive in researching and identifying the risks they may face in the markets in which they operate. They should also have sufficient knowledge of third-party individuals and vendors who represent and perform services on behalf of them.

Organisations are responsible for communicating policies and procedures to their employees and to third parties who represent and perform services for the organisation. This includes mandatory training procedures. Finally, organisations should take steps to ensure that the anti-corruption and anti-bribery internal controls framework is adequate, effective and reflective of current and emerging risks.

An organisation that has implemented adequate internal controls prior to the occurrence of an offence can shield itself from corporate liability (responsibility for the offences of an employee or a third party acting on its behalf).

5. Political risk

Political risk refers to the risk an organisation may face as a result of political changes or a political instability in a country. Country sanctions are an example of such risk.

Political risks are extremely hard to predict and manage (as insurance may not always be available), are more common in developing economies and can lead to substantial strategic, financial and employee (labour) losses for an organisation.

A high degree of political freedom in a country does not always directly translate into the low level of political risk. An authoritarian government country may be more politically stable than a democratic country.

Political risks are often grouped into two categories: macro and micro risks. The consequences of macro risks are not organisation-specific and will affect the whole country. For example, the Syrian civil war affected all organisations operating in the country. Micro-political risks are specific to an organisation or a project carried out by an organisation. The 2019 order from the Nigerian government that forced foreign oil and gas companies to pay nearly $20 billion in taxes to local states, industry and government is an example of a micro risk.

International sanctions are political and economic decisions against governments, organisations or individuals meant to protect national security interests, international law and defend against threats to international peace and security. These decisions typically include the temporary restriction of economic trade with sanctioned targets that is lifted when the motivating concerns no longer apply. The US sanctions against Iran selling its oil is a recent example.

Organisations manage political risks by first defining the appetite for such risks within their strategic framework. It is important to conduct the appropriate cost benefit analysis of political risks, as some risks may be worth taking. Risks that cannot be mitigated (through insurance, for example) should be monitored and regularly reviewed by both management and the board.

It is also important that policies and procedures related to political risks are clearly communicated and enforced within the organisation. Necessary training should be provided to employees and third party representatives and vendors.

6. Corporate gifts

The giving and receiving of gifts has always been a part of corporate life. However, the business ethics of such activities has been questioned in recent years. To ensure that a corporate gift does not constitute a bribe, the Bribery Act 2010 guidance put significant restrictions on the value and the timing of corporate gifts and related hospitality actions.

Because of the reputational risk attached, some organisations completely prohibit or significantly limit the amount an employee can spend on client hospitality. Organisations typically have a relevant policy, training and monitoring processes in place to mitigate the risk of employees receiving inappropriate gifts.

7. People risk

Behavioural risk management is focused on managing the individual and collective behaviour of an organisation's employees. Behavioural risk management targets the attitudes, perceptions and relationships of an organisation's employees, promoting 'good' behaviours that help the organisation to achieve its objectives and preventing 'bad' behaviours that can lead to a variety of risks.

Cultural factors can influence behaviours (see Chapter 10) but behaviours are not only determined by culture. Education, a person's upbringing, professional training and personal attitudes and perceptions can all influence employee behaviour.

7.1 Behavioural risk

Behavioural risk arises from negative employee behaviours. Negative behaviours may include:

◆   negligence and criminal behaviours;
◆   aggression and bullying;
◆   lack of concern for health and safety or environmental protection;

- a focus on short-term rewards over long-term benefits;
- ignoring policies and procedures;
- an unwillingness to communicate or to listen to the advice of others; and
- pursuing personal objectives at the expense of organisational ones.

Behavioural risks are sometimes known as conduct risks in sectors like financial services.

7.2 Common sources of behavioural risks

Bullying
Bullying behaviours are not restricted to young people or the school playground. Bullying in an organisation must not be tolerated.

Bullying may involve physical and psychological threats, including coercive and controlling behaviours. Bullying may take place between a line manager and their direct report or between colleagues.

Negligence
Negligent behaviours might include:

- refusing to follow a policy or procedure;
- neglecting assigned duties and responsibilities;
- a general lack of care and attention;
- lack of concern for others and their needs; and
- not following the instructions of a line manager or other figure of authority.

Information leaks
Information leaks can be accidental, but employees may decide to leak information to damage the reputation of the organisation or for personal financial gain.

Criminal activity
Employees may engage in a range of criminal activities, including:

- health and safety or environmental non-compliance;
- fraud;
- theft; and
- the facilitation of financial crime, including money laundering and terrorist financing.

Criminal activities may be the result of employee dissatisfaction with the organisation (such as a perception of low pay), personal problems (a gambling habit, for example) or pressures from organised criminal gangs.

7.3 Effects of behavioural risk

Bad employee behaviours can result in a wide range of risk events and effects. Table 14.1 summarises the common effects of behavioural risk events.

Implication	Description
Financial	Behavioural risks such as theft and fraud can cost significant amounts of money. Related compliance breaches can lead to large fines.
Legal and compliance	Bad employee behaviours can result in a range of legal and compliance effects, including court cases, supervisory intervention, the loss of an operating licence, fines and criminal sanctions.
Morale of employees	Bad behaviours can affect employee morale across the organisation. Behaviours like bullying can be especially damaging to employee morale.
Reputation	High profile behavioural risk events can lead to extensive adverse media attention. Socially aware stakeholders may also be reluctant to engage with organisations that allow bad behaviours in areas like bullying, financial crime or health and safety management.

Table 14.1 The effects of behavioural risk

7.4 Managing behavioural risk

Behavioural risk can be managed using a range of common risk controls including training, segregation of duties or whistleblowing arrangements. Specific behavioural risk controls include:

◆ recruitment controls;
◆ codes of conduct; and
◆ risk culture.

Recruitment controls

Effective recruitment controls reduce the potential for recruiting employees likely to exhibit bad behaviours.

Psychometric tests may be used to test the psychological tendencies of employees, such as their attention to detail. References and criminal record checks may reveal applicants with a previous history of bad behaviour. Probation periods may be used to address actual bad behaviours during the initial months of employment.

Codes of conduct

Codes of conduct make clear the standards of behaviour that are expected. Non-compliance with a code of conduct may lead to disciplinary action and ultimately dismissal.

Risk culture

The risk culture of an organisation is a subset of its wider organisational culture. Risk culture can relate to many different types of behaviour and attitude in relation to risk taking and risk management (see Chapter 9).

Assessing and controlling the risk culture of an organisation can help to manage behavioural risks. Examples of risk culture controls that can influence employee behaviours include:

◆ the tone from the top, where senior managers and directors reinforce the standards of behaviour that are expected;

◆ disciplinary and grievance processes, providing they are followed correctly and consistently;

◆ performance reviews, which focus on behaviours as well as operational performance; and

◆ training initiatives that look to influence employee behaviours.

Test yourself 14.2

Explain the adverse implications of behavioural risk for organisations.

8. Climate change risk

In 2018, the Bank of England (BoE) launched a consultation into how financial services organisations based in the UK are managing climate change risk.

As per the BoE view, climate change presents financial risks which can impact organisations through two main channels: the physical effects of climate change and the impact of changes associated with the transition to a lower-carbon economy.

Physical risks arise from changing climate conditions and extreme weather events, such as hurricanes, droughts, floods, storms and sea-level rises. These can potentially result in large financial losses for organisations, especially if these losses are not insured.

Transition risks, on the other hand, arise from the process of organisations adjusting towards a greener (lower-carbon) state. Changes in government climate policy, technology or market sentiment could prompt a reassessment of the value of a large range of assets as changing costs and opportunities become apparent. The speed at which such re-pricing occurs is uncertain but could be important for financial stability and the safety and soundness of organisations.

Organisations should form a strategic response to the financial risks arising from climate change to ensure their financial stability now and in the long run. This response should consist of granular research into organisational-level exposures to physical and transitional risks, including stress testing and business model analysis, as well as relevant disclosures.

The BoE expects organisations to identify a senior manager with responsibility for managing the financial risks posed by climate change, with clear board-level engagement (a designated board member to oversee climate change related risk management and disclosures).

9. Asymmetric risk

The asymmetric threat is a low resource attack that has large consequences. A cyber security attack launched by one person or a small group of individuals that causes a significant operational disruption for a target (organisation) is an example of such threat. In this context, the perpetrator has an unfair (asymmetric) advantage over its victim. Over the past few years, asymmetric cyber-attacks have become more frequent and common due to their low cost and readily available equipment.

In 2017, A.P. Møller – Mærsk A/S, the shipping giant which transports around 15% of global container trade, suffered a major cyber attack caused by the NotPetya malware. The incident was triggered by the Mærsk's employee responding to an email that featured NotPetya virus and occurred despite Mærsk having cyber security measures in place. The attack significantly affected operations, with the estimated cost of the attack between $250 and $300 million.

Organisations are more exposed to the risk of an asymmetric attack than they were in the past due to the twin trends of utilising different information sharing processes while shifting large chunks of highly sensitive data to cloud storage solutions.

Asymmetric threats are treated and managed in a similar way to natural disasters. Organisations should assess and monitor their vulnerabilities, then create mitigating strategies and contingency plans.

10. Reputation and resilience

Much risk management activity is focused on anticipating risk events, their causes and effects, with the aim of reducing their probability and impact. In the case of emerging risks there may not be sufficient information to anticipate and control all possible events.

Where risks cannot be anticipated, the alternative is to build resilience. A resilient organisation is able to respond to unanticipated risk events to help mitigate their effects. The aim is not prevention but effect reduction. At its most effective the adverse effects of unanticipated events can be reduced to near zero. It may even be possible to turn the event into a positive opportunity, by exploiting the good publicity that may be associated with an effective response to an adverse event.

Resilient organisations:

◆ accept that they cannot anticipate every risk event, especially when dealing with emerging risks;

◆ prepare for the unexpected by designing effective crisis management and business continuity arrangements;

◆ react quickly when surprised by new events, taking action immediately;

◆ invest in effect reduction tools, including effect public relations management to control media reaction; and

◆ learn from past events, including their successes and failures in managing these events.

10.1 Reputation

A key part of resilience is effective reputation management. Organisations affected by unanticipated events can find that they are subjected to significant scrutiny by their stakeholders and the media. How the organisation reacts to the event can have a significant effect on its reputation, as illustrated by Case study 14.1.

Case study 14.1

In 2017, the WannaCry ransomware virus affected organisations around the world. The virus was a new type of sophisticated ransomware that made files impossible to decrypt. Many organisations and households lost large amounts of data. Even if a ransom was paid, files were not decrypted.

One organisation affected by the virus was the National Health Service (NHS) in the UK. The attack caused 6,900 NHS appointments to be cancelled and it is believed that around 19,000 appointments were disrupted.

The cancellation of so many appointments led to major media coverage that damaged the reputation of the NHS trusts that were affected. The ability of these trusts to help prevent and respond to attacks was criticised heavily. The event triggered a detailed 'lessons learned' review and steps have been taken to improve crisis planning and communication across the NHS.

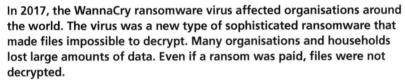

11. The changing balance between tangible and intangible risks

In 2015, Wells Fargo became the largest bank in the US by total assets, citing its famous product cross-selling culture as a key driver. By 2018, it slipped to the third place as the bank became embroiled in a scandal that saw its employees creating over 2 million fake bank accounts to meet internal targets. Following the scandal, both the CEO and the chairman have left, the board has been reshuffled, a large number of employees departed, and US regulators hit the bank with multiple fines and balance sheet growth restrictions.

This is just one example of how an intangible risk (loss of reputation) can trigger a series of tangible (fines, balance sheet growth constraints) and intangible (loss of talent) risks.

While organisations and boards worry about tangible risks like HR issues, fires, employee security, faulty products, very little attention is paid to less obvious items such as talent, intellectual property and reputation. Over the past few decades, as more and more companies have become globalised, technologically agile and services-driven, intangible assets have become more valuable than physical assets.

As a result, a growing number of organisations are now incorporating intangible risk assessments as a part of their risk management frameworks, with in-depth discussions happening on a senior management and board levels.

12. Shareholder activism

Shareholder activism has been on the rise over the past few years, often taking organisations by surprise.

Shareholder activism refers to a range of activities by one or more of a publicly traded organisation's shareholders that are intended to result in some change in the organisation. A wide range of investors participate in activism, including traditional asset managers, mutual funds, pension funds and individuals.

The extent of requested changes is driven by the type of the activist shareholder. Examples of activism-related changes include:

◆ changes to the board's governance policies or practices, or a change to the board composition (such as increasing board diversity or replacing a specific board member);

◆ changes to executive remuneration plans;

◆ change to the oversight of certain functions (such as audit or risk management);

◆ change to the organisational behaviour (such as environmental and climate change practices and disclosures, natural resource management, employment practices);

◆ changes to the share buyback and share dividend programmes (a request to pay a higher or a special one-off dividend); or

◆ changes to the divestment strategy (such as a request to divest a certain asset deemed non-core under the overall strategy).

Typically, pension funds and assets managers are more concerned with the environmental, social and governance (ESG) topics whereas hedge funds seek to effect a significant change in the organisation's strategy through their shareholder value proposals.

Fending off an attack from activist investors can be a time consuming, destructive and widely publicised exercise. Without a proper evaluation of the shareholder proposal, organisations run a high risk of prioritising short-term gains over long-term health and growth. To prepare for shareholder activism, organisations need to better understand whether they can be at risk of an activist event. Common risk factors include:

◆ a low market value relative to the book value;

◆ prolonged underperformance relative to peers;

◆ excessive cash on hand that has not been re-invested;

◆ parts of the business that do not align with the overall strategy;

◆ failure to meet basic corporate governance and ESG practices (such as lack of board diversity, lack of environmental disclosures).

Resistance is an appropriate response when the activist purely intends to transfer immediate value to the shareholder at the detriment of the organisation's attempt to create a long-term value. In other words, when time horizons and risk tolerance differ substantially between the organisation and the activist investor.

12.1 Role of the board

Well-advised and informed boards will take a less reactive response when dealing with activist shareholders; instead finding opportunities to better control the overall process and leverage their key stakeholders. Well-handled activist campaigns will maintain the credibility of the board in the face of often negative publicity.

It is crucial that the board members are engaged with the executive team and key stakeholders. They should also be capable of understanding and clearly articulating the organisation's strategy and performance relative to its peers.

Chapter summary

◆ Crime can occur in the workplace and leave an organisation facing financial and reputational losses.

◆ Crimes can be committed by employees and non-employees such as third party vendors, customers and cyber criminals.

◆ Continuous employee training and zero tolerance messages from the top can help to reduce the occurrence of crimes.

◆ The prevention of financial crime is an important trend in risk management. Laws relating to the prevention of money laundering and terrorist financing now extend beyond the financial services sector. Many organisations that support customer transactions or receive/donate large amounts of cash must comply with these regulations.

◆ In terms of identifying, assessing and controlling financial crime risks, an organisation should determine how their operations may be used to launder money or support the funding of terrorism. This will include identifying the products, services, stakeholders (customers and third parties) and physical locations that are most at risk of money laundering and terrorist financing activities, then assessing the level of exposure in terms of probability and impact.

◆ Where money laundering or terrorist financing is suspected, most regulatory regimes require that these suspicions are reported to the relevant authorities. The relevant authority in the UK is the National Crime Agency (NCA).

◆ The UK Bribery Act 2010 established a liability for organisations whose employees commit an act of bribery of public officials or business-to-business bribery anywhere in the world. Organisations that have implemented adequate internal controls prior to the occurrence of an offence can shield themselves from corporate liability.

◆ Political risk refers to the risk an organisation may face as a result of political changes or a political instability in a country. Organisations manage political risks by defining the appetite to such risks within their strategic framework and proactive monitoring.

◆ Corporate gift giving and hospitality should be limited to a minimum, so they are not perceived as a bribe.

◆ Behavioural risk management is focused on managing the individual and collective behaviour of an organisation's employees. Behavioural risk management targets the attitudes, perceptions and relationships of an organisation's employees to promote 'good' behaviours, which help the organisation to achieve its objectives, and prevent 'bad' behaviours that can lead to a variety of risks.

◆ Behavioural risk can be managed using a range of common risk controls including training, segregation of duties or whistleblowing arrangements. Specific behavioural risk controls include recruitment controls, codes of conduct and risk culture.

◆ Climate change presents financial risks which can impact organisations through two main channels: the physical effects of climate change and the impact of changes associated with the transition to a lower-carbon economy, It is the expectation from certain regulators that organisations will form a strategic response to the financial risks arising from climate change to ensure financial stability now and in the long run.

◆ An asymmetric threat is a low-resource attack that has large consequences. A cyber security attack launched by one person or a small group of individuals that causes a significant operational disruption for a target (organisation) is an example of such threat.

◆ Over the past few decades, as more and more companies have become globalised, technologically agile and services driven, intangible assets have become more valuable than physical assets.

◆ Shareholder activism is a new emerging risk for publicly listed organisations.

Chapter fifteen
More trends and future developments for risk management

Contents

1. Introduction

This chapter outlines more trends and expected future developments for risk management, particularly digital risks. The following trends and developments are outlined in this chapter:

- the growing complexity of modern markets and environments;
- advances in information technology (IT), focusing on big data and automated decision making;
- changing knowledge and skills; and
- managing digital risks.

These trends and developments are already affecting, or will soon affect, most organisations.

2. Complex and connected risks

As organisations and the environments within which they operate change, new risks can emerge or the probability and impact of existing risks may increase significantly.

The emergence of new risks or a significant increase in an existing risk can cause significant problems for an organisation. Existing risk management procedures and controls may not be sufficient to detect, assess and ultimately mitigate these risks. New risks bring new opportunities but these will not be exploited effectively without risk management arrangements that are adapted to support the achievement of these opportunities.

A common feature of modern organisations and their environments is complexity. Complexity can come with large, multinational and multiproduct organisations. It can also come with developments in IT, production processes, consumer expectations and growing levels of regulation in areas like health and safety and the environment. Complexity adds to the potential for risks to emerge or for large increases in probability and impact.

Emerging risks may be completely new or a significant change in the nature or exposure to an existing risk. Emerging risks are characterised by high levels of uncertainty, meaning that it can be very difficult to precisely assess the nature of these risks, including the probability of occurrence and level of impact. There are many sources of emerging risks but a common theme is the level of economic, technical and social development of the modern world in which we live.

2.1 The modern world and the growth in emerging risks

Our world today is very different than the world a few decades ago. Technology, including smartphones and the internet, has caused major changes in how we communicate, consume media and carry out business. New social, economic and regulatory developments, such as greater levels of market liberalisation and cross-border trade agreements have also transformed the global landscape.

The 21st century brings many benefits to organisations and wider society but with these benefits comes new risks and changes to existing risks. An organisation should understand the causes of these risks if it is to deal with them in an effective manner. There are three primary and interrelated causes of these new or changing risks:

◆ complexity
◆ interconnectedness
◆ globalisation.

Complexity
Complexity is partly a function of globalisation and interconnectedness, but these are not the only sources of complexity. Complexity is increased by many factors, including:

◆ developments in IT, the internet and social media;
◆ developments in financial markets, such as new financial market instruments like derivatives;
◆ a general increase in the volume and scope of regulation, for example in areas such as corporate governance and environmental protection;
◆ the size and structure of organisations, for example organisations that serve multiple markets and product niches;
◆ consumer expectations regarding product characteristics and design, including a desire for more customisation options;

◆   long supply chains, especially when international; and

◆   the use of outsourced service providers.

In a complex environment, new risks may emerge but go undetected. New and unfamiliar combinations of existing risks may emerge. Where risks are identified, high levels of complexity may prevent an accurate assessment of probability and impact.

Case study 15.1

In March 2018, it emerged that data had been harvested from tens of millions of Facebook users to support political campaigning. The data was harvested by Cambridge Analytica using an algorithm developed by a Cambridge University academic.

During the investigation, it emerged that Facebook was not aware of the full extent of the data harvesting that occurred. As a result, Facebook was affected by a large public relations crisis with adverse media attention and a significant drop in the company's share price. In the past, Facebook had claimed that it was not responsible for how the application was used by people or companies. The scandal revealed that public and political opinion was that Facebook should be held at least partially accountable.

Facebook is a complex application with a wide variety of potential uses. The scandal revealed that even Facebook was not aware of the full extent of these uses or how users might react to concerns over the privacy of their information, despite the fact that they had posted this information on a public social media platform. The crisis threatened the sustainability of Facebook's current business model, which offers free access to the service in exchange for customer data that is used to inform bespoke advertising campaigns.

Interconnectedness

Events such as the Fukushima Daiichi nuclear disaster highlight the interconnectedness of the modern world. The disaster was caused by a tsunami event that was caused by an earthquake. The disaster damaged the Japanese economy, causing £360 billion of property damage, a significant drop in the value of Japanese financial markets and concerns over the stability of Japanese banks.

The event affected financial markets in other countries and changed energy policy in Japan and countries like Germany. Many similar reactors were closed because of the disaster, causing energy supply problems and energy price increases. Semi-conductor supplies were disrupted worldwide (the main semi-conductor factories were near the reactor), causing disruption to supply chains around the world and affecting production of products like aeroplanes and smartphones.

Interconnectedness can occur across country borders, across markets and across risk types. One risk (a geological event) can affect another (stability of the financial system). One market (the energy market) can affect other markets (the supply of manufacturing goods). An issue in one country can affect other countries, or even the whole world.

Some interconnections can be hard to detect or assess. For example, it is very difficult to predict how financial markets may react to events like a terrorist attack or earthquake. Financial markets are driven by human sentiment and this is affected by many different factors, including the tone of media reporting and public opinion. It is through these hard-to-detect and hard-to-assess interconnections that significant risk exposures may emerge.

Globalisation

Globalisation is the trend of increasing interaction between the various nations and people of the world. Advances in travel and communication technology, coupled with fewer restrictions on international trade and the free movement of people, have all contributed to globalisation.

Globalisation brings many benefits, and has helped to improve economic development around the world but it can also create risks. Risks include:

- cross-cultural misunderstandings, where a product name or marketing campaign may cause offence in certain countries;
- political extremism and even terrorism fuelled by concerns around a loss of regional, national or religious cultural identity;
- unbalanced economic development as labour and capital move to more desirable locations (such as where there is a highly educated and skilled workforce or where labour is relatively cheap);
- national businesses and organisations may find it hard to compete with multi-nationals;
- local IT infrastructures become vulnerable to attacks from around the world;
- protectionism, where governments attempt to insulate their local economy from global market forces; and
- increased levels of complexity and interconnectedness in areas like financial markets.

Globalisation is not a new trend. Ideas and goods have been traded across large areas of the globe for thousands of years, but the pace of globalisation is accelerating, largely due to the internet as well as faster and cheaper air travel.

3. Managing emerging risks

The high degree of uncertainty and unpredictability around emerging risks makes them hard to assess and control. It can be some time before an organisation discovers the existence of an emerging risk. Even when a risk is identified, there may not be sufficient data to assess probability and impact.

Techniques for assessing and controlling emerging risks include:

◆ board level strategic risk assessments;

◆ scenario planning and reverse stress testing;

◆ resilience and reputation risk management; and

◆ fostering a culture of creativity, mindfulness and situation awareness.

3.1 Board level strategic environment emerging risk assessments

Risks often emerge from the broader strategic environment as a result of factors like complexity, interconnectedness and globalisation. The board's knowledge of this environment makes it well placed to identify emerging risks. Board members may have experience in multiple organisations or sectors. They require a good understanding of the broad social, political, legal and economic environment in which the organisation operates to help support its strategy.

One technique that can be used to facilitate a strategic environment emerging risk assessment is a Political, Economic, Social and Technological (PEST) analysis. PEST analysis is a strategic tool that can be adapted to help identify emerging risks. It provides a structure for board level discussions about future trends and developments that may become a source of emerging risk, such as:

◆ political change and uncertainty, such as the risks associated with the UK leaving the EU;

◆ economic growth or recession;

◆ social change such as changing demographics or an aging population, or changes in social opinion about matters ranging from information privacy, the use of plastics or religion; and

◆ technological developments like artificial intelligence and automated decision making.

3.2 Scenario planning and reverse stress testing

Scenario planning is a structured way for organisations to understand their future, as well as the risks and opportunities that may be associated with this future.

Scenario planning can be as simple as a group of people discussing future risks and opportunities. Alternatively, it can be more complex and involve techniques like **systems thinking**. A degree of background and contextual information is useful to help stimulate discussion but large amounts of probability or impact data is not required. Scenario planning is very similar to scenario analysis (see Chapter 9, page 180).

Reverse stress testing is a particular application of stress and scenario testing. The purpose of reverse stress testing is to assess the circumstances under which the organisation will become non-viable. Reverse stress testing helps an

systems thinking
A structured thought process that involves mapping out systems and the relationships between systems, whether IT-based, social, political, economic or other system. The goal of systems thinking is to discover, in a systematic way, a system's dynamics, constraints, conditions and principles (purpose, measure, methods, tools and so on).

organisation to understand its vulnerabilities and how extreme future events may affect its ability to continue as a going concern. By understanding these vulnerabilities, an organisation may be able to better prepare for them and avoid taking decisions that may increase its exposure to these vulnerabilities.

Example reverse stress testing events include:

◆   a financial crisis, similar to the 2007–08 crisis;

◆   a major economic recession or a significant rise in inflation or interest rates;

◆   a major loss of assets (due to a fraud, fire and so on); and

◆   a public relations disaster that severely damages stakeholder confidence in the organisation.

Reverse stress testing events are made as extreme as necessary to determine the point at which an organisation will become non-viable. This will vary according to the balance sheet strength of an organisation and the ambitiousness of its strategic objectives.

Reverse stress testing is undertaken in a variety of organisations and sectors. It is especially common in financial services, where regulators such as the PRA and the Independent Commission on Banking (ICB), require financial institutions to undertake reverse stress testing.

Stop and think 15.1

Look for real world examples of reverse stress tests that are used by financial and non-financial organisations.

Test yourself 15.1

How does reverse stress testing differ from conventional stress testing?

3.3   Current examples of emerging risk

Current examples of emerging risks include:

◆   the networked economy

◆   social media and digital natives

◆   disruptive technologies.

The networked economy
Since the invention of the internet, the modern world has only become more connected. Computers are only the tip of the iceberg when it comes to online-capable devices: nowadays tablets, smartphones, televisions, cars, homes, fridges, toasters and coffee machines can all connect to the internet.

The growth in devices and appliances connected to the internet has resulted in what is called 'the internet of things'. The objective of the internet of things is to make our lives easier and more convenient. Milk or bin bags are ordered automatically when supplies are low. Homes are heated and monitored from a distance. Cars update their software automatically and react to changing traffic conditions while providing access to hands-free communication and music streaming services.

Organisational benefits from the internet of things include improved customer service, supply chain and operational efficiency and new forms of collective working via file sharing, video conferencing and augmented reality.

New risks have emerged with the growth of the 'internet of things'. Cloud-based computing creates new data security and integrity challenges. Hackers look for vulnerabilities in devices like homes, TVs and fridges, which may not be as protected as traditional computers. Fraudsters may be able to exploit security weaknesses to obtain financial rewards.

Social media and digital natives

Many people rely on social media to conduct their personal relationships, including any relationships they may have with work colleagues and organisations. Social media use has led to a range of new risks relating to:

◆ personal privacy and the security of personal identity;

◆ fake news; and

◆ social media reputation storms where videos, events and opinions may be spread around the world in a few hours.

Most people under 30 have grown up only knowing a world with the internet and associated technologies: today's children and teenagers do not remember a time when social media did not exist. Individuals born from the 1990s onwards are known as 'digital natives'. Research into the values and beliefs of digital natives has revealed that they have different attitudes to the use of social media and the nature of privacy. Digital natives are comfortable conducting their lives over the internet and are more likely to share personal, even sensitive, information and opinions via social media platforms.

One key risk that has emerged with the growth in digital natives is cyber bullying. This is where social media is used to bully individuals and groups. Cyber bullying is not restricted to schools and colleges. Organisations also have to address cyber bullying in the workplace.

Disruptive technologies

New technology like smartphones, the internet and social media have led to the emergence of disruptive technologies that threaten established organisations and business models. Examples include:

◆ crowdfunding to replace traditional finance via a financial institution;

◆ peer-to-peer lending;

◆ app-based product ordering and payment services;

◆ transportation (Uber);

◆ three-dimensional printing, which can include printing cars, houses and firearms; and

◆ price comparison services.

Disruptive technologies create strategic risks for established organisations who may find that they are superseded by new entrants that are better able to exploit modern technology. Organisations that try to exploit disruptive technologies can experience a range of implementation risks including legal challenges, hacking attacks, system failures or operational risks, especially if the organisation grows too fast for its operational processes.

Stop and think 15.2

Look for real world examples of risk events that have affected organisations which are linked to the above three examples of emerging risks.

Test yourself 15.2

What is an emerging risk? Provide three current examples of emerging risks.

4. Changing knowledge and skills

Human capital is one of the most important intangible assets an organisation has. These are the people who will be making decisions and driving business strategy in an increasingly turbulent business environment.

Attracting the right talent (skilled, educated and adaptable employees) should be a key priority of the senior management team and the board. In fact, talent management is a business strategy in itself. Over the last decade, there have been a number of structural changes in the workspace in general:

◆ With increased globalisation and advances in technology, more and more low to mid-level jobs are being outsourced to emerging markets or computers. For example, a number of studies suggest that London will lose one-third of such jobs in the next 20 years, specifically highlighting jobs such as retail, storage and transportation being at the highest risk of automation. Specialist jobs such as doctors and teachers are seen to be less at risk, although a certain level of disruption is expected.

◆ Rapid advances in technology requires continuous employee training in order to remain agile and up-to-date with the latest business intelligence tools.

◆ Millennials – who now account for the largest segment in the workforce – demand a purposeful and personalised type of employment.

◆   Reporting structures within organisations have become flatter in order to encourage innovation.

◆   The drive for diversity has created more inclusive working environments.

◆   With a significant increase in the use of flexible working arrangements and higher mobility of people in general, organisations have to rethink how they remotely manage and train their employees.

In addition, the gap between skills possessed by employees and the skills required by organisations is becoming wider. Employees' skills and experience are becoming less valuable faster than in the past, due to the speed of change in internal and external environmental business factors.

4.1   In-demand skills

With rapid advances in technology and a shift towards digital culture, skills like data science, application development, cloud computing, digital marketing and advanced statistical modelling are in demand.

In addition, many roles increasingly combine a need for in-depth specialist knowledge and an aptitude for 'big picture thinking'. Personality traits such as attitude, motivation, curiosity, collaboration, adaptability and agility are greatly sought after by prospective employers.

4.2   Talent sourcing

The traditional recruitment model involved organisations seeking applicants for base-level entry roles and then gradually promote them internally. Having 'a job for life' was common. However, as people have become more mobile, employee turnover rates have increased dramatically – even in organisations that offer best-in-class training and development opportunities. This has forced organisations to tap into the market of external candidates across different managerial levels.

The traditional approach of simply advertising a vacant role on its own or through a specialist firm no longer guarantees that this position will be filled in a timely manner. Organisations have realised that hiring talent requires a well-thought-out process and creative sourcing tactics, such as:

◆   making use of social media platforms such as LinkedIn;

◆   forming partnerships with college communities;

◆   organising company insight sessions;

◆   creating talent referral programmes;

◆   building databases of prospective employees before vacancies are available;

◆   redesigning job specs to explain how a particular job opportunity can benefit the applicant instead of focusing on the needs of the employer. As a result, job ads are becoming more personalised and lighter on corporate jargon.

4.3 Talent management

The 'war for talent', a term coined by McKinsey consultants in the late 1990s, is not a new concept. It refers to the highly competitive landscape for attracting and retaining talented employees. Talent has become a form of currency: an intangible asset which directly contributes to an organisation's profits and losses. Talent management conversations now take place at board level. Even so, the skills gap has never been wider, despite organisations spending significant resources to find new talent.

To understand the impact of talent shortages, Manpower Group conducted a survey of 39,195 employers in 43 countries in 2018. The results were quite shocking: 67% of employers (with more than 250 employees) said they cannot find the skills they need. This feedback was consistent across different industries.

This survey also highlighted the fact that talent shortages have been growing over the past few years and are now at a 12-year high, with larger organisations facing greater challenges. The survey listed multiple reasons for why organisations are not able to fill open roles, with 27% of employers saying that applicants either lack professional skills or personal characteristics.

One of the drivers of the skills gap is the need for organisations to redefine jobs more frequently as business requirements change to reflect a new environment. Likewise, organisational talent planning and talent management strategies need to change to remain relevant.

Organisations have realised that short-term 'plug-in' or 'one-size-fits-all' talent solutions are not very effective, as they ignore the need to structurally reconfigure talent needs in a sustainable way. Talent management has therefore become a strategic tool within human resource planning, aimed at creating value by means of aligning the organisation's business strategy with its workforce.

At its core, talent management as a business discipline sees employees as the only assets that innovate in an organisation, and innovation as the only path to sustain long-term performance. Proactively managing talent should create a competitive advantage for the organisation. Furthermore, talent management practices themselves are also meant to be continuously reviewed so that the organisation is able to capitalise on its talented employees in order to grow and expand into new markets.

The key components of talent management are:

◆   strategic employee planning that clearly connects the organisational strategy to talent needs;

◆   talent acquisition and retention that recognises the importance of in-house development;

◆   performance management that aligns the right person with the right role and aligns roles with the strategy;

◆   learning and career development programmes that are aligned with the organisational culture and strategy;

◆ compensation structures that recognise and reward employees based on their contributions towards maximising the long-term value of the organisation;

◆ succession planning that ensures the sustainability of the strategy execution process.

Talent management programmes are typically developed and managed by human resources. However, many organisations now employ a designated talent management executive tasked with developing strategies to attract, empower and retain talent. This executive typically has a direct communication line to the board.

4.4 Talent training

Due to the increasing rate at which skills and knowledge become outdated, it is essential that organisations understand the importance of continuous training and development programmes in the workplace. Although expensive, training offers an opportunity to expand the knowledge base of all employees for the benefit of improved performance, job satisfaction and morale.

Employees who receive formal training are more confident, engaged and better able to perform their roles. Better performance increases productivity and reduces employee turnover which benefits the overall organisation. It enhances the organisation's reputation and profile, which in turn makes it easier for this organisation to attract top talent.

Corporate mentoring schemes are an increasingly popular way to engage and train employees. It gives more senior employees an opportunity to give back to the organisation and be directly involved in developing talent, while mentees benefit from valuable advice and access to important networks.

Some organisations also promote reverse mentoring initiatives, in which senior executives are mentored by younger employees on topics such as new technology and media trends. Jack Welch, former CEO of General Electric, has been widely credited with helping to promote reverse mentoring, when he committed himself and other senior executives to reverse training sessions dedicated to the internet in the 1990s.

Over the past few years, blended learning – a combination of classroom learning and online training – has become a popular and more affordable option for developing employees.

4.5 Talent risk management frameworks

Talent risk is a business risk. Talent risk management is the process of assessing the organisation's employee needs and its hiring capacity, compared to what skills are available internally and externally.

This process typically begins with an assessment of the business need for specific skills given the organisation's strategy. This can be due to an urgent need or a part of a long-term planning process. Residual talent risk should then be prioritised, mitigated, measured and monitored.

The central elements of talent risk assessment focus on organisational and employees' alignment, capability, cost, capacity, connection and compliance. Issues include:

◆ Potential misalignments between the current business strategy and the available internal talent pool.

◆ The ability to develop talent internally in order to meet future needs, including the breadth and depth of skills, qualities and unrealised potential of current employees.

◆ The cost of developing the existing workforce versus hiring external talent, including whether overall cost of the existing workforce is appropriate given the organisation's long-term strategy goals.

◆ The identification of critical roles, the retention of critical employees and the risks surrounding the succession into these roles. This includes considerations such as the ability to obtain required regulatory approvals. For example, organisations regulated by the FCA have to comply with the 'Approved Persons' regulation. This requires all employees who perform a governing function to seek a regulatory approval to become an 'approved person'.

◆ The risk of an organisation's top talent becoming disengaged, possibly due to a lack of cross-functional training opportunities, weak emotional connection with the company's leadership or lack of belief in the organisational mission.

◆ The risk of employees participating in talent programmes not complying with relevant laws and regulations.

For example, a US company may be looking to expand to the UK market in the next two to three years. This means the company must undertake a risk assessment of its talent to understand who it can source internally and who it will have to hire externally. Given that the project is two to three years away, the company may decide to launch a specialised training programme or prioritise certain training programmes over another to create a bigger pool of internal candidates. This reduces the cost of looking for senior executives externally. The company can also conduct an external market scan to evaluate the cost of 'plugging the gap' between internal candidates and the number of employees required to successfully execute the expansion.

4.6 The workforce of the future

Automation and artificial intelligence technologies are changing the nature of work. Certain skills are becoming obsolete in favour of new skills of the future as employees increasingly interact with machines in the workplace.

A 2018 survey by McKinsey concluded that advanced technologies will require people who understand how these technologies work and can be improved. Occupations such as data scientists, IT professionals and programmers, technology designers, engineers, advanced technology maintenance workers and scientific researchers will be in demand in the next few years. On the other hand, jobs that are built around skills such as basic data input and processing are expected to decline.

Organisations will need to execute multiple complex restructurings in order to adapt to the new digital world. In addition, demand for social and emotional skills such as entrepreneurship, leadership and managing others, as well as cognitive skills such as creativity, critical thinking and decision making will also increase.

4.7 The role of the board

The board plays a key role in overseeing the implementation of appropriate talent strategies and managing talent risks as per the overall business objectives.

This role should not be underestimated. A 2016 KPMG survey identified senior leaders' lack of interest in connecting and engaging with their employees, poorly designed performance management processes, an insufficient budget for managing and developing talent and a weak future leadership pipeline as key contributors to talent gaps.

The board should ensure that the organisation has an effective and robust talent management process in place which is capable of delivering value for stakeholders. Talent management oversight should not be delegated to management. To more effectively oversee talent risks, the board should ensure that:

◆ the organisation has an effective talent risk assessment and management framework in place. This framework should cover business, reputational, regulatory and compliance risks that are related to talent;

◆ the organisation has incorporated contingency planning and crisis management scenarios within its talent management framework, such as the sudden departure or illness or death of critical employees, poaching of entire critical teams by competitors and so on;

◆ Board members should have a direct oversight of how the CEO's and executive members' compensation packages are structured relative to overall strategy and performance;

◆ senior leadership should be directly accountable for the execution of talent strategies;

◆ issues such as diversity (gender, ethnicity, nationality and age) and pay gaps should be incorporated within the talent management framework;

◆ the organisation should maintain a strong leadership pipeline with a succession planning process in place;

◆ board members should have regular access to talent-related KPIs and risk discussions;

◆ The board should appoint a designated talent management director or executive to address talent-related issues and risks.

It is essential that the board understands and receives assurance from management that the talent risk is being proactively assessed, monitored and managed. These risks will only become more important as the business world becomes more complex and interconnected.

5. Digital transformation

Digital transformation is the modernisation of an organisation's internal and external processes using the latest technology. Reaching out to consumers by digital marketing is an example of an external process, whereas using cloud technology to store and process data is an example of an internal process.

As well as being a source of emerging risk, advances in technology provide significant opportunities for enhancing risk management practices in organisations.

5.1   Big data

With the development of computers, the internet and social media, the volume of data that are available for analysis has grown exponentially. New data collection, aggregation and visualisation techniques have been developed to help cope with the volume and variety of available data. The term 'big data' is used to refer to these techniques. Big data incorporates:

1. The analysis of extremely large and complex data sets, which cannot be analysed using traditional data analysis techniques (statistics and relational databases).
2. Techniques for coping with rapid changes in data (social media trends).
3. The use of data collection algorithms to 'mine' data. These algorithms look for hidden patterns and relationships between variables and sources of data.
4. The analysis of quantitative and qualitative data, including social media tone and trends.
5. Tools for visualising complex relationships between data sources.
6. Behavioural analysis to investigate human attitudes and sentiment.
7. Predictive analysis to identify future trends in human behaviour.

From a risk management perspective, big data can be used to help identify and assess risks, especially emerging risks where there is comparatively little statistical data on probability or impact. It can also be used to help identify connections and correlations between risks.

Stop study 15.2

Big data and the Scottish independence referendum

Just before the vote on Scottish independence in 2014, the BoE was preparing to pump money into the Scottish banking system to help mitigate the risk of capital flight from Scotland. The Bank of England was concerned that, in the event of a yes vote, confidence in the Scottish economy might be lost and capital would flow out of Scotland. This was because the Westminster government had ruled out a single currency should Scotland declare independence, as well as concerns over the creditworthiness of an independent Scotland.

To help determine whether or not to inject cash into the Scottish economy, the BoE used big data techniques to monitor both financial markets and social media feeds. The BoE was looking for patterns in the data that might indicate capital flight, such as adverse social media commentary on the Scottish economy that could be linked to financial market movements.

5.2 Automated decision making

Automated decision making is where decisions are made by a computer rather than a human. Automated decision making can be used to reduce costs and to speed up decision-making processes.

Automated decisions can be used to support risk management decision making. For example, a computer might decide to turn on a sprinkler system in the event of a fire or it may decide to trade stocks and shares on financial markets to exploit price increases or falls. Computers can do this faster than a human decision maker, potentially saving lives or generating higher investment returns.

There are threats as well as opportunities with automated decision making. The advantages and disadvantages, and governance and compliance implications, are explored below.

Automated decisions may be based on decision algorithms that are pre-programmed by human operators or they may be given greater levels of freedom as part of an artificially intelligent system.

Algorithmic decision making

Algorithmic decision making is where a human operator provides a system with one or more programmed responses to specific situations, such as activating a sprinkler system when heat or smoke is detected for more than a few seconds. Algorithmic decision making is used in the prevention of fraud and financial crime to detect and block suspicious transactions.

Algorithmic decision may be limited to one simple response or a series of responses to a variety of situations. Human operators set the parameters but are not required to be present at all times. Algorithmic systems are usually closely monitored and human intervention is possible where necessary.

Artificial intelligence

Decision-making systems that use artificial intelligence (AI) have greater decision-making autonomy. Artificial intelligence systems are often combined with big data techniques to support the collection and processing of large amounts of data.

Artificial intelligence decision systems are in their infancy but they are used to manage market risks within financial markets. In this context, AI systems monitor financial market movements for patterns that can be exploited for profit. These systems do not require monitoring by human operators but it is possible to do so and for humans to intervene where necessary. Human monitoring may become harder as the complexity of AI systems increase.

Advantages and disadvantages

The primary advantage of automated decision making are speed and consistency. Decisions can be made faster than a human operator, as well as when operators are not available.

The speed of automated decisions is particularly important in the case of market risk management. Investments can be bought or sold very quickly, allowing the system to be one of the first to take advantage of any rise or fall in price.

In the case of AI-supported automated decisions, it is possible for computers to process data much more quickly and to spot more complex patterns and relationships in the data. The human brain is far more adaptable than that of a computer but slower and less capable of spotting complex data trends. This can further speed up decision making.

Errors in decision making are the main problem with automated decision systems. In the case of algorithmic decision making, this is likely to be caused by human error when programming the decision algorithm. For example, a HR manager developing a candidate assessment and elimination algorithms may unconsciously introduce gender or graduation school preferences into the algorithm, rather than prioritising skills needs. In the case of AI-supported decisions. It could be that the computer makes its own mistakes based on any flaws or limitations in its ability to learn.

Whether automated decisions are algorithmic or AI-supported, it is vital that human operators monitor these decisions and intervene if necessary to ensure that mistakes are not made. This can be difficult where automated decisions are made very quickly or where humans struggle to see the patterns and trends in the data that an AI system can see. There are no solutions to this problem to date.

Governance and compliance implications

Most legal and regulatory regimes are based on the notion of human agency – where humans are responsible for their own decisions and actions, individually or as a collective (a board of directors, for example).

The assumption of human agency and responsibility becomes less reliable with the automation of decision making. It is possible to identify the human element in the case of algorithmic decisions but this is less clear for AI decision systems.

One current area of focus is on data protection laws. In the UK, Ireland and the rest of the EU, the GDPR includes articles relating to automated decision making and the automated profiling of personal data to evaluate individuals (such as for the purposes of marketing or political canvassing). Where an organisation uses automated decision making and profiling, they are required to:

◆ make the use of these systems clear to stakeholders;

◆ allow stakeholders to challenge automated decisions and to require human intervention – challenging the automated refusal of credit, for example; and

◆ carry out regular checks to ensure that systems are working as intended.

Stop and think 15.3

Identify one organisation that uses big data and one that uses automated or AI decision making.

Relevant sectors include: online retail, banking and credit cards, telecommunications, food retailers, restaurant chains and entertainment streaming services.

Test yourself 15.3

Provide a definition of 'big data'. How can big data be managed?

5.3   Other new technologies

There are a number of other rapidly emerging technologies which are also having a major impact on business and wider society. These include:

◆ *Blockchain technology* centralises data records in real-time in a verifiable and permanent way. It offers multiple opportunities, including faster and more efficient payment processing, money transfers and securities settlement services, a more effective management of supply chains and retail loyalty reward programmes, digital voting capabilities, ability to optimise paper trail processes such as real estate, land and vehicle title transfers, and more besides.

◆ *Quantum computing* utilises quantum-mechanical phenomena such as superposition and entanglement to perform computation, empowering machine learning by enabling artificial intelligence programmes to search through large-scale databases consisting of consumer behaviour surveys, financial market records and medical research;

◆ *Robo-advisor technology* offers low-cost digital consumer service with little or no human interaction. A number of financial services and tourism businesses use this technology to service their clients.

◆ *Facial recognition systems* are capable of identifying or verifying a person from a digital image or a video frame. It is extensively used by businesses conducting payment processing, security solutions and medical diagnosis.

◆ *Voice or speaker recognition* understands and carries out spoken commands. This technology is widely used in the consumer space to enable hands-free requests such as playing a specific music video or turning consumer appliances on and off.

◆ *Augmented reality* offers an opportunity to experience a real-world environment where the objects are augmented by computer-generated perceptual information. This technology can be used by a furniture distributor to help its consumers to visualise a specific item within their home environment;

◆   *Self-driving software* is the application of artificial intelligence technologies to enable autonomous vehicles that can be controlled, navigated and driven without a human operator.

Organisations face difficult choices in this environment. Do they embrace every new technology at a price of high cost and potentially irrelevance, or incur the risk that rejecting one of these new technologies will make them unprofitable or even extinct in the long run?

5.4   Managing risks in a digital world

Embracing digital transformation is a way for organisations to increase their value. On the flip side, organisations that ignore digital transformation are at risk of having their value significantly eroded and, in some cases, completely destroyed. A digital transformation strategy is a necessity for organisations. This involves not only embracing new technologies, but also understanding how these technologies affect consumer behaviours. This requires a shift in corporate culture.

One industry that has been significantly affected by digital transformation is the publishing business. The circulations of 'old media' paper newspapers have fallen significantly around the world due to the availability of news through the internet. Newspaper companies that did not embrace online publishing at an early stage are either extinct or struggling.

New businesses automatically have an advantage over established players because most start-ups do not need to consider digital transformation; it is already embedded in their DNA. For example, companies like Airbnb and Deliveroo based their business models on mobile technology, rather than adapting a legacy model to new technology.

The new digital economy is built on the following 12 pillars:

1.   *Knowledge*: knowledge is the key driver, with organisations increasingly focusing on attracting and retaining high calibre human capital.

2.   *Globalisation*: knowledge has no boundaries and enables organisations to become global players much faster.

3.   *Digitalisation*: knowledge can be easily stored and moved around the globe in a matter of seconds; customers can also be reached in new and more rapid ways.

4.   *Integration and online working*: organisations are flattening their hierarchical structures in order to stay agile and speed up decision making processes.

5.   *Disintermediation*: technology reduces the reliance of organisations on a traditional middleman to connect to their customers.

6.   *Convergence*: communication, computing and content are all converging to create an interactive multimedia environment.

7.   *Innovation*: the new economy is powered by innovation and disruption.

8.   *Virtualisation*: organisations can convert tangible assets into virtual resources.

9. *Immediacy*: customers in the new economy are more informed, demanding faster and more personalised service and solutions.

10. *Prosumption*: the distinctions between producers and customers are breaking down, with customers directly shaping products through real-time feedback.

11. *Molecularisation*: traditional organisational structures are moving towards a more flexible work environment.

12. *Discordance*: there is always resistance to change, with some parties adapting slowly. The gap between the technologically literate 'haves' and the 'have-nots' is growing.

5.5 Digital risks

Risk management frameworks and techniques must be redesigned to avoid unintended consequences of digital transformation. Digital risks can be split into four key types:

◆ The risk that an emerging technology will significantly impact the future profitability of an organisation:

- Organisations should look out for structurally disruptive technologies that can put their business models and future revenue generation capabilities at risk.

◆ The risk that new technologies are adopted too early or are irrelevant to the business model of the organisation, resulting in significant costs and very little benefits:

- Organisations should be mindful of the development and/or integration costs versus monetary benefits and organisational culture readiness. Organisations should carefully evaluate all the alternatives in the context of short-term and long-term strategy.

◆ The risk that the newly adopted technologies create additional risks for the organisation that are not well understood and/or properly captured within the existing risk management framework:

- Organisations should assess the ability of their current risk management framework to capture risks arising from the integration of new technology. For example, implementation of new workspace-sharing technologies to increase productivity can introduce new cyber-security risks and challenges that may require new risk mitigation techniques.

◆ The risk that the new digital economy enables almost immediate dissemination of negative information globally through various sources that cannot be effectively managed or controlled, and that this information can remain in the form of a digital record forever:

- Growing interconnectivity and news travelling at a speed of light, it is becoming an ever more challenging task for organisations to manage reputational risk.

5.6 The role of the board

Board members need to understand that traditional risk management techniques alone are not sufficient to deal with risks arising from the digital age.

Organisations are operating in an environment where a teenager can completely shut down the operational system of a major corporation from the comfort of their home, where an iconic consumer brand can disappear in seconds and where a small start-up is able to secure a substantial market share for minimal investment. Board responsiveness to emerging threats has never been more important

Good governance and regular discussions around emerging risks that arise in the face of digital transformation are essential activities. Transforming organisational agility and culture, and putting risk management at the heart of decision making must also be a top priority for any organisation and its board members.

Chapter summary

◆ Emerging risks may be completely new or a significant change in the nature or exposure to an existing risk. Emerging risks are characterised by high levels of uncertainty, meaning that it can be very difficult to precisely assess the nature of these risks including the probability of occurrence and level of impact.

◆ Emerging risks are emerging faster and more often. This is linked to increasing levels of environmental complexity, economic, social and technological interconnectedness and globalisation.

◆ Emerging risks may be identified and assessed using techniques like scenario analysis, reverse stress testing and PEST analysis.

◆ Current examples of emerging risk events include the networked economy, social media and disruptive technologies.

◆ With increased globalisation and advances in technology, organisations spend more resources to attract and retain their talent. Talent risk management frameworks help organisations to forecast, prioritise and manage their talent gaps according to the strategy.

◆ The board plays a key role in overseeing the execution of appropriate talent strategies, and that talent risks are managed as per the overall business objectives.

◆ With the development of computers, the internet and social media the volumes of data available for analysis have grown exponentially. New data collection, aggregation and visualisation techniques have been developed to help cope with the volume and variety of data that is available. The term 'big data' is used to refer to these techniques.

◆ Automated decisions can be used to support risk management decision making. Computers may be able to do this faster than a human decision maker, potentially saving lives or generating higher investment returns.

- Automated decisions may be human-controlled via algorithms or more independent using AI systems. Automated decisions speed up decision making. Artificial intelligence systems can cope with complex data trends and relationships that humans cannot process.

- There are risks with using automated decision making and automated decisions can go wrong. Regulators are only just starting to address the governance and compliance implications of automated decision making.

- The 21st century has brought with it unprecedented technological growth and new types of risks. These risks are forcing organisations to re-evaluate their current business models and adopt new technologies to increase organisational productivity and effectiveness.

Test yourself answers

Chapter 1

Test yourself 1.1

Identify the key risks that the following stakeholder groups will wish to have managed effectively:
- *creditors*
- *customers*
- *employees.*

Creditors are primarily exposed to the risk that an organisation will default on its loan repayments. This will mean a loss of some of or the entire loan amount, plus the loss of interest payments.

Customers face three possible risks – the risk of injury as a result of their use of products or services, the failure of a product or service (such as a breakdown) and the loss of a guarantee or warranty. Guarantees and warranties may be lost if an organisation goes bankrupt.

Employees face health and safety-related risks, plus the loss of their economic livelihood in the event that an organisation becomes bankrupt or has to make staff redundant due to unforeseen losses.

Test yourself 1.2

Explain the conflict of interest that can exist between shareholders and creditors.

The primary conflict of interest that can exist between shareholders and creditors relates to their preference for short-term profits. Creditors need organisations to make a positive return in order to pay back a loan with the agreed rate of interest. However, creditors will not want organisations to chase short-term profits at the expense of the long-term viability of the organisation. In contrast, shareholders may value short-term profits more, since this will provide them with larger dividend payments. It may also result in an increase in the value of their shares, which they might then sell for a profit before the share price is hit by any adverse risk events.

Test yourself 1.3

Explain why the existence of asymmetric information may require risk management regulation.

Asymmetric information between the organisation and its stakeholders may mean that stakeholders are less able to assess the level of risk that they are being exposed to by the organisation (such as the level of risk associated with being an employee or consumer). Stakeholders may be exposed to excessive amounts of risk because they cannot properly price the cost of risk into their relationship with the firm (such as their salary or the price they pay for a product or service).

Test yourself 1.4

Identify the reasons why international environmental risk management regulation is needed.

International environmental risk management regulation is needed to help ensure that environmental risk events in one country do not affect stakeholders in other nations.

Events such as air, river or maritime pollution can quickly spread across national borders. Issues like excessive CO_2 production are proven to cause global warming, a major international problem that requires co-ordinated risk management regulation.

Furthermore, a level playing field should be created so that companies that do not have to adhere to stricter regulation cannot undercut the ones that do, thus introducing unfair competition.

Test yourself 1.5

Why is an international standard on risk management needed?

An international standard primarily helps to share good risk management practice from around the globe. An international standard is also needed because organisational stakeholders may come from around the world, and because organisations are becoming more international.

Chapter 2

Test yourself 2.1

Corporate governance is concerned with how organisations are directed and controlled. Explain how risk management can be used to support the control and direction of organisations.

In terms of how organisations are controlled, effective risk management should help an organisation to achieve its strategic objectives. Many risks may affect the achievement of an organisation's objectives. These might be external risks such as political or technical change; they may also be internal risks, such as systems and process failures; or people-related risks such as misconduct, negligence, fraud and so on. Risk management provides a range of tools and techniques that organisations can use to identify, assess, monitor and ultimately control these risks to ensure that they do not disrupt the achievement of an organisation's objectives, whatever they are (profit, social or environmental objectives and so on).

In terms of how organisations are directed, effective risk management can help organisations to make better strategic decisions. All organisations need a strategy to help them create value into the long term. Developing an appropriate strategy will involve exploiting opportunities and avoiding highly damaging risks. In both cases, an organisation needs to understand the risks to which it is exposed, their significance and its ability to manage these risks. Organisations should be able to develop a strategy that helps them to exploit the best possible opportunities, while remaining a going concern.

Test yourself 2.2

Explain the advantages and disadvantages of a 'comply or explain' approach to corporate governance regulation.

The primary advantage of a 'comply or explain' approach is that it allows organisations a degree of flexibility when deciding how to implement specific regulations.

Organisations often differ in size, organisational structure, corporate form and ownership (public or private limited companies), stakeholder needs, strategic objectives and so on. This means that a single set of prescriptive rules may not be appropriate for all organisations. It may even create unnecessary compliance costs.

A 'comply or explain' approach also makes the board and associated senior management responsible for deciding how to comply. Prescriptive approaches can hinder creativity and lead to a 'tick box' style of corporate governance and risk management.

However, the 'comply or explain' may also allow organisations to avoid complying with specific regulations to the detriment of their stakeholders. A 'comply or explain' approach can only work where stakeholders have the necessary skills and authority to assess compliance and enforce change where necessary. This may not always be the case. Organisations may also find that 'comply or explain' approaches create uncertainty. It may be hard for an organisation to decide not to comply when it is unsure how stakeholders will react.

Test yourself 2.3

What are the main risk management related principles within the UK Corporate Governance Code?

The main risk management principles are as follows:

◆   Boards are responsible for identifying, assessing and controlling the principal risks to which an organisation is exposed.

◆ Boards, in particular the NEDs, are responsible for ensuring that effective risk management and internal control systems are in place. This will include regular monitoring of these systems and a formal review of effectiveness at least annually.

◆ A board audit committee or a separate board risk committee should normally be in place.

◆ Information on the organisation's principal risks and the soundness of its risk management and internal control systems should be provided in the annual report.

◆ The board's work on risk management should include consideration of the organisation's appetite for risk, as well as embedding the desired risk culture.

Test yourself 2.4

Why do organisations like the EU and OECD need to provide regulations on corporate governance and risk management?

As markets, organisations and their stakeholders become globalised, there is a need to ensure consistent corporate governance arrangements around the world. Organisations operating in countries with comparatively weak corporate governance and related risk management regulations can have significant negative effects on organisations, stakeholders and markets in other countries and make for an uneven playing field. The global financial crisis is an example of this.

Effective corporate governance and related risk management regulations also help to raise the quality of management in organisations. This should support global value creation and stakeholder equality. For example, effective regulation should help to prevent managerial opportunism and misconduct, which may lead to the loss of financial capital, health and safety risk events, environmental risk events or some other form of exploitation (for example, human rights violations).

Test yourself 2.5

What are the problems with a voluntary corporate governance code?

Voluntary codes are not legally enforceable, either via criminal or civil sanction. This means that where an organisation chooses not to comply with some or all of the contents of a voluntary code, stakeholders may not be able to take effective enforcement action. The ability of stakeholders to take action will depend on the degree of market power that they possess. For example, large institutional shareholders that hold a significant percentage of company shares may be able to enforce compliance with voluntary codes via a vote at an annual general meeting or by simply threatening to sell their shares and devalue the company. Minority shareholders will have much less power. Other stakeholder groups may find it hard to take enforcement action (such as employees concerned about their health and safety or creditors concerned about loan repayment) where an organisation is large and powerful.

Chapter 3

Test yourself 3.1

Which organisations does the ECB regulate?

The ECB regulates systemically important financial institutions whose operations are located within any country that is a member of the Eurozone.

A systemically important financial institution is any bank, insurance company or other financial institution whose failure may affect the stability of the financial system and potentially trigger a financial crisis. Most large banks, insurers and investment firms are systemically important.

Test yourself 3.2

Compare and contrast the objectives of the PRA and FCA.

The objectives of each regulator are summarised in the following table:

PRA	FCA
To promote the financial safety and soundness of the firms it regulates	Consumer protection
For insurers, securing an appropriate degree of protection for existing and potential future policyholders	Protect the integrity of financial markets from misconduct
Facilitate effective competition	Promote competition in financial markets to ensure that consumers get a fair deal

These objectives are very similar, but there are differences. The PRA is primarily focused on prudential regulation and the FCA on conduct of business regulation. In other words, the PRA is focused on financial stability and the FCA is focused on ensuring that consumers are protected against misconduct on the part of financial institutions. Sometimes these two areas of focus can conflict. For example, the PPI mis-selling compensation provided to consumers ensures that they get a fair deal, but the costs involved could potentially threaten financial soundness.

Test yourself 3.3

Why are market-based incentives for health and safety risk management often thought to be insufficient?

Market based incentives such as wages or prices may be insufficient because of asymmetric information and public good problems.

Asymmetric information between the organisation and its stakeholders may mean that these stakeholders are unable to assess the level of health and safety risk to which they are exposed by the organisation. Stakeholders may be exposed to excessive amounts of risk because they cannot properly price the cost of risk into their relationship with the firm (their salary or the price they pay for a product or service). This problem can be particularly acute in longer term (known as latent) health and safety risks, such as exposure to cancer-causing chemicals.

Public good problems arise where the costs associated with exposure to health and safety risks are not fully internalised by the organisation and its more immediate stakeholders such as consumers and employees. Third parties (such as local residents) may be exposed to health and safety risks as a result of pollution, but they have no market mechanism available to help them obtain compensation for such risks. Legal liability claims do not count as a market mechanism, as they rely on laws and regulations to make then enforceable.

Test Yourself 3.4

Describe the regulatory powers of a typical environmental regulator.

Environmental regulators have a range of roles. They typically have the authority to:

- issue rules and guidance on the management of environmental risks
- ensure that the activities of organisations do not breach any international treaties that the country has signed up to (such as carbon dioxide emissions)
- inspect the premises of organisations
- licence activities that may be a source of environmental risk (such as chemical use)
- take enforcement action (issuing fines, for example).

Chapter 4

Test yourself 4.1

Should every organisation implement an identical risk management framework?

The short answer to this question is no. Organisations differ in terms of the nature, scale and complexity of their activities. Even organisations of a similar size or from the same sector may implement risk management frameworks that are designed differently. Many factors will influence the design of a framework. This might include:

- the structure and reporting lines of the organisation;
- its culture;
- the human and financial resources it has available; or
- the regulations with which it is expected to comply.

That said most organisations should make use of elements such as the risk management process and should generally have a risk management policy and risk reporting arrangements.

Test yourself 4.2

Why should an organisation follow the principles and guidance within ISO 31000?

ISO 31000 is not a regulatory document. Organisations are not required to comply with the standards that it contains.

ISO 31000 provides a universal benchmark for risk management practice. Organisations that choose to use the standard can use it to identify gaps between their current risk management framework and the good practice provided in the standard.

An ISO 31000 gap analysis that is accompanied by action planning will help to improve the effectiveness of an organisation's risk management practices. This should enhance the operational and financial performance of the organisation and deliver value to its stakeholders.

Test yourself 4.3

What type of organisation is the Orange Book aimed at?

The Orange Book is aimed at government organisations and departments but it contains much that is of use to other types of organisation. The Orange Book's approach to risk management is relatively simple, so it is less useful for large complex organisations. Small to medium-sized organisations may find much that is of use.

Test yourself 4.4

Explain how exposure to risk may prevent an organisation from achieving its objectives.

All organisations have objectives. They might be business objectives such as increasing profit or market share, or they may be social and environmental objectives, such as delivering a local public service or protecting the environment.

Risk events which occur may have a variety of adverse consequences. There may be financial losses, due to the damage or destruction of assets, or people may have been killed or injured. In addition, an organisation may find that its normal operations are disrupted or that it suffers bad publicity and reputation damage.

All of these adverse consequences may affect an organisation's ability to meet its objectives. The replacement of lost or damaged assets will hit organisational cash flows and profitability, reputation damage might lead a loss in demand for the organisation's products or business disruption may prevent the organisation from producing sufficient quantities of its goods and services.

Test yourself 4.5

Why are governance processes included as part of the COBIT 5 IT risk management framework?

Any risk management framework needs governance processes to be effective. These processes ensure that the framework is implemented fully and consistently by the organisation's managers and employees. They also ensure that the framework considers the needs of the organisation's stakeholders.

In addition, governance processes help to ensure that a risk management framework remains up to date through regular effectiveness reviews, audits and the identification and implementation of framework enhancements.

Chapter 5

Test yourself 5.1

How are risk and uncertainty linked?

The terms risk and uncertainty are often used interchangeably. Both describe a situation where a decision or action may result in two or more outcomes.

The term risk is generally used where it is possible to assign probability and impact values to these outcomes. Uncertainty arises where there is no data to allow the estimation of probability and impact.

In reality, there are very few situations within an organisational context where the probabilities and impacts of the outcomes associated with risky activities or decisions are known with complete confidence. This does not mean that there is only uncertainty, but there are degrees of uncertainty. The concept of the confidence interval allows us to express the degree of uncertainty.

Test yourself 5.2

Provide three examples of pure risk and three examples of speculative risk in organisations.

The table below lists some examples.

Pure risks	Speculative risks
Injury at work	Research and development
Pollution of any kind	Mergers and acquisitions
Production of faulty products	Major change projects, such as implementing a new IT system
Fires, floods and so on	Fluctuations in consumer demand
IT systems failure	Economic cycle (boom or bust)

You will notice that the pure risk examples tend to be much more specific than the speculative ones. This is because it is usually necessary to frame risks in a restrictive way in order to create pure risks. The risk of injury is part of the wider operational processes of an organisation and these processes may result in both positive and negative outcomes. Some of these negative outcomes could be worker injuries.

Test yourself 5.3

What is the purpose of classifying risks using the common categorisation approach?

Categorising risk helps an organisation to understand the range of risks to which it may be exposed. It also supports the management of risk: different types of risk may require different management approaches.

Test yourself 5.4

What risk perception factors may cause decision makers to underestimate the level of risk?

The following risk perceptions may cause risks to be overestimated:

◆   voluntarily choosing to take a risk;

◆   feeling in control of a risk activity (such as driving);

◆   being familiar with a risk because it has been taken before; and

◆   the ultimate outcome associated with taking a risk is a long way in the future (smoking risks, for example).

Chapter 6

Test yourself 6.1

What is a black swan event?

A black swan event is an event or occurrence that deviates beyond what is normally expected of a situation and is extremely difficult to predict. The term was popularised by Nassim Taleb, a professor of finance and former Wall Street trader. Black swan events are typically random and are unexpected.

Chapter 7

Test yourself 7.1

Provide one-sentence explanations of the following:
• risk identification
• risk assessment
• risk monitoring
• risk control.

◆ Risk identification: activities associated with identifying the actual risks to which an organisation is exposed.

◆ Risk assessment: activities concerned with assessing and prioritising an organisation's exposure to identified risks, in terms of probability and impact.

◆ Risk monitoring: activities used to monitor and report on potential changes in risk exposure or the effectiveness of risk controls and risk management activities in general.

◆ Risk control: application of tools and techniques to manipulate specific risk exposures, in terms of probability and or impact.

Test yourself 7.2

Explain the benefits of ERM for an organisation's board or equivalent governing body.

The benefits of ERM for the board are as follows:

Improved reporting to support strategic decision making	By promoting a holistic understanding of the risks that may affect the organisation boards should be able to make better strategic decisions that balance risk and opportunity.
Improved profitability and organisation value	Better strategic decisions through ERM should ensure that organisations are successful in achieving their objectives. In the case of commercial organisations, this should mean improved profitability and equity values. For non-commercial organisations, it might mean improved surpluses and service delivery. In addition, ERM should be able to further protect profitability/surpluses by helping to reduce the impact that risk may have on the assets and cash flows of an organisation.

Test yourself 7.3

Explain the purpose of drafting an ERM policy

An ERM policy is needed to ensure that risks are managed in a consistent manner across an organisation and that risk exposures are kept within the organisation's exposure to risk. An ERM policy will also be needed to make clear roles and responsibilities for risk management, at an organisation-wide and a local business unit or subsidiary level.

Test yourself 7.4

Compare the role of the company secretary or governance professional with the internal audit function in relation to risk management.

The role of the internal audit function in relationship to risk management is clear – to provide assurance on the effectiveness of the design and implementation of an organisation's risk management process and associated policies, procedures and activities.

The role of the company secretary or governance professional may vary. In some organisations the company secretary or governance professional will have direct responsibility for risk management. In others they will play more of a supporting role.

Where company secretaries have direct responsibility for risk management, they will be involved in the oversight of risk management activities across the organisation. In contrast, internal audit has an assurance role.

Where the company secretary or governance professional is not directly responsible for risk management, their role will move closer to that of audit. However, the company secretary or governance professional will be focused on the role of the board in relation to risk management and ensuring that the board fulfils its risk management responsibilities. This might include conducting board effectiveness reviews, reviews of board member skills and experience in terms of risk management, and advising the board on its risk management responsibilities.

Test yourself 7.5

Contrast the role of the risk function and the finance function in relation to risk management.

The role of the risk function is to oversee, co-ordinate and facilitate risk management activity across an organisation. In fulfilling its role, the risk function will help to write risk management policies and procedures, produce risk reports and provide training and advice to other organisational functions.

The role of the finance function in relation to risk management is to ensure that it manages the risks associated with its activities in a manner that is consistent with an organisation's risk management policy and procedures. It must also ensure that these risks are managed within the organisation's risk appetite. In addition, the finance function will normally provide a range of financial information to the risk function to support risk monitoring and reporting.

Chapter 8

Test yourself 8.1

How are governance, risk and compliance activities complementary?

There are a range of potential examples. Each are related to the following issues:

◆ Weak governance or non-compliance with laws and regulations can create significant risks for organisations. These risks need to be identified, assessed, monitored and controlled using risk management tools and techniques.

◆ Organisations that have risk management frameworks need to ensure that these frameworks are compatible with all applicable laws and regulations (compliance). They also need to ensure that that they meet the needs of their stakeholders (governance) and support the achievement of their objectives. This relates to the design and implementation of risk management frameworks.

Test yourself 8.2

Why are compliance standards needed? When might a degree of compliance of less than 100% be acceptable?

Laws and regulations are rarely 100% prescriptive; this means that organisations will often have a degree of discretion when it comes to deciding how they should comply. In addition, compliance can cost significant amounts in financial and other resources (such as management time). Organisations need to prioritise their limited compliance resources appropriately, especially when strict compliance is not required.

For example, an organisation finds that it has asbestos on its premises, a harmful carcinogenic substance if particles are breathed into the lungs. To eliminate the risk of asbestos exposure, the organisation could remove the asbestos completely or close off the affected area, but such a strategy might be very expensive and may cause significant disruption to its workplace. An alternative but riskier solution is to seal in the asbestos. This type of solution may not be fully effective and a degree of risk will remain, but it may be considered acceptable by the organisation and its regulator on cost and efficiency grounds.

Test yourself 8.3

Assess whether compliance management is the equal responsibility of all employees within an organisation.

All employees should make every effort to comply with internal organisational policies, external laws and regulations but that does not mean that each employee has equal responsibility. In particular, line managers are responsible for ensuring that appropriate incentives are in place to ensure compliance and that their staff have the training and support they need to behave in a compliant manner. An organisation's board has responsibility for overseeing the operation of the whole compliance management framework, supported by the compliance function where present.

If an employee behaves in a non-compliant manner, it is often not their fault. Non-compliance is usually the result of ineffective management or weak organisational compliance management arrangements.

Test yourself 8.4

Compare and contrast the three lines of defence approach with the five lines of assurance.

Both approaches separate front line risk taking and control from risk management oversight and risk management assurance.

The five lines of assurance approach makes more explicit the role of the board, the CEO, other executive directors and senior managers. The five lines of assurance approach also replaces the word defence with assurance. This re-emphasises that risk management is not simply about reducing risk. Risk management is about pursuing risky upside opportunities as much as reducing the risk of downside losses.

Test yourself 8.5

Explain the benefits of implementing a GRC management framework.

Governance, risk and compliance management frameworks help to prevent management of GRC issues in silos. This can help to reduce management time and other resource costs, such as the costs associated with maintaining different governance, risk and compliance IT systems. Governance, risk and compliance management frameworks can also help to create more integrated reporting, allowing managers at all levels to make connections between governance, risk and compliance activities and issues.

Chapter 9

Test yourself 9.1

Compare the costs and benefits of using the judgement of one expert versus a focus group.

Using one expert is cost effective in terms of time. But there is the possibility that the expert might miss something important or that they exhibit some form of perceptual bias (Table 5.1, page 106). Focus groups cost more in terms of time but are more likely to identify all of the relevant risks.

Test yourself 9.2

What is a near miss and why should they be investigated?

Near misses are events that should have resulted in a financial or non-financial loss, but for one reason or another did not. Luck often plays a part in near misses. For example, monies that are lost may be recovered or a serious accident is narrowly averted.

Near misses are important learning opportunities. The next time they occur, an actual loss may be incurred. It is important to learn from the near miss to help prevent future occurrences.

Test yourself 9.3

Provide a definition for emerging risk and two current examples of potential emerging risks.

Emerging risks are either significant new risks, or risks that were known about previously but which were not considered to be significant. Emerging risks are characterised by high levels of uncertainty and may be ignored or underestimated because of this.

Current examples of emerging risks include cyber risks such as ransomware and adverse social media coverage. Other examples are linked to political uncertainty (such as Brexit) and global warming (the rise in severe weather events).

Test yourself 9.4

Compare and contrast the strengths and weaknesses of quantitative and qualitative risk assessment approaches.

Quantitative approaches are more scientific and use statistical methods to ensure consistent and objective assessments of risk. Quantitative approaches are theoretically superior but require large amounts of data which may not be available in practice.

Qualitative approaches do not need data, but they are much more subjective. They can only provide an order of magnitude for probability and impact rather than a precise measurement.

Test yourself 9.5

What are the differences between risk, control and performance indicators?

Risk indicators provide information on an organisation's inherent risk exposures to one or more risks.

Control indicators provide information on the effectiveness of controls. These indicators can help organisations to understand how their residual risk exposures may be changing.

Performance indicators provide information on how efficiently an organisation is operating, indicators may look at financial performance or operational efficiency.

Note that performance indicators may also be risk or control indicators in some circumstances. For example, staff absence rates is a common performance indicator but it may also be a risk indicator. High levels of staff absence will put pressure on systems and processes, increasing the chance of failure.

Chapter 10

Test yourself 10.1

How can using the concept of risk appetite add value to an organisation?

Organisations that determine their appetite for risk should be able to make better strategic and risk management decisions, as well as improve governance and internal control.

Better strategic decisions should mean that an organisation:

◆ does not enter into investments or activities that may expose it to an 'excessive' amount of risk; and

◆ is not overly conservative (stifling innovation or instating excessive bureaucracy) and thereby passing up investments or activities that should add value.

Better risk management decisions should ensure that an organisation can allocate its limited risk management resources more efficiently – targeting them where they are most needed. In addition, it should help to improve buy-in for risk management activities by highlighting the consequences of not maintaining appropriate levels of risk exposure.

Better governance and internal control should come from the fact that decision makers have a clear understanding of the risks that the organisation is willing to take and those that it is not willing to take. This should reduce the chance of making inappropriate risk management decisions.

Test yourself 10.2

Compare and contrast risk appetite, risk tolerance and risk capacity.

Risk appetite denotes the overall level of risk that an organisation is willing to take (or is prepared to accept). Risk appetite may be expressed for an organisation's total exposure to risk, but it is more commonly applied to broad risk categories, such as market risk, credit risk and operational risk.

Risk tolerance is sometimes confused with risk appetite, especially where the focus is on the acceptability of risk. Risk tolerance is more commonly applied to specific types of risk event, such as a tolerance for data inputting errors or customer complaints. It is used to express a clear limit of exposure to risk events that will generally have no upside.

Risk capacity relates to the total maximum level of risk that an organisation can be exposed to before risking its long-term financial viability. The strength of an organisation's balance sheet is a major determinant of risk capacity.

Test yourself 10.3

Why should risk appetite be expressed quantitatively as well as qualitatively?

Not all risks can be quantified. Where categories of risks can be quantified to a degree, it is usually appropriate to have quantitative expressions of risk appetite for these risks.

Where risks cannot be quantified, either because of a lack of data or because historical trends are an unreliable indicator of the future, it is necessary to express risk appetite in a qualitative way.

Test yourself 10.4

What is the difference between culture and risk culture?

The culture of an organisation represents the general beliefs, values and assumptions that influence how people dress, communicate, behave and make decisions. The risk culture relates specifically to how people talk about risk, behave in relation to risk taking and control and make risk management decisions.

Test yourself 10.5

How often should organisations attempt to assess, monitor and control their risk culture?

There is no agreed rule on frequency, but organisations should look to assess, monitor and control their risk culture on a regular basis. Cultures and risk cultures are fluid and change on a regular basis, sometimes in surprising ways. It is important that organisations respond to any inappropriate changes in their risk cultures, such as excessive risk taking or negative views on risk management and compliance. Organisations like Barclays and VW, who failed to respond to inappropriate changes in their risk cultures, have suffered major and costly scandals.

Chapter 11

Test yourself 11.1

What is compliance risk and what are the consequences of compliance risk events for organisations?

Compliance risk refers to the risk of legal or criminal penalties as a result of an organisation's failure to comply with applicable laws and regulations.

Compliance risk events can have serious consequences for organisations, including:

◆   fines that can run into thousands, millions and even hundreds of millions;

◆   the imprisonment of key staff in relation to corporate manslaughter convictions or fraud and financial crime convictions;

◆   the forced closure of the organisation: for example, financial organisations that fail to meet minimum financial solvency standards may have their licence to operate withdrawn;

◆   lengthy and costly legal disputes,

◆   liability claims and other compensation costs for third parties that have suffered from non-compliance (such as from pollution);

◆   negative media coverage contributing to a loss of reputation; and

◆   a reduction in the share price of quoted companies, where investors will factor in the other costs above when determining the value of the organisation and its investment potential.

Test yourself 11.2

Are all staff members within an organisation equally responsible for compliance management, irrespective of their role and responsibilities?

All employees within an organisation are responsible for conducting their duties in a way that is not knowingly non-compliant with applicable laws and regulations, but that does not mean that they are equally responsible. Responsibilities vary according to the function they work within and their job role.

Broadly speaking, there are four levels of responsibility:

1.   Board members, who must assure themselves that all necessary compliance management arrangements are in place to maintain an appropriate level of compliance with applicable laws and regulations.

2.   Compliance, risk and governance specialists, who must ensure that the design and implementation of an organisation's compliance management arrangements are appropriate.

3.   Line managers, who must follow the instructions of the compliance, risk and governance specialists and ensure that their direct reports support the effective operation of the organisation's compliance management arrangements.

4.   All other staff members, who must follow the instructions of their line manager to support the effective operation of the organisation's compliance management arrangements.

Test yourself 11.3

Does the concept of risk-based compliance monitoring mean that organisations do not need to comply in full with laws and regulations where the level of compliance risk is low?

No. Risk-based compliance monitoring definitely does not mean that an organisation may choose to not comply in full where the level of compliance risk is low.

Risk-based compliance monitoring only relates to the level of time and resources that is devoted to monitoring compliance. Organisations should ensure that policies, procedures and controls are in place to maintain full compliance with all applicable laws and regulations.

That said, where the level of compliance risk is low an organisation may decide not to devote scarce time and resources to monitoring the implementation and operation of these policies, procedures and controls. This will free up additional time and resource for monitoring more significant compliance risks, where the probability or impact of non-compliance is high.

Test yourself 11.4

Why does an organisation need compliance policies, procedures and codes of conduct?

Organisations need compliance policies, procedures and codes of conduct to emphasise the importance of complying with applicable laws and regulations and to explain what staff members must do to ensure compliance.

Compliance policies explain roles and responsibilities, as well as the basic principles and values that underpin an organisation's compliance management activities. Procedures outline the actions that must be taken and how decisions should be made to ensure compliance. Codes of conduct outline how staff should behave to ensure compliance.

Test yourself 11.5

What role do HR controls, and whistleblowing policies and procedures, play in controlling compliance?

Human resources controls, and whistleblowing policies and procedures, have a very similar role – they exist to prevent and mitigate compliance breaches.

The presence of HR controls and whistleblowing policies and procedures may deter staff members from deliberate acts of non-compliance, because of a higher likelihood of detection and also because of the consequences of detection. Where a staff member still chooses to act in a non-compliant manner these controls should increase the chance that they are detected and disciplined as quickly as possible.

Chapter 12

Test yourself 12.1

What are the common causes and effects of loss events?

The causes of loss events are typically due to one or more of the following:

◆ people (human error, negligence and criminal acts);

◆ processes (poor process design, excessive reliance on fallible human input or breakdown);

◆ systems (systems failure); and

◆ external events (weather politics, terrorism and economic events).

The effects of loss events are:

◆ loss of resources (asset damage or loss of cash);

◆ loss of human resources (injury, ill health or death); and

◆ loss of reputation, including customer goodwill.

Test yourself 12.2

Under what circumstances may risk be tolerated? Contrast this with termination.

Risks may be tolerated where they are known and accepted. Usually this will mean that the level of risk exposure is considered to be within the agreed appetite for the risk in question. Alternatively, a risk that exceeds appetite may be tolerated because it is not cost effective to control the risk further and termination is not an option.

To accept a risk, it is important to have a good understanding of the level of exposure, in terms of probability and impact. The decision to tolerate should be approved by management. The greater the level of exposure to be tolerated the more senior should be the level of management approving the toleration.

Termination is the decision to terminate exposure to the risk in question. Termination often means that operational activities or premises are closed down. This may not be possible where these activities or premises are important to the organisation and necessary for it to achieve its objectives.

Test yourself 12.3

Categorise the following controls using the PCDD approach:
* *smoke alarm*
* *financial reconciliation*
* *internal audit action plans*
* *insurance*
* *building security*
* *IT acceptable use policy*

- smoke alarm – Detective
- financial reconciliation – Detective
- internal audit action plans – Directive
- insurance – Corrective
- building security – Preventive
- IT acceptable use policy – Directive

Test yourself 12.4

Distinguish funded from unfunded risk finance.

Funded risk financing means putting in place arrangements (such as provisions or contingency loans) to help fund the financial effects of loss events before these financial effects are incurred. Funding may take place before a loss event has occurred. It may also take place afterwards when there is a gap between the occurrence of the event and the realisation of any financial effects.

Unfunded risk financing means that arrangements are not put in place to fund the financial effects of loss events. Unfunded risk financing relies on cash flows and any capital in the balance sheet to pay for any financial effects. Unfunded risk financing may be accidental – for example, where a financial effect is not identified or assessed inaccurately. Unfunded risk financing may be deliberate where the level of financial effect is considered to be small relative to cash flows or capital or where funded risk financing is not possible or too expensive.

Test yourself 12.5

How does business continuity planning fit with crisis management?

Crisis management addresses all stages of a crisis from the emergence of the causes of the crisis (which may emerge days, weeks or years before the crisis event), through to the crisis event and its aftermath.

Business continuity plans help with containment and damage control, and support business recovery. Rapid recovery should ensure that the continuity of organisational activities is maintained with the minimum disruption. Business continuity planning is an important control in the crisis management process.

Chapter 13

Test yourself 13.1

Define operational risk management and explain its benefits for an organisation.

Operational risk management exists to control the risks which may have an adverse effect on the operations of an organisation. Risks such as fires, process breakdowns or employee misconduct may all affect the efficiency, continuity and cost effectiveness of an organisation's operations.

Operational risk management can help to prevent such risks and reduce the impact of any loss events that occur. In turn, this should help to improve operational efficiency, prevent any long-term disruption and reduce costs; all of which adds value to the organisation and its stakeholders.

Test yourself 13.2

How do people-related controls help to prevent cyber risk events?

People-related controls, such as recruitment controls, HR policies and procedures and training help to prevent a range of cyber risk events. This may include:

◆ succumbing to a 'phishing attack' by inadvertently clicking on spam emails;

◆ sharing passwords;

◆ losing confidential information;

◆ criminal activities, such as data theft;

◆ unauthorised use of IT equipment and networks; and

◆ cyber bullying or harassment.

In the 21st century, cyber risk events are not always technical in nature (such as hacking, systems failures and so on. With the growth of the internet, cloud computing and social media, new types of cyber risks are emerging. Many of these risks have a human element that requires the use of people-related controls.

Test yourself 13.3

What are the key risks associated with projects?

Projects are always concerned with making change to an organisation and its strategy or operations. With any change comes risk. From a project management perspective, there are three key risks:

1. the project's goals are not met (the desired changes are not implemented in full);

2. the project's goals are not met within the required time scale (the risk of a project over-run); and

3. the costs associated with the project are higher than budgeted (the risk of over-spend).

Test yourself 13.4

How can risk management support an organisation's CSR and sustainability objectives?

The management of CSR and sustainability is about:

◆ sharing the economic value created by organisations in a fair way across all relevant stakeholders; and

◆ minimising the adverse consequences of an organisation's economic activities (such as pollution or health and safety events).

Risk management can help to:

◆ protect the economic value that can be shared to all stakeholders though the prevention and mitigation of loss events, many of which can destroy economic value (fires, fraud and so on);

◆ identify, assess, monitor and control the risks arising from its economic activities, including pollution and health and safety events; and

◆ protect the reputation of the organisation, which might be damaged if the occurrences of loss events are linked to weaknesses in its CSR or sustainability management activities.

Test yourself 13.5

Explain the five activities that make up an effective regulatory reporting process.

The five activities are:

1. understanding and implementing the regulatory reporting requirements (ensure the organisation knows what needs to be reported and is capable of producing the necessary reports);

2. fulfilling the specific regulatory reporting requirements (collecting the required information for the reports);

3. managing the risk of process failure (ensuring that reports are submitted on time and are complete and accurate);

4. managing the reputation and financial impacts of reporting risk events (escalation procedures to ensure that any incidents of late, inaccurate or incomplete reporting are identified and mitigated); and

5. managing legal and resource requirements (ensuring that the necessary legal and compliance expertise is in place to support reporting and that people, systems and processes exist to complete the required reports).

Chapter 14

Test yourself 14.1

What types of organisation are required to comply with AML and CFT regulations?

A wide variety of organisation types are required to comply with AML and CFT regulations. AML and CFT regulations are most common where organisations:

- make, receive or facilitate large cash transactions (in the UK and Ireland this means transactions that exceed €10,000);
- provide credit (such as loans and sometimes trade credit);
- offer products that provide investment returns; and
- provide certain types of insurance service.

Organisations subject to AML and CFT regulations include:

- accountancy firms
- auctioneers
- banks
- bureau de change
- estate agents and rental agencies
- housing developers
- insurers and insurance agents
- investment firms
- lawyers
- motor vehicle sales
- pawn brokers.

Test yourself 14.2

Explain the adverse implications of behavioural risk for organisations.

Behavioural risks such as poor employee conduct, criminal activities or negligence can have a variety of adverse implications. Key implications include:

- potential financial loss (due to fraud, for example);
- legal and regulatory compliance breaches that could lead to lengthy court cases, supervisory intervention, enforcement action and criminal sanctions;
- damage to employee morale, (as a result of bullying, for example); and
- adverse media coverage, leading to reputation damage.

Chapter 15

Test yourself 15.1

How does reverse stress testing differ from conventional stress testing?

Conventional stress testing examines the effect of low probability and high impact risk events on an organisation. Examples include a large change in interest rates (such as a 2% increase in borrowing costs), a significant fall in asset values or a large financial loss.

Reverse stress testing goes further to examine destructive events that threaten the solvency of an organisation. The idea is to determine the financial breaking point of an organisation.

Reverse stress testing helps an organisation to understand its vulnerabilities and how extreme future events may affect its ability to continue as a going concern. By understanding these vulnerabilities, an organisation can prepare for and hopefully avoid them.

Test yourself 15.2

What is an emerging risk? Provide three current examples of emerging risks.

Emerging risks are one of the following:

◆ a completely new risk that has only recently emerged; or
◆ an existing risk that increases in significance (probability and impact).

Emerging risks are characterised by high levels of uncertainty and change. This means that they may be difficult to identify and assess based on current knowledge. Examples of emerging risk include:

◆ cyber risks, such as new types of hacking or denial of service attacks or attacks targeted at security weaknesses created by developments like the 'internet of things';
◆ social media-related risks, including cyber bullying and social media legal risks;
◆ disruptive technologies and organisations who threaten existing business models (such as Uber, peer to peer lending and crowd funding);
◆ extreme political change (such as Brexit); and
◆ climate change.

Test yourself 15.3

Provide a definition of 'big data'. How can big data be managed?

Big data is datasets that are so voluminous and complex that they cannot be managed using traditional data processing techniques. Data is created on a continuous basis and may be quantitative (numbers) or qualitative (words and opinions).

Big data can be managed using sophisticated data capture and analysis techniques that can cope with a variety of data types and large volumes of rapidly increasing data. Big data techniques include the use of search algorithms and artificial intelligence.

Data visualisation is an important aspect of big data management. A variety of visualisation tools can be used, including:

- 3D scatter plots
- Gantt charts
- heat maps
- networks
- stream graphs
- tree maps.

Directory of web resources

Association of Chartered Certified Accountants
www.accaglobal.com

Association of Insurers and Risk Managers
www.airmic.com

Bank for International Settlements
www.bis.org

Bank of England
www.bankofengland.co.uk

British Standards Institute
www.bsigroup.com

Business Continuity Institute
www.the bci.org

Committee of Sponsoring Organizations of the Treadway Commission
www.coso.org

CRO Council
www.crocouncil.org

CRO Forum
www.thecroforum.org

Financial Action Task Force
www.fatf-gafi.org

Financial Reporting Council
www.frc.org.uk

Financial Stability Board
www.fsb.org

GRC2020
www.grc2020.com

Health and Safety Executive
www.hse.gov.uk

Institute of Chartered Accountants in England and Wales
www.icaew.com

Institute of Operational Risk
www.ior-institute.org

Institute of Risk Management
www.theirm.org

International Labour Organization
www.ilo.org

International Monetary Fund
www.imf.org

International Organization for Standardization
www.iso.org

Organisation for Economic Co-operation and Development
www.oecd.org

Project Management Institute
www.pmi.org

Quoted Companies Alliance
www.theqca.com

The Green Book
www.gov.uk/government/publications/the-green-book-appraisal-and-evaluation-in-central-governent

The Orange Book
www.gov.uk/government/publications/orange-book

The World Bank
www.worldbank.org

United Nations Conference on Trade and Development
www.unctad.org

World Economic Forum
www.weforum.org

Glossary

Asymmetric information – Present when one party to a transaction has more material knowledge than the other. Almost all economic transactions (contract agreements, investments or the purchase of goods and services) involve an element of asymmetric information.

Asymmetric returns – Present when the gains or losses from a risky investment or other economic decision are not equal. For example, the gains associated with positive outcomes may exceed the losses associated with negative ones, or vice versa.

Cognitive bias – An influencing factor that causes someone's judgement to deviate from a norm or rationality. Cognitive biases are directly connected to how people perceive and process information.

Compliance risk – The risk of criminal sanction or a financial or reputation loss as a result of actual or perceived non-compliance with all applicable laws, regulations, standards, guidelines and codes of conduct.

Conduct of business regulation – Regulation that governs the conduct of financial organisations, including financial institutions and any financial intermediaries which support the sale of financial products. Conduct of business regulation covers the production and supply of financial services (such as product mis-selling) and the conduct of financial market participants (such as insider dealing). Financial crimes such as money laundering and fraud also fall under conduct of business regulation.

Downside risks – Risks which have no upside and can only impact negatively on an organisation.

Emerging risk – A risk that does not yet affect an organisation but may develop to become a principal risk in future. Also known as disruptive risk.

Enterprise risk management – Enterprise risk management is a process, effected by an entity's board of directors, management and other personnel, applied in strategy setting and across the enterprise, designed to identify potential events that may affect the entity, and manage risk to be within its risk appetite, to provide reasonable assurance regarding the achievement of entity objectives.

Hazard – Anything that may cause physical or mental harm to an organisation's stakeholders. Common hazards include poisonous chemicals, electricity, working at height, working excessively long hours, trip hazards such as an open drawer and the utilisation of machinery.

Hedging – An investment to reduce the risk of adverse price movements in an asset. Normally, a hedge consists of taking an offsetting position in a related financial derivative. Many organisations use derivatives to hedge risk. For example, farmers might use forwards and futures to help hedge the risk of commodity price fluctuations (to fix the price they will receive for crops they produce in the future), as do food processing companies to help stabilise their input costs. It is common for airlines and other transport related organisations to look to hedge oil price risks. Energy intensive manufacturing companies may seek to hedge energy price risks. Organisations which have loans may use interest rate swaps when they are concerned about the financing costs associated with increasing interest rates.

Indemnity – Financial security or protection from the financial effects of a loss event. Full indemnity ensures that a person or organisation is put back in the same financial position that they were in pre-loss. Partial indemnity means that they will receive only a fraction of the money they have lost.

Inherent risk – The level of risk exposure with no controls applied. Also known as gross risk.

Internal control – The systems and processes used by an organisation to ensure that organisational objectives are fulfilled and that related policies and procedures are complied with. In this context organisational objectives may include maintaining operational efficiency, protecting financial, social, and environmental performance, and ensuring compliance with legal and regulatory requirements.

Loss event – A risk event that results in some form of loss for an organisation. This may be a financial loss, such as asset damage or a regulatory fine, or a non-financial loss, such as a loss of customer goodwill or reputation. Loss events may also involve the death or injury of employees, customers and third parties.

Organisational culture – The values, beliefs and assumptions that are shared by the employees of an organisation and which influence how these employees perceive the world around them, behave and make decisions.

Principal risks – A single risk or a combination of risks that affects the performance, future prospects or reputation of an organisation to a significant degree. These include risks that could threaten the business model, future performance, solvency or liquidity.

Principles and outcome-based regulation – Regulation that relies on high-level principles and desired regulatory outcomes, such as 'consumer protection' or 'maintaining financial stability'.

Prudential regulation – Regulation that governs the financial soundness of financial institutions in order to protect the customers of these institutions and maintain financial stability.

Public good – A good, service or some other benefit that is non-exclusively available to all members of a society. Examples include air and water.

Pure risk – Risks that may only have neutral or negative outcomes, such as fire risk, risk of a physical injury or risk of illness.

Residual risk – The level of risk exposure with controls in place. Also known as net risk.

Risk attitude – A chosen state of mind or a response to a single decision or an action that could result in more than one potential positive or negative outcome (risk event).

Risk averse – A reluctance to take or to be exposed to risk. Individuals, groups or organisations that are risk averse will, all things being equal, prefer certainty to risk and will typically require some form of financial premium in order to take risk.

Risk culture – The values, beliefs and assumptions that are shared by the employees of an organisation and which influence how these employees perceive risk and make risk management decisions.

Risk event – A random discrete occurrence which may affect, positively or negatively an organisation.

Risk neutral – An indifference to risk. A risk-neutral individual, group or organisation will be unconcerned about exposure to risk and is indifferent to risk or certainty, providing the expected returns from these two different states is identical.

Risk preferring – A liking for risk and risk taking. Individuals, groups or organisations that are risk preferring will, all things being equal, prefer risk to certainty and will typically pay a financial premium or suffer some other kind of non-financial cost (such as to their health) in order to take risk.

Risk premium – The rate of return required for risk taking. The higher the level of risk exposure, the higher the risk premium.

Risk profile – An organisation's risk profile refers to the number and types of risks to which it is exposed, as well as the size of these exposures.

Securitisation – The practice of grouping risky assets into an investment vehicle (known as a financial instrument) for sale to one or more third parties. When an asset is securitised, the third party obtains the rights to any cash that flows from these assets (such as investment returns) but they are also liable for any losses that arise. Debt is a common securitised asset. An organisation sells debts that are outstanding to a third party who gains from all future interest payments but will also lose out if the relevant creditors default.

Segregation of duties – An internal control designed to prevent error and fraud by ensuring that at least two individuals are responsible for the separate parts of any task or activity. Segregation of duties involves breaking down tasks that might reasonably be completed by a single individual into multiple tasks so that no one person is solely in control.

Speculative risk – Risks that may have three outcomes: positive, neutral or negative. Gains are usually financial but they can also be non-financial human welfare or social gains such as improved health, happiness or environmental benefits.

Systems thinking – A structured thought process that involves mapping out systems and the relationships between systems, whether IT-based, social, political, economic or other system. The goal of systems thinking is to discover, in a systematic way, a system's dynamics, constraints, conditions and principles (purpose, measure, methods, tools and so on).

Index